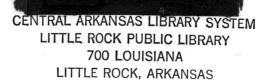

DOROTHY L. SAYERS

by Ralph E. Hone

DOROTHY L. SAYERS

 A Literary Biography

The Kent State University Press

Frontispiece: Portrait of Dorothy L. Sayers by Sir William Oliphant Hutchison 1950 (*National Portrait Gallery*)

Library of Congress Cataloging in Publication Data

Hone, Ralph E
    Dorothy L. Sayers.

    Includes bibliographical references and index.
    1. Sayers, Dorothy Leigh, 1893-1957.   2.   Authors, English—20th century—Biography.
PR6037.A95Z73   823'.9'12   [B]   79-9783
ISBN 0-87338-228-5

To DOROTHY HANBURY ROWE
Christchurch, Bournemouth

and CLYDE S. KILBY
Wheaton, Illinois

AMICI USQUE AD ARAS

CONTENTS

Illustrations

Preface

Every biographical study is an interim report, for the simple reason that each biographer measures another's foot by his own last. Like translation, biography ineluctably comes short of the subject. "Who do you say that I am?" was a question that of necessity elicited several points of view. One approaches accuracy only insofar as adequate data, ability to interpret, rapport, and readiness are at his disposal: this is as true of biographical study as it is of many other kinds of investigation.

The reflection is properly humbling. In an age of facile impatience with the facts, distortion and injustice appear all too frequently. Moreover, we tend too often to hold men's persons in admiration merely because of advantage; a calculating self-interest in producing a biography will deprive both the subject and the reader of some measure of integrity.

Dorothy Leigh Sayers clearly knew all this. She herself had been addressed by American and Continental university students, for example, who announced that they had chosen her as the subject of a literary thesis, and they invariably asked if she would "kindly supply details" of her life, opinions, personal idiosyncrasies and what she "meant" by her books! She had dismissed them abruptly: "I tell them to go away & learn to do their own work for themselves." People who lightly passed over the writer's work and merely wished to chat about the author she simply condemned out of hand. "A lot of so-called 'criticism' to-day is just glorified and pretentious gossip-column." She inveighed against them: "I would have all *that* lot fried in boiling oil!"

Her objection to people of shallow interests is understandable. Shallowness and sensationalism are close cousins. Clearly it was the sensationalists she had in mind when less than a year before her death she wrote to a friend that "people should be forbidden to write biographies & psychological analyses" of authors until the subjects had been fifty years dead: "by which time all the people who might reasonably be pained or irritated will probably be dead too, & past minding." Nowadays, she fumed, "the vultures don't even wait till one is dead!"[1]

Sayers was not opposed to biography. In 1928, when she announced that she was preparing to do a critical biography of Wilkie Collins, she did not even observe her own dictum of fifty-years-dead. In a sense, her fiction and her dramas made use of biographical method.

While she lived, Dorothy L. Sayers controlled the outlines of her own life revealed to editors and compilers of directories. In some of her lectures, she incorporated autobiographical snippets about her childhood and youth, her education, her career, her interests and tastes. And both before and after her death some of her friends and acquaintances published vignettes which captured aspects of her life: her school and university days; her postgraduate days in Oxford; her brief career in France; her work in radio broadcasting; her lecturing and writing. (Vera Brittain, Vera Farnell, Charis Barnett Frankenburg, Val Gielgud, Ivy Phillips, Barbara Reynolds, Doreen Wallace, and Eric Whelpton must be included in this number.)

In the last two decades there have been numerous "interpretations" of Sayers, including prefatory lives (not always accurate). But until recently there was no separate biography, and to date there is nothing like a balanced, critical biography. At the risk of being hoist with my own petard, I have tried to present as complete a portrait of Dorothy L. Sayers as was possible. For upwards of ten years I have read Sayers, pursued her through libraries and archives, interviewed several people who knew her personally, visited her haunts, and written innumerable letters to try to establish adequate perspective.

She was a public figure, at ease with scholars, bishops, businessmen, fellow writers. She made her mark as novelist, dramatist, journalist, essayist, lecturer, translator, and poet. She was also a private person. Like most private persons, she did not welcome Nosy Parkers, gossip-mongers, pretentious critics. Of course she had some things she wished to keep private. What private person doesn't? That attitude, also, is a part of character. There were intensities of contrast and ironic similarities between Sayers as writer and Sayers in the flesh.

If I have to some extent succeeded in my purpose, it is because I have been aided and encouraged by a host of wonderful people who shared my fascination and delight with the mind of Dorothy L. Sayers the writer. Indeed, I can think of nothing more rewarding than to encourage more and more readers to become familiar with the full corpus of her writings.

My study, however, is not a bibliography. (James Sandoe, and Robert B. Harmon and Margaret A. Burger have made very decent steps in that direction.)[2]

I should like to acknowledge the kindness and assistance of many people. Among the friends of Miss Sayers, the following have been most generous and gracious in assisting me at various times: Miss Dorothy Hanbury Rowe, Dr. Barbara Reynolds, the late Professor Lewis Thorpe, Miss Norah Lambourne, Mrs. Charis Barnett Frankenburg, Mr. C. W. Scott-Giles, and Miss Muriel St. Clare Byrne. To many libraries and their efficient staffs I must express my gratitude: The Armacost Library of the University of Redlands; Bodleian Library, Oxford; Boston University Library; British Museum Library and Colindale Annex; Honnold Library, Claremont, California; Houghton Library of Harvard University; Library of Congress; Los Angeles Public Library; National Library of Scotland, Edinburgh; New York University Library; Northwestern University Library, Evanston, Illinois; Occidental College Library, Eagle Rock, California; Princeton University Library; Sion College Library, London; University of Arkansas Library; University of California Library, Los Angeles;

University of Texas Library, Austin; Wheaton College Library, Wheaton, Illinois; and Yale University Library.

Numerous individuals have given me courteous and timely aid: Prof. G. W. Allen, Oradell, N.J.; BBC's Miss Mary Hodgson and Mrs. Jacqueline Kavanagh, Written Archives Centre, and Miss Winifred Phillips, Programme Correspondence Section; Ms. D. J. Beaumanoir Hart, London; Mrs. Evelyn Bedford, Christchurch, Wisbech, Cambridgeshire; Mr. R. A. Bevan, Boxted House, Colchester, Essex; Rev. Peter R. Blackman, Ratby, Leicestershire; Mr. John Bush, Director, Victor Gollancz, Ltd.; Mrs. Eileen Bushell, Witham, Essex; Dr. Maurice Campbell, London; M. A. C. Charpentier, Relations Extérieures, Ministére des Affaires Culturelles, Paris; Lt. Col. and Mrs. R. L. Clarke, Witham, Essex; Mrs. Barbara Denise Craig, M.A., Principal, Somerville College, Oxford; Mrs. G. F. Cunningham, Edgehill, Alva, Clackmannanshire; Mr. Philip Dalton, Hon. Secretary, The Sherlock Holmes Society, London; Rev. Oscar Keith Deberry, Oxford; Dr. James Denholm, Witham, Essex; Rev. L. J. Derrett, Witham, Essex; Miss Mary Judith Dunbar, Santa Clara; Rev. L. R. Fawcett, Tittleshall, King's Lynn, Norfolk; Mr. Val Gielgud, O.B.E., Wychwood, Barcombe, Lewes, Sussex; Mr. A. R. Green, Wisbech, Cambridgeshire; Prof. Peter Green, University of Texas; Mrs. Heather Harper, S. H. Benson, Ltd.; Prof. Carolyn Heilbrun, Columbia University; Rev. John Hester, Rector of Soho; Mr. S. W. Hobson, Chief Education Officer, Kingston upon Hull; Rev. Walter Hooper, Jesus College, Oxford; Mr. Stanley Horrocks, F.L.A., Reading; Miss Dorothy Horsman, former Director, Victor Gollancz, Ltd.; Mr. J. A. Huitson, M.Litt., Principal, Darlington College of Education, Darlington, Durham; Mr. R. E. Hutchison, Keeper, Scottish National Portrait Gallery, Edinburgh; Mr. W. Elmer Kingham, Redlands; M. Daniel Labrosse, Los Angeles; Mrs. D. M. Lennie, Secretary, The Oxford Society; Prof. Bruce McAllister, Redlands; Prof. Josette Melzer, Redlands; Rev. Aubrey Moody, Colchester, Essex; Mr. W. Morrow, Chief Clerk, University of Durham; Mr. Alexander Muirhead, Witham, Essex; M. Félix Paillet, Ecole des Roches, Verneuil, Normandy; Mrs. Sheila Patton-Smith, Clevelands, Felsted, Essex; Miss V. I. Phillips, St. Morvah, Throwleigh, Okehampton, Devon; Mr. C. A. Potts, Ministry of Defence Library, London; Miss Kathleen Richards, Witham, Essex;

Mr. Paul H. Rohmann, Director, The Kent State University Press, Kent, Ohio; Prof. Glenn Sadler, Long Beach; Miss Mildred Salivar, Harcourt, Brace, Jovanovich, New York; Prof. James Sandoe, Boulder, Colo.; Prof. Alfred Satterthwaite, Haverford, Pa.; Mrs. Ann Fleming Schreurs, Danvers, Mass.; Sir Sacheverell Sitwell, Weston Hall, Towcester, Northamptonshire; Dr. R. C. Smail, Sidney Sussex College, Cambridge; Mr. G. W. Sparrow, Witham, Essex; Prof. Rosamond Kent Sprague, Columbia, S.C.; Prof. Robert L. Stuart, Redlands; Mr. Wolf Suschitzky, London; Rev. John A. Thurmer, Exeter; Miss Molly Walker, British Council, Paris; Miss Doreen Wallace, Diss, Norfolk; Mr. Eric Whelpton, Rye, Sussex; Mr. Leonard Wibberley, Hermosa Beach; Mr. Julian Wolff, Baker Street Irregulars, New York.

To The University of Redlands I owe particular thanks. To the President and Trustees I acknowledge the helpfulness of a sabbatical in the spring of 1971; to the Faculty Research Committee and the Wilcox Fund I am grateful for assisting grants; to former secretaries Mrs. Magdalene Hester, Mrs. Linda Hunt, and Mrs. Eleanor Finlay Otte I owe immeasurable patience and expert assistance.

To my wife and children who have constantly encouraged this work by their enthusiastic interest I express my devotion.

Redlands, California
23 August 1978   Ralph E. Hone

Acknowledgments

All excerpts from the writings of Dorothy L. Sayers appear by arrangement with Anthony Fleming, through his agents David Higham Associates Ltd., London.

Published Works: " '. . . And Telling You a Story': a Note on *The Divine Comedy*," *Essays Presented to Charles Williams* (London: Oxford University Press, 1947); *Begin Here: A War-Time Essay* (London: Gollancz, 1940); "Biographical Note Communicated by Paul Austin Delagardie;" "Charles Williams: A Poet's Critic," *The Poetry of Search and the Poetry of Statement* (London: Gollancz, 1963); "The Church in the New Age," *World Review*, March 1941, pp. 11-15; *Clouds of Witness*; "Constantine—Christ's Emperor," *Everybody's Weekly*, 16 February 1952, pp. 15, 20; *Creed or Chaos?* (London: Methuen, 1947); *The Comedy of Dante Alighieri the Florentine: Cantica I: Hell*, ibid., *Cantica II: Purgatory*, ibid., *Cantica III: Paradise* (Harmondsworth, Middlesex: Penguin, 1949, 1955, 1962); *The Devil to Pay* (London: Gollancz, 1939); "The Dogma Is the Drama," *Strong Meat* (London: Hodder & Stoughton, 1939); "Dorothy L. Sayers Reveals Origins of Lord Peter Wimsey," *The Harcourt, Brace News*, 15 July 1936; "A Drama of the Christian Church," *International Review of Missions*, XXXIV (1945), 430-32; *The Emperor Constantine* (London: Gollancz, 1951); "The English War," *Times Literary Supplement*, 7 September 1940, p. 445; "Eros in Academe," *Oxford Outlook*, I (June 1919), 110-15; *Even the Parrot* (London: Methuen, 1944); "The Faust Legend and the Idea of the Devil," *Publications of the English Goethe Society*, XV (1945), 1-20; "The Fen Floods: Fiction and Fact," *The Spectator*, 2 April 1937, pp. 611-12; "For Albert, Late King of the Belgians," *Life and Letters To-*

day, XXVI (July 1940), 36; *Further Papers on Dante* (London: Methuen, 1957); *Gaudy Night*; "Gaudy Night," D.K. Roberts, ed. *Titles to Fame* (London: Nelson, 1937), pp. 73-95; "The Greatest Drama Ever Staged," *Sunday Times*, 3 April 1938, p. 20; "The Great Mystery," *Sunday Times*, 6 January 1957, p. 8; *Have His Carcase*; "Helen Simpson," *Fortnightly*, 155 n.s. 149 (January 1941), 54-59; *He That Should Come* (London: Gollancz, 1939); "Introduction," Charles Williams: *James I* (London: Arthur Barker, 1953); *Introductory Papers on Dante* (N.Y.: Harper, 1954); *The Just Vengeance* (London: Gollancz, 1946); Letter to the Editor, *Daily Sketch*, 5 March 1946, p. 2; Letter to the Editor, *Daily Telegraph and Morning Post*, 6 January 1942, p. 4; Letter to the Editor, *John o' London's Weekly*, 7 April 1944, p. 16; ibid., 19 May 1944, p. 77; Letter to the Editor, *The Spectator*, 1 December 1939, p. 782; Letter to the Editor, *Times*, 24 November 1938, p. 15; ibid., 26 August 1941, p. 5; ibid., 26 November 1952; Letter to Editor, *Times Literary Supplement*, 21 January 1928, p. 468; *The Lost Tools of Learning* (London: Methuen, 1948); "The Church's Responsibility," *Malvern, 1941: The Life of the Church and the Order of Society* (London: Longmans, Green, 1941), pp. 57-78; *The Man Born to Be King* (London: Gollancz, 1943); *The Mind of the Maker* (N.Y.: Harcourt, Brace, 1941); *Murder Must Advertise; The Mysterious English* (London: Macmillan, 1941); "Night Bombing," *Fortnightly*, 155 n.s. 149 (June 1941), 559; *The Nine Tailors*; "Notes on the Way," *Time and Tide*, 15 June 1940, pp. 633-34; "Obsequies for Music," *London Mercury*, III (January 1921), 249-53; *Op. I* (Oxford: Blackwell, 1916); "Fair Erembours," *Oxford Poetry 1917* (Oxford: Blackwell, 1917), pp. 52-53; "Vials Full of Odours," "For Phaon," *Oxford Poetry 1919* (Oxford: Blackwell, 1919), pp. 52, 50; *The Other Six Deadly Sins* (London: Methuen, 1943); "Playwrights Are Not Evangelists," *World Theatre*, I (1955), 61-66; "The Poem," *London Mercury*, III (October 1921), 577; "Ignorance and Dissatisfaction," *Latin Teaching: The Journal of the Association for the Reform of Latin Teaching*, XXVIII (October 1952), 69-92; "Poetry, Language and Ambiguity," "The Translation of Verse," *The Poetry of Search and the Poetry of Statement* (London: Gollancz, 1963), pp. 263-86, 127-53; "The Present Status of the Mystery Story," *London Mercury*, XXIII (November 1930), 47-52; "The Psychology of Advertising," *The Spectator*, 19 November 1937, pp. 896-98; articles in *Punch*, 2 November 1953, 6 January 1954, 13 January 1954, 20 January 1954; "The Religions behind the Nation," *The Church Looks Ahead: Broadcast Talks* (London: Faber and Faber, 1941), pp. 67-78; *The Song of Roland* (Baltimore: Penguin, 1957); *Strong Meat* (London: Hodder & Stoughton, 1939); *Strong Poison*; "Three Good Crime Novels," *Sunday Times*, 9 September 1934, p. 8; "A Resolution for the New Year," *Sunday Times*, 30 December 1934, p. 6; "Target Area," *Fortnightly*, 161 n.s. 151 (March 1944), 181-84; "Technicalese," Herbert Brean, ed. *The Mystery Writer's Handbook* (N.Y.: Harper, 1956), pp. 64-65; "The Triumph of Easter," *Sunday Times*, 17 April 1938, p. 10; "Towards a Christian Aesthetic," V.A. Demant, ed. *Our Culture: Its Christian Roots and Present Crisis* (London: S.P.C.K., 1947), pp. 50-69; *Unnatural Death; The Unpleasantness at the Bellona Club*; Foreword, "Are Women Human?" "Christian Morality," "Creative Mind," "Divine Comedy," "Forgiveness [and the Enemy]," "The Gulf Stream and the Channel," "They Tried to Be Good," "The Human-Not-Quite-Human," "How Free Is the Press?" "Living to Work," "A Vote of Thanks to Cyrus," *Unpopular Opinions* (London: Gollancz, 1946), pp. 7, 106-16, 9-12, 43-

58, 20-23, 13-17, 59-66, 97-105, 116-22, 127-33, 122-27, 23-28; "Vocation in Work," A.E. Baker, ed. *A Christian Basis for the Post-War World* (London: Student Christian Movement, 1942), pp. 88-103; "What Is Right with Oxford?" *Oxford* (Summer 1935), 34-41; *Whose Body?; Why Work?* (London: Methuen, 1942); ed. Wilkie Collins: *The Moonstone* (London: J.M. Dent, 1944); "Wimsey Papers," *The Spectator*, 26 January 1940, p. 104; *The Zeal of Thy House* (London: Gollancz, 1937).

Unpublished Writings: Poem, "Fatima;" Letters (©1979, Anthony Fleming) (a) from the BBC Written Archives Centre, Caversham Park, Reading, by arrangement: DLS to Mr. Ackerley, 5 December 1931; DLS to Antony Brown, 19 May 1954; DLS to Eric Fenn, 4 April 1941, 14 December 1942, 16 May 1943; DLS to Mr. Fielden, 28 March 1934; DLS to Val Gielgud, 18 November 1938, 24 February 1941, 1 April 1941, 22 July 1941, 13 January 1942, 27 January 1942, 9 February 1942, 16 February 1942, 22 September 1942, 2 January 1943, 16 August 1943, 12 December 1945, 19 June 1946, 13 January 1947; DLS to Miss M. Jenkin, 22 November 1940; DLS to Mr. Lambert, 4 February 1931; DLS to Sir Richard Maconachie, 13 July 1940; DLS to D. McCulloch, 25 October 1940, 28 November 1940; DLS to Mr. Nichols, 22 October 1942; DLS to Dr. James Welch, 23 July 1940, 5 November 1940, 28 November 1940, 7 December 1940, 21 December 1940, 2 January 1941, 20 May 1943, 20 November 1943; DLS to Rev. J.G. Williams, 19 May 1941; (b) by permission, Boston University Library, DLS to Robert Speaight, 24 July 1943; (c) by permission of The Trustees of the National Library of Scotland, DLS to Sir Herbert J.C. Grierson, 26 April 1948; (d) by permission of Humanities Research Center, The University of Texas at Austin, DLS to Leonard Green, 29 August 1919; DLS to R.A. Scott-James, 2 November 1938; DLS to Sir Hugh Walpole, 13 January 1940; DLS to "King Juan," July 1957; (e) by permission of C.S. Kilby, Curator, Marion E. Wade Collection, Wheaton (Illinois) College Library, DLS to Michael Williams, 2 December 1947; DLS to Michael and Mrs. Charles Williams, 24 May 1948, 28 June 1948, 29 September 1948, 5 May 1950, 23 December 1953, 4 January 1956; DLS to Canon Wright, 21 March 1946; (f) personal letters by permission of the recipients, DLS to Mrs. C. Frankenburg, July 1948; a friend, 24 August 1950; DLS to Norah Lambourne, 27 August 1946, 26 April 1949, 11 May 1949, 8 May 1952; DLS to Kathleen Richards, before 13 June 1946; DLS to Dorothy Hanbury Rowe, 8 October 1915, 15 April 1937, 25 April 1937, before 12 June 1939; DLS to C.W. Scott-Giles, 15 April 1936.

I am also grateful to authors, editors, publishers, and literary executors respectively for permission to cite extracts as indicated below.

Carolyn G. Heilbrun, "Sayers, Lord Peter and God" in *The American Scholar*, XXXVII, No. 2 (Spring 1968), © 1968 by the United Chapters of Phi Beta Kappa. By permission of the publishers.

John Heath-Stubbs, *Charles Williams* [Writers and Their Work] (London: The British Council, 1955).

Letters of C.S. Lewis, ed. W.H. Lewis, © 1966 by W.H. Lewis and Executors of C.S. Lewis; Curtis Brown, Ltd., London, on behalf of the Estate of C.S. Lewis; reprinted by permission of Harcourt Brace Jovanovich, Inc.

Vera Brittain, *Testament of Youth*, © 1933; by permission of Victor Gollancz, Ltd., London, and the author's literary executors, Sir George Catlin and Paul Berry. Vera Brittain, *The Women at Oxford*, © 1960, by permission of George G. Harrap & Co., Ltd., London, and the author's literary executors, Sir George Catlin and Paul Berry.

Cambridge University Press for permission to quote from Mrs. Q.D. Leavis, "The Case of Dorothy Sayers," *Scrutiny*, VI (1937); and permission to quote from C.S. Lewis, "De Descriptione Temporum," *Selected Literary Essays*, 1969, ed. Walter Hooper.

Bernard Palmer, ed. *Church Times*, for permission to quote from various issues from 8 April 1938 through 27 December 1957.

Syndication International, Ltd., for permission to quote an extract from *Daily Mirror*, 26 April 1952.

Iain Mackie for permission to quote from articles in *Daily Sketch*, 27 February 1946 and 5 March 1946.

Terence Dalton, Ltd., and the author to quote extracts from Charis Frankenburg, *Not Old Madam, Vintage*, 1975.

Wm. B. Eerdmans Publishing Co. and the author for permission to quote from Rosamond K. Sprague's *A Matter of Eternity*, 1973.

Martin Dodsworth, ed. *English*, for permission to quote an extract from Volume XII (Spring 1958).

David Higham Associates, Ltd., for permission to quote from Val Gielgud, *Years in a Mirror* (London: The Bodley Head, 1965).

Val Gielgud for permission to quote from *Years of the Locust* (London: Nicholson and Watson, 1947).

P.G. Wodehouse: A Portrait of a Master by David A. Jasen. Copyright 1974 by David A. Jasen. Used by permission of the author.

Eric Whelpton, *The Making of a European*, 1974. By permission of the author and Johnson Publications, Ltd., London.

Longman Group, Ltd., for permission to quote from B. Causton's "The Scene of the Conference," *Malvern, 1941: The Life of the Church and the Order of Society*, 1941.

Mary Ellen Chase, "Five Literary Portraits," *The Massachusetts Review*, III (Spring 1962), © 1962 by permission of The Massachusetts Review, Inc.

New English Library Ltd., London, for permission to quote from Janet Hitchman, *Such a Strange Lady: A Biography of Dorothy L. Sayers*, 1975.

Oxford University Press for permission to quote from *Somerville College 1879-1921* by Muriel St. Clare Byrne and Catherine Hope Mansfield (1922) and from C.S. Lewis's Preface to *Essays Presented to Charles Williams* (1947).

R.E. Hutchison, Esq., Keeper, Scottish National Portrait Gallery, for permission to reproduce the portrait of Miss Sayers made by his father, Sir William Oliphant Hutchison, 1950.

Pantheon Books, a Division of Random House, Inc., and Routledge & Kegan Paul, Ltd., for permission to quote from Noel Stock, *The Life of Ezra Pound*, © 1970.

The late professor Lewis Thorpe, for permission to quote from *Nottingham Mediaeval Studies*, Volumes II (1958) and IX (1968).

Times Newspapers, Ltd., for permission to quote from articles in *The Times, Times Literary Supplement,* and *Sunday Times* as indicated in the Notes.

Robert Graves and Alan Hodge for permission to quote from their book *The Long Week-End: A Social History of Great Britain 1918-1939* (London, 1940).

Popperfoto, London, for permission to reproduce the photograph of Dorothy L. Sayers following p. 110.

chapter one

Adventurers All

There were no special portents accompanying the birth of Dorothy Leigh Sayers such as intrigued her when as a child she read about the life of Cyrus the Persian. The circumstances of her birth, however, were a bit unusual. Her father was almost forty, her mother over thirty, when she was born. Her birth place was Oxford, and she was a Monday's child, born on 13 June 1893 with the promise that she should be fair of face. She was an only child, and although she did not lack a certain amount of privilege, she had less than an ideal childhood.[1]

Her first home was Number 1, Brewer Street, St. Aldate, just across the road from the portal to Christ Church College. Her father was the headmaster of the Cathedral Choir School, and it was part of his duty, as Sayers later wrote, "to instruct small demons with angel-voices in the elements of the ancient Roman tongue." Back of him lay an impressive clerical and schoolmasterly career. He had served as headmaster of St. Michael's College, Tenbury, a school with a reputation for excellence in musical training, and he had been concurrently chaplain of Christ Church. He had also been at one time headmaster of the Cathedral Choir School, Hereford, and chaplain of New College, Oxford. He was a devout and learned man, a High-Churchman, and he took great delight in music. The home in Brewer Street was provided by the school, and surely Dorothy grew accustomed to the sounds of church and college bells, the regulators of her father's life.[2]

Her mother, Helen Mary Leigh Sayers, was the daughter of a solicitor who resided in Ratby, Leicestershire, where Henry Sayers's father was (from 1881) the vicar of the parish church of St. Philip and St. James. The Leighs had earlier come from Hampshire. Dorothy's mother was a patient, kindly wife and mother, self-effacing and charitable.[3]

In 1893 Victoria, queen of England and empress of India, was seventy-three years of age and approaching both the Diamond Jubilee of her accession and the end of her reign. The child born to the Sayerses in that year was destined to finish her own career as a supporter of sovereign and church under another queen. Moreover, Oxford was to become for her greater in significance than simply the place of her birth.

When Dorothy was past her fourth birthday, her father was appointed rector of the parish church of Bluntisham cum Earith, in the Fen country. After many years of service to Christ Church College and the Cathedral Choir School, Mr. Sayers went to serve in Bluntisham because the rectory and the parish church were in the patronage of Christ Church College. The rectory was to be "home" for Dorothy for the next twenty years.

She vividly remembered the circumstances of the arrival in Bluntisham. The parents had moved into the rectory before their daughter and the rest of the family arrived.

> When I was four-and-a-half years old, [Father] was presented with the living of Bluntisham-cum-Earith, in Huntingdonshire—an isolated country parish, which was one of the ancient ports or bridges to the Isle of Ely, and which contains to this day the bulwarks of a Roman camp. I recollect very well my first arrival at the Rectory, wearing a brown pelisse and bonnet trimmed with feathers, and accompanied by my nurse and my maiden aunt, who carried a parrot in a cage. It was January [1898], and the winter must have been mild that year, for the drive near the gate was already bright yellow with winter aconites—a plant which is said never to grow except where the soil has been watered by Roman blood.

What she wore, with whom she traveled, the parrot, January, the drive near the gate bright yellow with winter aconites: here was little Dorothy already totting up "the shapes and appearances of things."[4]

The home was spacious, the central portion containing three floors with wings two-stories high. It was neoclassic in style, the doorway late seventeenth-century—coming from Old Slepe Hall, St. Ives. In the lintel were large crossed palm leaves. The building was surrounded by spacious lawns bordered with trees and shrubs. This lovely large dwelling in an isolated country parish was indeed expansive after the serried quarters across from Christ Church College. There was room for the rector's library, room for entertaining the parishioners and other friends—there was a fine paneled dining room, room for Mr. Sayers's mother, room for Aunt Mabel Leigh (who remained a member of the Sayers household, wherever the family resided, until she was eighty-five), room for servants, room for a nursery.[5]

The nursery was the scene of at least one clearly etched memory.

> I do not know whether my father missed his small choristers amid the new duties of a country parish, or whether he was actuated only by a sense of the fitness of things and a regard for his daughter's intellectual welfare. I know only that I was rising seven when he appeared one morning in the nursery, holding in his hand a shabby black book, which had already seen some service, and addressed to me the following memorable words: "I think, my dear, that you are now old enough to begin to learn Latin."

The daily Latin lessons were pleasant to her; they gave her, according to her own reckoning, a sense of superiority over her mother, her aunt, and her nurse, but not over her grandmother, who was a "lady of parts, and had at least a nodding acquaintance with the language." There did not seem to be anything perplexing about acquainting herself with the unEnglish oddities of the language. The "complications of the morphology and syntax," she wrote much later, "released in me some kind of low cunning which today finds expression in the solving of crossword puzzles."[6]

A photograph of Dorothy at the age of eight reveals a healthy, dark-haired, round-faced child, open and responsive, a touch of the pert already dominating the mouth and the clear blue eyes. One can appreciate from the photograph a hint of what she was to write later to Dr. James Welch, Director of Religious Broadcasting for the BBC, during the years of World War II: "When I was a child I liked a bit of mystery and the sense of something larger than life."[7] In facial features she resembled her mother; in personality she resembled her father.

Did the bulwarks of the Roman camp in Bluntisham serve as the foundation for simple history lessons about England's ancient past? Did the doorway, retrieved from Oliver Cromwell's old home at St. Ives, become the portal for lessons about the Establishment?

One aspect of Dorothy's childhood reading in history is certain. In a children's magazine entitled *Tales from Herodotus,* she made the acquaintance of Cyrus the Persian, illustrated in the fashion of Kingsley's *Heroes.* He was "dressed in a short tunic very like the garment worn by the young Theseus or Perseus." She learned the usual details about Cyrus: he was brought up by a herdsman of King Astyages; he overcame Croesus, "that rich king of whom Solon had said, 'Call no man happy until he is dead' "; he moved in fairy tale— "his mother dreamed," "the oracle spoke"; he moved also in history—he commanded his soldiery "to divert the course of the Euphrates, so that they might march into Babylon along the river-bed." Then one day, "with a shock as of sacrilege," she realized that he had marched "clean out of Herodotus and slap into the Bible." It was he of whom Daniel warned after the mysterious finger wrote on the palace wall *Mene, mene, tekel upharsin.* She was reluctantly forced to recognize that history and the Bible could not be kept in separate pigeonholes. Here—in history—was God, "the fierce and dishevelled old gentleman from Mount Sinai," bursting into Greek affairs "in a most uncharacteristic way," and "taking an interest in events and people" that seemed to her "altogether outside His province."[8]

In due time, Dorothy was also given lessons in French and German by governesses. She rapidly became adept enough to converse with the governesses. "By the time I was thirteen," she later wrote, "the French had hauled up hand over fist upon the Latin, and overtaken it." She first read *The Three Musketeers* at the age of thirteen. She said that in her early teens she could read and write French "almost as quickly and correctly as English," and she was "not far behind in German."[9]

Life was not all devoted to lessons. There were holiday excursions, such as visits with her parents to Broadstairs in Kent or to Hunstanton on the Wash. Her father, with training and delight in music, often provided some musical diversions. In her youth, she herself began to play the piano and the violin. She liked to sing, especially certain types of hymns:

> When I was a kid, did I like singing about "The King of Love my Shepherd is"? or "We are but little children weak"? or "Jesus meek and gentle"? Not on your life. I liked "Christian, dost thou hear them?"—especially the bit about "prowl and prowl around," "The Church's one foundation"—good swinging, thick stuff, with a grand line or two about heresies and schisms—quite unintelligible, but gloriously rending and distressful; and "Lo! He comes with clouds descending"—that was *fine,* with all the sinners deeply wailing; and "Ride on, ride on in majesty" with the angel armies looking on, and the Father on His sapphire throne—that was something *like* a throne!—and the "lowly pomp" . . . and the donkey and the palms and all the rest of it. And all the Good Friday hymns, wallowing in a voluptuous gloom.[10]

At the turn of the century, the parish of Bluntisham-cum-Earith numbered about nine hundred, mostly farmers. The church was half a mile to the east from the rectory and stood on a slight rise. It had a remarkable polygonal apse, and the nave roof stood on stone corbels, mostly of angels with shields or musical instruments. Henry Sayers, during his incumbency, had bells erected in the church tower (although some of the bells had been cast and presented to the parish long before), and change ringing similar to that in Sayers's *The Nine Tailors* must have been familiar to the parish.[11]

There were garden parties in the summertime for Sunday-school children and their mothers. There were surely morning and evening prayers with the family and servants. There were explanations of the traditional church festivals and, occasionally, interesting reports of the parish-calling done by the Sayerses. There was also modest catechetical training. Dorothy remembered that in childhood she had been embarrassed by what seemed to her at the time "a serious blot," a fatuity even, in a verse of the Athanasian Creed:

> It was, I felt, quite unnecessary to warn anybody that there was "one Father, not three fathers; one Son, not three sons; one Holy Ghost, not three holy ghosts." The suggestion seemed quite foolish. It was difficult enough to imagine a God who was Three and yet One; did anybody exist so demented as to conceive of a ninefold deity? Three fathers was a plurality even to absurdity. I found myself blushing faintly at the recitation of words so wildly unrelated to anything that the queerest heathen in his blindness was likely to fancy for himself.

5

At the same time, however, the language of the Creed was overwhelming:

> I know I should never have dared to confess to any of my grown-ups the over-mastering fascination exercised on me by the Athanasian Creed. They were kind . . . , and I felt instinctively that they would be surprised and amused, and say, "Surely you can't understand that," and tell each other about it as a quaint thing I had said. So I hugged it as a secret delight.[12]

She had thought it was a mild winter when she first arrived in Bluntisham. But Dorothy knew other winters. Many years later, after publication of *The Nine Tailors,* she suddenly found herself among the company of the prophets, and she wrote about the flooding of the Fens.

> As a child I was thoroughly accustomed to the phenomenon of winter floods. Year after year, someone would regularly observe at breakfast: "We've been having a lot of rain; they'll be letting the water out." Year after year, we could see from our front windows the overflowing of the upper Ouse, that turned plough and pasture into standing water; and could thereafter take a walk to the Seven-Holes Bridge or the Hermitage Sluice at Earith, and watch the flood come swirling and eddying through the opened gates into the Old and New Bedford Rivers. Year by year, Earith parishioners from outlying places excused lateness at church by the natural explanation that the water was over the causey and they had to wait for the ferry. Year by year, a journey by train in almost any direction found us looking from the carriage-window over a sheet of sullen water, broken only by the lines of sunken hedges and the tops of willow and poplar trees. Year by year, the prospects of skating on the Fen were discussed; and once the Ouse froze hard, so that the Fen people could run from Earith to Ely on the characteristic Fenland running-skates, with the blades curled up at the toes. When we first came to the parish in 1898, the memory of the ancient marsh agues was still vivid, and old women still smoked opium in clay pipes as a prophylactic.[13]

The Fen country, furrowed by winter floods, became part of Dorothy's temperament. Her isolation as an only child was relieved somewhat by her studies, but her first sixteen years were virtually cloistered. She did not lack security, yet dwelling in fairly untrodden ways had made her introspective. The first flush of "the poetic age," as she later categorized it, was the "difficult age." Self-centered, she yearned to express herself. She specialized in being misunderstood. She was restless and tried to achieve independence. Talented, observant, imaginative, keen-minded, studious, she needed more guidance than her parents and governesses could continuously supply in order to develop the signs of creativeness, to satisfy her "eagerness to know and to do some one thing in preference to all others."[14]

Her parents were not unmindful of her needs. She *must* go to school. In January 1909 they took her out of the Fens and down to Wiltshire, so that she could become a boarding student at Godolphin in Salisbury.

The Wiltshire hills and Salisbury, even in January, were a delightful change from the Fens. Godolphin School at the top of Milford Hill, north and east from the cathedral with its lofty spire, high above the railroad and the commercial activity of New Sarum, could have been to Dorothy a place where every prospect pleases. But there were occasional inhibitions.

It was a school with traditions. The Commemoration was held shortly after the opening of the autumn term every year; and governors, mistresses, old girls, and lesser Godolphinites remembered not only the Cornish foundress, Elizabeth Godolphin and her bequest some two hundred years earlier, but also the continuing providence of God during the interim since last meeting. Competitive games brought the Houses into traditional rivalry. A Mark Reading Day was also regularly observed each term to announce the girls' achievements. The school motto, in Cornish out of respect for the Godolphin family, was *Franc ha leal eto ge* ("Frank and Loyal Thou Art").

About two hundred girls attended Godolphin, over half of them boarders. The headmistress was Miss Mary Alice Douglas, the acrostic of whose initials was often noted by those who misunderstood her stern seriousness.

Dorothy entered in the spring term, 17 January 1909, the second term of the year.[15] She was nearing sixteen, and most of the other girls had already been in school for three years and had acquired comfortable friendships. She was a member of Oakhurst, the small House which later became known as Hamilton. She was neither skilled nor interested in games. Furthermore, the uniform appearance of pigtails and pinnies was a threat of anonymity. One also *marched* into Hall, the assembly room, and, upon occasion, into the city for some function. The loneliness of the tall, slender girl, who by now had become obliged to wear glasses, was intensified in the midst of a large number of peers already settled in, and also in the midst of a cloud of mistresses who could not easily become surrogates for father, mother, aunt, nurse, and governesses.

7

In addition to continued study of languages, she had classes in English, history, and mathematics. She also continued her study of piano, under Fräulein Fehmer, who returned to Germany before World War I and in a later generation became a Nazi. She keenly recollected Miss Fehmer's appearance—she was "stiffly built, with a strong square face, lionish, slightly blunted, as though the hand of the potter had given a gentle push to the damp clay; she wore eye-glasses, and a shawl round her shoulders in cold weather; her hair was straight and dark, combed back over a pad; she had strong square hands, grasping the keys easily from middle C to the major third above the octave, blunt finger-tips and wide flat knuckles; she used a rather unorthodox and very powerful action of the whole forearm, so that the wires sang under her touch like bells." She remembered such details as Miss Fehmer's inscribing the date neatly on every new piece started and the "tart, rebuking voice" when the learner made mistakes, "stumbling feverishly among the accidentals"—"Na, na!" Nor could she ever forget that Miss Fehmer's music room was named Chopin, after her favorite composer; nor the recitals of Chopin Miss Fehmer gave in the Hall after supper: "There is a particular Nocturne that I cannot hear to this day without thinking of her; when it is rendered by celebrated musicians over the ether I see the red-brick walls, the games trophies, the rush-bottomed chairs, the rows of aspidistras that garnished the edge of the platform, and Fräulein Fehmer, gowned in an unbecoming dark-blue silk, lifting the song from the strings with a squaring of her strong shoulders."[16]

Although there was "no nostalgic glamour" in her later memories and she was "not happy at school," Dorothy derived more from Godolphin than she could or would acknowledge. She could hardly have avoided, for one thing, being influenced by the precept and example of the religious work-ethic of the headmistress. From first to last, with Miss Douglas it was *angusta ad augusta*. On the day school opened in that spring term 1909, Miss Douglas spoke about the spice and novelty in the change from holidays to systematic work, and she underscored the joy of work for its own sake. "The blade is not made in the fight, but in the forge," she said. The theme did not vary much from term to term. It was now Joan of Arc's *En avant, tirez!* It was then "Fight the good fight!" Lent brought discipline and prayers to "Help us to further fruitfulness," or a reminder that "He that overcometh shall inherit all things." Miss Douglas must have had some early cumulative effect upon her, for Dorothy was among the twenty-eight Godolphinites who were candidates for confirmation in the spring of 1910.

She participated in several extracurricular activities during her days at Godolphin. She may have found it silly stuff, but within little more than a month after her first term had begun she became involved in a House entertainment, portraying the wolf in an unusual version of *Red Ridinghood:* the wolf "turned into a prince only just in time." She also attended a performance of *L'Avare* by a French company in County Hall on 13 October 1909, and she reviewed the production for the *Godolphin School Magazine.* She witnessed productions by M. Roubaud's Company of Molière's *Le Bourgeois Gentilhomme* on 4 November 1910 in the school Hall and Labiche's *La Poudre aux Yeux* and Molière's *Précieuses Ridicules* at the Picturedrome on 28 October 1911, all of which she reviewed for the school magazine. There were also concerts and guest lecturers in nearly every term. There were excursions of various sorts: to Grovely for a picnic; to Old Sarum to see the evidences of ancient Roman occupation; to County Hall to hear Sir Ernest Shackleton lecture on Antarctica. The excursions became opportunities for Dorothy to write and publish additional items in the school magazine. She also served as a sublibrarian for the school Modern Language Library. She became involved in the Godolphin Debating Society. She was a house-prefect for a while. She finally became editor of the *Godolphin School Magazine* for two terms.

Patriotic events, of course, duly involved the school. Dorothy walked with the other girls, "four abreast" in forms, to the marketplace to celebrate Empire Day on 24 May 1909; the girls joined all the schools of the city of Salisbury to salute a flag sent to the children of the city by the children of Salisbury, New South Wales. The death of Edward VII, the subsequent memorial service in Salisbury Cathedral, and the accession of King George V were properly noted, the school going down to the city in customary "fours." When Bishop Ridgeway succeeded Bishop Wordsworth, the school marched down to the Cathedral close to participate modestly in the investiture.

Needless to say, Dorothy did not waste her time academically at Godolphin. Each autumn, as Miss Douglas read publicly the results of the Oxford and Cambridge Joint Board Higher Certificate Examinations, Dorothy's name acquired more luster. On 17 September 1909 Miss Douglas announced that "Six full certificates had been gained, and six distinctions, three by one girl, D. Sayers." In the autumn term 1910, announcement was made that she had again earned distinction. At the opening of spring term 1911, Miss Douglas "announced the delightful news that Dorothy Sayers had passed Group B in the Cambridge Higher Local Examination and was distinguished for written French and spoken French and spoken German, and that she had done better than any other candidate in England who had taken both languages."

But the Godolphin years were not unalloyed. In spring term 1911, a note was inserted on the verso of the title page of the *Godolphin School Magazine* by Miss Douglas;

> The readers of the Magazine will, we know, sympathise very much with the Editor, Dorothy Sayers, who has had a long illness, measles followed by pneumonia. They will, however, rejoice to hear that she is much better, and will, we hope, soon be able to go home to complete her recovery.

Each term seemed to bring some such announcement about an outbreak of an infectious disease. After a stay in a nursing home in Salisbury, Dorothy did return home to recuperate, and she returned for autumn term 1911. But before the term ended on 20 December, illness came again, and she was obliged to return home. Miss Ivy Phillips recalls taking some of the senior members of the House to say goodbye to her. Miss Douglas said on the next Mark Reading Day, "It was a great disappointment that Dorothy Sayers had to leave on account of illness. She is going to try at home to win her scholarship." Miss Douglas's expressed disappointment was indeed sincere, for she recognized that Dorothy was a scholar. She also surely sympathized with the discomfiture that seized the girl as a result of her illnesses and her exhausting work. All of the initial loneliness upon arriving at Godolphin in January 1909, of course, was aggravated by a miserable stroke of fortune: Dorothy lost all her hair because of the illnesses, and she was obliged to wear a wig during her last school days. The chagrin of facing herself in the mirror in this condition, especially at this time of her life, must have been hardly bearable.

Dorothy did win her scholarship, the coveted Gilchrist Scholarship in Modern Langauges at Somerville College, Oxford. It was a distinct achievement, won in an open competition. That she won is a tribute to her brilliance and hard work. Her success was duly commemorated by the placing of her name on a plaque in Hall.

No doubt Dorothy's later aloof attitude toward Godolphin was evoked in part because she had entered the school at an advanced age, but in even greater part by the humiliation which she endured from illness in her last days. Peripherally, also, institutional regimentation annoyed her. During World War II she wrote to her friend Dr. Welch of the BBC with a lightness which does little to disguise the pain: "in my youth I rather wallowed in gloom, and liked to have the myrrh along with the gold."[17]

Nevertheless, from that dark backward abysm of time there lay a pattern of inspiration which included the faces, however dim, of Fräulein Fehmer, house-mistress Ethel E. Jones, headmistress Mary Alice Douglas, and gentle fellow students like Ivy Phillips, in whose autograph album Dorothy filled a page in 1911.

Family feelings kept pace with Dorothy during those opening months of 1912. Solicitude over her health and the ensuing baldness; gratitude for the academic standing; elation over the results of the scholarship examination; anticipation of her next move—to Oxford. A mingling of comfort, exasperation, counsel, and misgiving surely arose in the household during the summer around the young lady who not too many years previously had strutted from the nursery to the kitchen in order to show off her Latin declensions. Here she was now equipped with school publications, letters and certificates, and the Gilchrist Scholarship in Modern Languages at Somerville College, Oxford.

Coming up to Somerville in 1912, Dorothy would find herself, as a Scholar, obliged to take the degree course and to read for honors even though women students in Oxford were not yet admitted to degrees. This requirement at Somerville was a wise anticipatory regulation established by the Council of the College. From 1911 to 1920 it was almost compulsory at Somerville to qualify for the degree. As a consequence, when women were finally admitted, Dorothy was among the first to receive degrees from the University of Oxford.

Both Lady Margaret Hall, closely connected with the Church of England, and Somerville Hall (as it was first known), deliberately established "in favour of an undenominational foundation," had been opened in 1879. More than a dozen years of pioneer work on behalf of higher education for women had preceded this important event. This Hall was named in honor of the gifted mathematician Mary Somerville and adopted the arms and motto of her family as its seal. It became a college under the Companies Acts in 1881. In 1910, the university had established by statute a Delegacy for Women Students, including, of course, Somerville College.

Examination of women students above the age of eighteen started in 1875. In 1886 women students had been officially admitted to responsions; in 1888, to the Honour School of Literae Humaniores, or "Greats." By 1894, all the examinations qualifying for the B.A. degree had been opened to women. But it took another quarter of a century, until the final statute was brought forward in 1920 and passed convocation without opposition, before women were admitted to matriculation and graduation as full members of the university.

Behind this effort were such people as Mrs. Humphrey Ward, Professor and Mrs. T. H. Green, Professor Gilbert Murray, Arthur Sidgwick, and the first three principals of Somerville—Miss M. Shaw Lefevre (1879-1889), Miss A. C. Maitland (1889-1906), and Miss Emily Penrose (1907-1926).

> Somerville College was born . . . of enlightened ideas, and in particular of a progressive conception of woman, which clothed itself discreetly in the hereditary feminine garb of modest manners and watchful tact. To live at the gates of a venerable and conservative University, with support and encouragement from some of its most liberal members, was to be perpetually conscious both of deference due to ideas of the past and the beckoning promises of the future.

The number of College buildings had been augmented by the time of Dorothy's arrival. Maitland Hall, named for the previous principal, was opened with ceremonies on 4 October 1913, in her second year in residence. The library, erected in 1904, had received some outstanding acquisitions, among them the personal libraries of Mark Pattison and John Stuart Mill.[18]

Within a radial sweep of less than a mile to the south and east of Somerville stretched all the colleges (except St. Hugh's and Lady Margaret's), museums, libraries, and churches.

Immediately adjoining Somerville to the north, between Woodstock Road and Walton Street, was Radcliffe Infirmary.

Some patterns of life in college, to be sure, resembled school. The number of students in residence was about one hundred. Prayers were said daily. Students were required to consult the principal before accepting invitations from friends, and might not go to dances in Oxford during term. No student was allowed to be out of the college after dinner without leave. No girl was to bicycle alone; at least two must be together. No girl was to go to a lawn-tennis party on foot, because it was considered unseemly to be seen carrying a racket through the streets. (In earlier days, however, no girl could even attend lectures without a chaperone.) There was also a college song in resonant Latin which must be learned by heart. Everyone was addressed as *Miss* with the surname.

Even male undergraduates in Oxford, until well after World War I, were expressly forbidden to visit the bar or lounge of any hotel, public house, or restaurant; to play billiards before 1:00 P.M. or after 10:00 P.M.; to give dances at public rooms or to take part in public subscription dances; to loiter about the stage door of the theatre; to attend any public race-meeting; to take part in pigeon shooting, coursing, or similar sports; to take part in any game or amusement "which is scandalous or offensive"; to take any part in aviation; to smoke in public in academic dress; and so forth. How often the regulations were observed in the breach rather than in performance remains an incompletely told tale.

Many entering students were obliged in the early part of the century to attend "coachings" in order to pass responsions, once the most usual of several examinations admitting students taking the degree course to the university. Dorothy was coached by a Mr. Herbert May, who "lived in Wellington Square and gallantly thrust whole battalions of imperfectly trained recruits through the Hot Gates of Responsions." He lived

in a perpetual atmosphere of snuff. With this he refreshed himself all through his coachings; and I would not grudge him a single pinch of it, for his life must have been a hard one. So far as I know, he spent all his time with people like me. He was the indefatigable seagull, forever winging his way through the clanging rocks of Latin Prose and Greek Unseens with a fleet of dismal and inexperienced Argonauts thrashing the seas at his tail. A kindlier and more imperturbable man I never met.

She found it necessary to spend two terms under Mr. May's tutelage, pounding her way through the *Hecuba* and the *Alcestis;* "we coped with the *Aorist;* we mowed down under our feet that weedy growth of repulsive particles with which the Greek language is infected."[19]

Dorothy's tutor at Somerville was Mildred Katherine Pope (1892-1956), a former Somerville student and the recipient of a doctorate from the University of Paris. To Miss Pope, Dorothy dedicated her own translation of Thomas the Anglo-Norman's *Tristan in Brittany* in 1929, and in the acknowledgments prefacing her translation of *The Song of Roland,* published in the year of her own death, Dorothy wrote:

> My first debt of gratitude is, of course, to my old tutor, the late Mildred K. Pope, with whom I read the *Roland* at Oxford, and to whom I owe such Old French scholarship as I possess. Unhappily, she did not live to see this translation published, but she gave it every encouragement and much practical help.[20]

Miss Pope surely knew already from the scholarship examination how advanced her pupil was, and she would acquaint her with the requirements of the necessary examinations to follow, suggest a course of reading, recommend certain lectures to attend, and then establish a schedule for meeting in a series of tutorials.

Only brief references to Dorothy's reading appear: "I was reading French, and the Old French required for the Langauge Papers demanded a minimum acquaintance with the Latin roots, morphology, and syntax." One had "to take some great story—such as the story of Tristan and Iseult, which had given inspriation to many conscious artists—and trace it back to its primitive origins." This type of reading required sufficient critical stance to be able to free the "real story" from successive "accretions," and thus to identify the "purer."

> This was an entertaining game; but the most curious part of it was that, invariably, by the time one had arrived at the "oldest and purest" form of the story, the story had somehow ceased to be great. "In its oldest and purest form," we said in our Oxford essays, *"Tristan and Iseult* is one of the many 'marriage-by-capture' legends in which Celtic folk-lore abounds." Quite so: but what has now become of the strange power and poignancy that have made of that story one of the great stories of the world? The greatness and the power were not in the story, but in the imagination and the conscious art of the poets who made it their own.[21]

She also recorded that, when presented by the Schools examiners at the end of her course of study with a sonnet to render into English, she was "tackled at the viva about a miserable sprig of rue that had crept into the rhyme in place of heliotrope, and was obliged to confess with blushes that it was the only plant that fitted the rhyme." The examiners shook their heads, but forgave her. (Even at Godolphin and during the scholarship examination she had shown discontent in simply translating a poem: she felt compelled to render the translation in strict poetic form, thus occasionally jeopardizing accuracy for effect.)[22]

Dorothy does not refer to the outstanding Oxford figures of her day. There is no published Sayers recollection of the Regius Professor of Greek, Gilbert Murray; of the Rawlinson and Bosworth Professor of Anglo-Saxon, Arthur Sampson Napier (who was simultaneously a Merton Professor of English Literature); of Walter Alexander Raleigh; of David Nicoll Smith. She *does* pay tribute to Alfred Denis Godley, the Public Orator, a Fellow of Magdalen, as the author of a "noble poem" which begins:

> What is it that roareth thus?
> Can it be a motor-bus?
> Yes! The reek and hideous hum
> *Indicant motorem bum.*[23]

There were, of course, sufficient academic matters to occupy Dorothy's attention. She *was* a Scholar. And one of the published regulations of Somerville was that "Any student may be required to withdraw whose residence whether for want of industry or other reasons, is, in the opinion of the Principal, no longer desirable."[24]

During summer vacations she welcomed classmates in Bluntisham. Dorothy Hanbury Rowe remembers being entertained there and, in return, greeting Dorothy at the Rowe home, St. Anne's, in Bournemouth.

The advent of World War I thrust troubled dimensions upon the lives of all Oxford students. On the one hand, the policies of Herbert Asquith and David Lloyd George stood for sweeping measures aimed at social betterment. Laws dealing with workmen's compensation, national insurance, and minimum wages were passed by Parliament. The agitation for Home

Rule at that time in Ireland created an ambivalent presentiment of future discontent and disaster. There was, moreover, an epidemic of strikes in 1911-12, the most distressing of which were the transport workers', the railwaymen's, and the miners'. International relations were deteriorating, under murkiness of policy, until the assassination of the Austrian Archduke Francis Ferdinand at Serajevo in June 1914 finally plunged Europe into war.

Dorothy's experience indicates that the lot of the young single woman in England during World War I could be relatively immune from distress. Her first volume of verse, which appeared in the very midst of the war in 1916 after she had left Oxford, contains a singularly undiscerning dedication ("To the Stage-Manager of 'Admiral Guinea,' the Conductor of the Bach Choir, and the Members of the Mutual Admiration Society"), and the poems themselves reveal no awareness beyond her fairly sheltered life in Oxford. The second volume of her verse, published in 1918, also shows an individual insulated from the larger world. It is the utterance of a provincial girl largely protected against contemporaneity.[25]

Not that all undergraduate women at Oxford were alike. Vera Brittain, for example, who entered Somerville in 1914, shows increasing concern over the advance of the war and a poignant sense of involvement. But then she had an only brother and a highly talented young gentleman friend who both had entered training and were to die on foreign soil before the war's end. Vera Brittain joined the War and Peace Society. Yet even so, the excitement of being an Oxford student tended to diminish for her also, for a while, the significance of nations at war.[26]

The involvement of Oxford male undergraduates in the war was another matter. C. S. Lewis, who later was to become one of Dorothy's friends, went to Oxford late in the winter term 1916 to take his scholarship examination. He wrote:

> Boys who have faced this ordeal in peace-time will not easily imagine the indifference with which I went. This does not mean that I under-estimated the importance (in one sense) of succeeding. . . . What blunted the edge of it now was that whether I won a scholarship or no I should next year go into the army; and even a temper more sanguine than mine could feel in 1916 that an infantry subaltern would be insane to waste anxiety on anything so hypothetical as his post-war life.[27]

Increasingly, moreover, with the development of the war, the men's colleges saw fewer and fewer undergraduates (and fewer young tutors), and more and more conversion of quarters into hospitals under the direction of the Royal Army Medical Corps.

Dorothy had by temperament and training a sense of detachment which had not yet matured into discrimination. She was as yet only an observer touched with a degree of flamboyancy. Vera Brittain recorded in her diary when she entered Somerville that "There are . . . two classes of second and third-year people, (1) those who thoroughly examine every atom of you, (2) those who do not look at you at all; and appear perfectly oblivious of your presence even if you get in their way."

> I took an immediate liking to Dorothy Sayers, who was affable to freshers and belonged to the "examine-every-atom-of-you" type. A bouncing, exuberant young female who always seemed to be preparing for tea-parties, she could be seen at almost any hour of the day or night scuttling about the top floor of the new Maitland building with a kettle in her hand and a little checked apron fastened over her skirt.

Vera Brittain, however, knew nothing about Dorothy's Godolphin days. How could she sense anything beyond the bizarre, therefore, when she remarked that Dorothy's "thin, straight dark hair became an excuse for extravagant indoor head-gear, which varied from shrill colours by day to gold or silver by night"?[28]

Charis Frankenburg (née Barnett) was also one of Dorothy's Somerville friends. Charis, Margaret Chubb, Amphilis Middlemore, Dorothy Rowe, and Dorothy Sayers—all 1912 freshmen—arranged weekly meetings throughout their university years in order to read aloud their literary efforts and to subject their work to one another's criticism. Naming themselves "The Mutual Admiration Society," they adopted a motto: "The best of what we do and are, Just God forgive." Mrs. Frankenburg has written that it was Dorothy Sayers who gave the group its name, saying "if we didn't . . . , the rest of College would." One of the items Dorothy read to the M.A.S. was a conversation of the Magi, and to Charis it became her "most interesting recollection . . . , an anticipation of *The Man Born to Be King.*"[29]

Was it flamboyancy that led to the eccentricity remembered by another contemporary and friend? Vera Farnell recalls that Dorothy

> appeared at breakfast one morning, previous to an early lecture at the Taylorian, wearing a three-inch-wide scarlet riband round her head and in her ears a really remarkable pair of ear-rings: a scarlet and green parrot in a gilt cage pendant almost to each shoulder and visible right across the hall. Miss Penrose, shocked, but ever mindful of the rights and liberties of the individual student, was loth to abuse her authority by direct interference, but deputed to me, as a fellow student of D.L.S., the delicate task of effecting the removal of the offending bedizenment by gentle persuasion.[30]

It may very likely have been such well-meaning restraint upon her individuality that later led Dorothy Sayers upon occasion to favor attire which was bound to excite comment.

Vera Brittain had the distinct impression that Dorothy "dominated her group at college" and "made the most lasting impression both on her contemporaries and on the outside world" of Somerville students in the years immediately preceding World War I. She detected a bit of *Schwärmerei* and a good sense of humor in Dorothy. A member of the Bach Choir, singing with the altos, Dorothy had an "unconcealed passion" for Dr. (later, Sir Hugh) Allen, the director, that was "a standing joke in college."

> During the practices of the Verdi Requiem, which we were preparing to sing in the Easter term, she sat among the mezzo-contraltos and gazed at him with wide, adoring eyes as though she were in church worshipping her only God. But a realistic sense of humour saved her from becoming ridiculous, and at the Going-Down Play given by her Year the following summer, she caricatured her idol with triumphant accuracy and zest.[31]

Amateur theatricals "had a permanent place in college life." Dorothy was ready and eager to participate. In February 1913 the entering students had been entertained by *Hamlet, the Pragger-Dagger* ("Pragger-Wagger" was contemporary slang for the Prince of Wales), and the skit employed Shakespearean phrases in topical allusions to a case of measles in college. It "elicited such loud and prolonged explosions of laughter" that the cast had to repeat the performance before the whole college.[32]

In December 1913, the Second Year offered W. E. Henley and Robert Louis Stevenson's *Admiral Guinea* and Granville Barker and Laurence Housman's *Prunella*. Dorothy played the role of John Gaunt in the former and frequently signed herself "J. G." in letters to her classmates—especially to Dorothy Rowe, who had been stage manager of the production.

The Going-Down Play, "produced by the Third Year in the exuberance of having completed Schools," was constructed again on local and topical allusions.[33] Entitled *Pied Pipings, or the Innocents Abroad,* it was presented in Skimmery Quad, Oriel College, because Somerville had been evacuated to make room for increased convalescents, an overflow from adjoining Radcliffe Infirmary. Dorothy Rowe was the director, and Dorothy Sayers enacted the leading role, Dr. H. P. Rallentando. She not only caught the pose of Dr. Hugh Allen (preserved in a photograph) but also some of his phrases:

> My good women, what kind of a noise do you call that? I want a beautiful, round, golden sound, like a poached egg for Schools People, and you make it exactly like College coffee at nine o'clock in the morning. Now! Two bars before you come in.

Gilbert and Sullivan tunes were appropriated, the girls composing pertinent lyrics. Dorothy good-naturedly allowed herself to be satirized for her energetic work as bicycle secretary:

> It's well to be methodical where culprits are concerned,
> So I've made a little list, I've made a little list
> Of members of this commonwealth who ought to be interned
> And who never would be missed, who never would be missed,
> The brutes who borrow bicycles without the owners' leave,
> Who get their own in pound and come and ask for a reprieve.

It was all great fun while it lasted.

She was generous enough to become involved in another sort of college activity, no matter what she later said about her motivation:

> In my Oxford days a bunch of Somerville charitables used to go round on Sunday afternoons and sing hymns to the sick at the Radcliffe Infirmary. One day they roped me in—I wasn't charitable, but I could sing alto. We sang all the cheerful and comforting hymns we could think of, and then, having some minutes to spare, asked the patients to choose some hymns for themselves. Their first choice was "A few more years shall roll", and the second was like unto it, namely, "Within the churchyard side by side".

She claimed that this experience taught her "all simple minds love gloom." She also passed judgment: "Since then I have been chary of considering what people may reasonably be expected to like, and have contented myself with observing

19

what they do, in fact, like; after which I please myself about giving or withholding it."[34]

In Trinity Term 1915 Dorothy's work at Somerville was completed. She received Class I Honors in French and, of course, the Degree Course Certificate, which was the then-equivalent for women to the university's Bachelor of Arts degree.

What Dorothy Sayers received intellectually from Oxford was more than the exhilaration of living in a community of scholars with ancient and revered tradition. Of greater importance was the total impact of discipline and of scholarly judgment, as she was to describe it twenty years later. "The integrity of mind that money cannot buy; the humility in face of the facts that self-esteem cannot corrupt: these are the fruits of scholarship, without which all statement is propaganda and all argument special pleading."[35]

She has also spoken—but in a different tone—about the "social wisdom" she acquired at Oxford.

> When I lived in Academe I should never have thought of going to one of its guardians for advice in any social difficulty. I should have feared, not unkindness or unwillingness to help, but just blank want of knowledge. "This kind of thing never happened to me," says the guide, philosopher, and friend; "to a nice girl social difficulties do not occur." That is a cowardly lie. Things do happen; it is monstrous to pretend that they do not or ought not.

She winced at the remembrance that at one time during her undergraduate years she could not look on a man reasonably "as a human being" but only as a "cataclysm of nature." No one had helped prepare her at that point, not even her favorite authors, to know, as she later said, that "love is in itself a passion which sooner seizes upon the heart than one is aware." No one had enabled her to realize that the man "leaves college still a lad"; the girl, when she goes down, is already a woman, and (with poignant allusion to her own imminent lot after Oxford)

> if she is still socially ignorant it is late for her to begin learning. If she goes straight to the cloister of a girls' school she never will begin; she will return perhaps later to a position of trust in Academe, as ignorant as a child, and hampered to boot by an intellectual acquaintance with the names of things which spoils her for the lessons of experience.

Coeducation, she maintained, did not mean sitting side by side with a male at the same lecture. Nor can a college woman "grow wise in an atmosphere in which going to tea with a youth ranks as a thrilling dissipation, and inviting the same man twice in a term is considered too desperately exciting for all concerned." It must be clear that when Dorothy spoke of "social wisdom" she meant "sexual wisdom." "It cannot be an accident," she wrote, "that the conversation of all my friends revolves so unerringly about one only[sic] subject."

> Flirtation was once a dignified and delicate affair, like whist; now it is more like poker. . . . We have advanced indeed so far that it is no longer considered indecent to understand Love (which we now call Sex), but only to enjoy it.[36]

Whatever may have been her reservations, Dorothy loved Oxford: "I that am twice thy child have known thee, worshipped thee, loved thee." She would return many times. Although she had now completed her work, she could not easily forswear her attachment. She composed a poem on going down and sent handwritten copies to her college friends:

> Now that we have gone down—have all gone down,
>   I would not hold too closely to the past,
>   Till it become my staff, or even at last
> My crutch, and I be made a helpless clown.
>
> All men must walk alone, not drowse, nor drown
>   Their wits, with spells of dead things overcast,
> Now that we have gone down, have all gone down,
>   I would not hold too closely to the past.
>
> Therefore, God love thee, thou enchanted town,
>   God love thee, leave me, clutch me not so fast;
>   Lest, clinging blindly we but grope aghast,
> Sweet friends, go hence and seek your own renown,
> Now that we have all gone down—have all gone down.[37]

Dorothy returned to Bluntisham after completing her work at Somerville. The almost inevitable consequence of such a formal education as she had acquired was an academic post of some sort, but the opportunity did not immediately arise. She read voraciously. She wrote poems. On 8 October 1915 she wrote from Bluntisham Rectory to her friend Dorothy Rowe, who had already started to teach English in Bournemouth High School.

> I have been meaning for days to write and tell you how I got on in London, but like a procrastinating ass I kept putting it off, & writing you out poems instead, which I am now sending. It is a bulky package, but you are not to feel bound either to read or to admire them. The rondeaux

especially are the merest technical exercises in most cases—trying different shapes and models with different lengths of line & arrangements of
rime & refrain— none original, as you will see. They are the sort of things
one either tears up when done, or keeps filed for reference in an alphabeti-
cal list. The last poem "Matter of Brittany" was written merely for
enjoyment. I thought I was tired of "Oxfords" & "Alma Maters" & "Going-
downs" & "To a Leader of Men's' " & things that meant a powerful lot, &
terseness & pregnancy & dignity & so on, so I thought I'd just revel a bit in
the dear old obvious glories of scarlet cloaks & dragons & Otherworld
Journeys, & in the clank and gurgle of alliteration, & the gorgeousness of
proper names. So you are to read it in this spirit, please, if possible at night
& by the fire.

She included in her letter an account of the trip to London,
where she had stayed with Charis Barnett. The trip had been
postponed longer than she had anticipated "because of a
violent cold." She stayed with Charis two nights, spending
part of the daytime shopping for a coat, skirt, and hat about
which she happily writes details.

I got my coat & skirt. . . . It is all black, with a short front & long straight
back to the coat & high collar; the skirt is simply fascinating—band, &
deep hip-yoke, & wide skirt with two most attractive little pleats in front &
full pleats at the back. . . . Then we bought a black velvet hat at Whiteleys
for 7/—a pink rose for eighteen pence, & Hilda did the trimming in a most
fetching manner.

The shopping tour provided Dorothy's first trip down an
escalator. She was fascinated until an old lady suddenly
pushed violently past her from behind, muttering, "I must get
down this thing quickly—I'm always sick if I don't." The
incident was at the time a bit disconcerting, but afterwards it
became a source of chuckling amusement. She even sketched
the old lady in action at the bottom of her letter.

She had managed also to talk with her friends late into the
nights: "we all lay on the floor, round a gas-stove with no gas
in it for fear of Zepps; & the eider-downs & pillows all over us,
. . . & pretended we were at college." Every odd minute during
the trip and throughout the time in London she had devoted to
reading Compton Mackenzie's *Sinister Street, Part II,* a novel
with an Oxford episode, published in 1913 and 1914. This, she
boasted, was "rather an achievement," considering the short
time involved. She invited Dorothy Rowe's comments on the
book by offering her own:

Isn't the Oxford part good? It is tremendously real—I do hate a book which
makes you feel the man's only read up Oxford in guidebooks, but whatever

one may think of the story or the style, it's so obvious that Compton M. has been there & knows it all through and through. I simply *love* the account of Michael's first day, & how he daren't call the scout, & tries to get information indirectly with a splendid carelessness. I don't like the last part so well—I get dreadfully sick of Lily—I always did—& I can't bear Stella. Further, I must say I find Michael a most interesting youth. But it's a wonderfully clever book. I only wish he wouldn't deal in adjectives like "fulaginous" & "immotionable".

Back in Bluntisham, Dorothy agreed to go with three other girls to the hospital in St. Ives to give a concert for the soldiers. She and one girl dressed as pierrots in black; the other two girls were pierrettes in white. "My genius for make-up," she wrote, "asserted itself again—I've got the regular Pierrot pointed chin, & with powder & scarlet lips & two black patches looked truly fetching." New clothes or an exotic costume gave her bubbling self-confidence. She still needed reassurance over the ordeal of those final Godolphin days. As for the hospital concert, she thoroughly enjoyed singing with her friends for the soldiers in St. Ives.

There was also a joyous bit of news about the future:

> Vera Farnell has just asked me to go up to Oxford on the 16th to help her with the library. Isn't it jolly? I shall be staying in college free of charge—& I hope I may be able to extend my visit among friends. I'm so awfully glad in one way that it is at the beginning of term, because I shall be able to settle Jim [Muriel Jaeger] in, who will be feeling a bit stranded, I expect, poor darling. Of course, if I had been arranging for myself, I should have preferred to go in, say, November, for one or two reasons, but it is so lovely to be able to stay in college for nothing!—I suppose that date is quite impossible for you to run up? I do so want to see you some time, but I suppose they are still keeping your nose to the grindstone là-bas.[38]

Two of the poems Dorothy wrote out for her friend were to appear in *Op. I* in 1916. For all her lighthearted disparagement of the poems, she was eager to publish them in due time.

A teaching position finally became available. She accepted an appointment at Hull High School for Girls. The school was housed at that time on Park Street (the school later moved to Tranby Croft). Her first assignment was to teach French.

Her teaching stint started with the autumn term of 1916 and was completed in July of 1917. In 1947 in Oxford, when she was speaking at a Vacation Course in Education, she facetiously made reference to the Hull experience:

> That I, whose experience of teaching is extremely limited, and whose life of recent years has been almost wholly out of touch with educational circles, should presume to discuss education is a matter, surely, that calls for no apology. It is a kind of behaviour to which the present climate of opinion is wholly favourable. Bishops air their opinions about economics; biologists, about metaphysics; celibates, about matrimony; inorganic chemists, about theology; the most irrelevant people are appointed to highly-technical [sic] ministries; and plain, blunt men write to the paper to say that Epstein and Picasso do not know how to draw.[39]

Again, in 1952, when she was speaking to a group of Latin teachers, she touched upon her teaching experience:

> And I remember, too, in my own school-teaching days, being confronted by a class of girls of fifteen or sixteen, who had to have some German pumped into them for an exam. They had done French in the ordinary way, but now had to offer a second language. I remember saying—stupidly and without thinking, for I was still young—"No, you can't say, 'Ich bin gegeben ein Buch'—'I have been given' isn't a true Passive." I remember their bewildered faces. And I remember realising that we had come to the Wood where things have no Names, and that everything would have to be laboriously thought out and explained from the very beginning. And they hadn't got much time.[40]

Whatever may have been the cause, Dorothy, however, turned aside from a classroom career in Hull. Conjecture prompts many possible reasons: administrative demeanor, personnel conflicts, odium of assignment, frustration or failure, cultural isolation, wartime atmosphere. She certainly considered the experience an unsatisfactory spell. Many years later, when she was writing weekly book reviews for the *Sunday Times,* she made a striking comment about teaching in private schools. It has the ring of personal witness:

> For some reason, nearly all school murder stories are good ones— probably because it is so easy to believe that murder could be committed in such a place. I do not mean this statement to be funny or sarcastic: nobody who has not taught in a school can possibly realise the state of nervous tension and mutual irritation that can glow up among the members of the staff at the end of a trying term, or the utter spiritual misery that a bad head can inflict upon his or her subordinates.

Sad to say, one of her own Hull students had overheard her saying, "I would rather sweep the streets than teach children!"[41]

After one year of teaching, for the third time Dorothy settled in Oxford, this time on Long Wall Street, where she lived on a meager income she earned as a reader for Basil Blackwell, the author, publisher, and bookseller. Her tasks were varied: she may have criticized submitted manuscripts; she probably did some proofreading; she certainly assisted in editing *Oxford Poetry* for the years 1917, 1918, and 1919.

It was in the autumn of 1917 that Doreen Wallace, then a Somerville student, met Dorothy. "Long and slim in those days"—Dorothy was five-feet, seven-inches tall—"small head held alert on slender neck, she loped round Oxford looking for fun." She would go "singing, springing down the Broad." The spectacled, blue-eyed young lady took "long elastic strides." She wore black frocks most of the time: that was practical. On one of them she appliquéd a Tudor rose of Doreen Wallace's design. However lonely and frustrated in the past, and whatever the slim promise of the present, Dorothy set out to make Oxford her demesne of joy. The walls and spires and bells of the colleges were a delight. Here she was a citizen in the world of learning and love of learning. She read, she wrote, she taught herself to play a wind instrument. She rejoined the Bach Choir. She learned a great deal about ancient music.

"I have never known anyone so brimful of the energy of a well-stocked mind: even at 24, when I first knew her," wrote Doreen Wallace, "she knew an enormous amount about all sorts of subjects unconnected with Old French literature, which was her alleged 'special', and nothing would content her but fact." The tone of her voice supported this reading of her character: it was "loud, clear and positive. Everything she said was a statement, almost an edict."[42]

Dorothy worked seriously during this period at becoming a poet, along with numerous other Oxford graduates and undergraduates. Her first volume, *Op. I,* had appeared late in the spring of 1916 while she was still at Hull. Published by Blackwell, it was Number 9 in the Adventurers All Series. Earlier young poets "unknown to fame" in the series included Wilfrid Rowland Childe, Elizabeth Rendall, Esther Lilian Duff, T. W. Earp, Frank Betts, Sherard Vines, Aldous Huxley, and Stephen Reid-Heymann.

The fifteen poems contained in *Op. I* are an early random harvest. Four of the poems had appeared previously, two of them ("Hymn in Contemplation of Sudden Death" and "Epitaph for a Young Musician") in *Oxford Magazine;* one ("Matter of Brittany") in the *Fritillary,* a magazine of Oxford women students; and one ("Lay") in *Oxford Poetry 1915*. (Two other early poems should be noted, both published in the *Oxford Magazine* in 1916 but not included in her collections: "To the Members of the Bach Choir on Active Service," 18 February 1916; "Icarus," from the French of Philippe Desportes, 5 May 1916.)[43]

There is a peripheral fussiness in the book. The dedication (to which attention has already been called) is girlish. There are epigraphs preceding two of the poems ("Alma Mater" and "Lay"), one in German and one in French, which are mere ornament, not at all essential to the matter of the respective poems.

The poems do show metrical and imagistic dexterity, but the majority of the lines are thin in thematic strength. They show her still partially wrapped up in a private world of French medieval romance—"the dear old obvious glories of scarlet cloaks & dragons & Otherworld Journeys." Nostalgia is prominent. In "The Last Castle," which is full of Oxford reminiscences, she aptly describes her own mood: "Those songs of ours were so fantastical / They held faint presage of the time at hand." Although she alludes to the war in one short section of the poem, she romanticizes and generalizes: "No sorrow can displace / The ordered beauty" of Oxford's face; the soldiers are only "lost lovers," and Oxford—like Iseult "looking oversea"—is "Straining to Tristram hard bested in far-off Brittany." She was not the only person, however, who later in life looked back upon youth as a series of separate music rooms, each with its own "private harmonies."[44]

Dorothy not only assisted in editing *Oxford Poetry* for the years 1917, 1918, and 1919, but she also contributed to each volume herself. Other contents were submitted by students from many of the colleges. (Some of the earliest work, for example, of Vera Brittain, Muriel St. Clare Byrne, Robert Graves, Aldous Huxley, and J. R. R. Tolkien appears in these volumes.) What Gilbert Murray wrote in the introduction to the one-volume edition of *Oxford Poetry* for the years 1910-1913 still applied later in the decade. He had noted that the poetry was widely varied in its themes: local poems, poems with a touch of classicism, poems "with a rather strong note of ecclesiasticism," poems of "extraordinary skilful parody and superingenious tricks of versification." While many of the writers were well read, "in touch with almost all the moving impulses of contemporary poetry," there were some—including the writers "of the most beautiful and delicate work"—who "with that curious negative strength that often lurks in delicate things" resisted "the main currents altogether."[45]

The poem submitted by Dorothy to the 1917 volume is entitled "Fair Erembours." It is a romantic ballad characteristic of twelfth-century French verse; it is also an ingenious expression of her own romantic longings. The six-stanza poem concludes:

> O then Count Reynault up by the stairs ran,
> Wide were his shoulders, and small his girdle's span,
> His hair close-curled, and very fair to scan,
> In all the world is not so fine a man.
> Erembours saw him, and so to weep began.
> Ha, Reynault, ha, true love!
>
> Count Reynault mounts into her highest towers
> And sets him on a bed of broidered flowers,
> And close beside him sits fair Erembours.
> Then they take up their loves of former hours,
> Ha, Reynault, ha, true love![46]

The poem by Dorothy which appears in the 1918 volume is entitled "Pygmalion."[47] Such writers as Ovid, John Marston, William Morris, W. S. Gilbert, and George Bernard Shaw had told the story of Pygmalion and Galatea previously—erotically or humorously or allegorically. Dorothy wrote an elegy on the death of Galatea. The creature who was cold marble, and into whom the gods breathed life, became again—to her lover's irreparable loss—as cold as stone.

In *Oxford Poetry 1919,* three of Dorothy's poems were published. "For Phaon" is another personal romantic statement, for all its stance as a dramatic monologue attributed to Sappho.

> Why do you come to the poet, to the heart of iron and fire,
> Seeking soft raiment and the small things of desire,
> Looking for light kisses from lips bowed to sing?
> Less than myself I give not, and am *I* a little thing?
> . . . .
> The insolent new nations shall rise and read, and know
> What a little, little lord you were, because I loved you so.[48]

"Sympathy," ironic in tone, sets forth levels of awareness between friends or lovers. One may be conscious of physical appearance, setting, conversation, sounds, and also the voice of the interpreter, who remembers the past, who distinguishes the truth, who sits in judgment. It is a poem lovely in its texture and imagery.[49] The third poem, "Vials Full of Odours," is frankly sensuous, and was surely created under the impulse of a new love:

> The hawthorn brave upon the green
> She hath a drooping smell and sad,
> But God put scent into the bean
> To drive each lass unto her lad.
>
> And woe betide the weary hour,
> For my love is in Normandy,
> And oh! the scent of the bean-flower
> Is like a burning fire in me.
>
> Fair fall the lusty thorn,
> She hath no curses at my hand,
> But would the man were never born
> That sowed the bean along his land![50]

Eric Whelpton was the man Dorothy Sayers met in 1918, and she fell in love with him. He had started his university work at Hertford College in the autumn of 1912 but left to join the Berkshire Territorials after the outbreak of World War I. He was transferred to a home service battalion employed for coastal defense but was released from the service because of ill health in September 1916. In the spring of 1918 he returned to Oxford, thin and weak, having suffered from polio. He found some "remarkable women" at Oxford, including Dorothy Leigh Sayers.

> Strictly speaking, she was far from beautiful, but her grey [sic] eyes radiated intelligence, her mobile features vividly expressed her thoughts and her emotions, and her voice, though rather high pitched, was a pleasant one. She usually wore black, but was given to large pendulous earrings and exotic strings of beads. From the first, her manner to me was protective and almost maternal. . . .

A few weeks after his return to Oxford, Whelpton moved to "the gabled house" at the bottom of Bath Place, which is off Holywell Street. "After a while," he writes, "Dorothy Sayers moved into rooms on the first floor, but we seldom visited each other, though we met very frequently at coffee parties which I could still find fairly entertaining because of the talk about books which I had not yet read."[51]

Like Dorothy, Whelpton was a child of a clergyman, although his father was a member of the nonconformist clergy. Born in France, associated with the Haute Société Protestant, bilingual, the product of a privileged education, widely traveled, handsome in appearance, an Oxford student, a war veteran with the rank of captain—he would have been especially attractive to Dorothy on many counts. He left Oxford in February 1919, unable to endure in his debilitated condition "the rigours of winter," and before spring had passed found employment in the Ecole des Roches near Verneuil in Normandy. There is no doubt that Dorothy regretted his departure. It is surely of Whelpton that she wrote in "Vials Full of Odours"—"woe betide the weary hour, / For my love is in Normandy. . . ."

Before the year was over, Dorothy and Whelpton were to meet again. But for the rest of the winter of 1919 and during the spring and early summer she had only poetry.

In April 1918 one of her poems was published in G. K. Chesterton's *New Witness*.[52] The poem is "Rex Doloris," and it was reprinted in her second volume of poetry, *Catholic Tales and Christian Songs,* published by Blackwell in September 1918. The title of the collection was appropriated from some lines by Hilaire Belloc, which are reprinted on the verso of the title page. (Interestingly, as an Oxford undergraduate Belloc occupied the very rooms in which Whelpton resided on Bath Place.) This surface relationship of Dorothy with Chesterton and Belloc suggests her affinity with the vestiges of the Oxford Movement current in her day; so also does the tone of the poems in the collection. Her interests in the tradition, however, were theological and devotional, rather than ecclesiastical.

The volume of poetry is unified, not because the poems are all topically religious but by virtue of their sustained hortatory and devotional quality. Over half of the twenty-five poems in *Catholic Tales and Christian Songs* follow epigraphs which in almost every case are Biblical phrases or adaptations. Such an apparatus implies the documentation of the idea, mood, or direction explicated in the poem. The contents of the poems, of course, chiefly exhibit the hortatory aspect. They represent stylistic and thematic reminiscences of Dorothy's reading of John Donne, George Herbert, Robert Browning, and Francis

Thompson. Dorothy demonstrated control of various metrical patterns, imagery, and nuances of diction in these poems.

The volume shows, however, that she resisted what Gilbert Murray referred to as "the main currents" of poetry. This was the same period that "Prufrock," "The Wild Swans at Coole," *Eminent Victorians,* and *Exiles* appeared. The *Times Literary Supplement* reviewer's judgment of *Catholic Tales* is understandable: "These pieces reproduce in graceful religious fantasies the childlike spirit and familiar intimacy with Christ characteristic of the Middle Ages."[53]

Dorothy was also responsible for contributions, primarily in verse, to the first two volumes of *The New Decameron* (1919, 1920), published by Blackwell. It has been claimed that she also wrote "The Prologue" to Volume I. Hers is the first tale, "The Journeyman," a poem very much in the style of the poems in *Catholic Tales.* In Volume II her contribution is "The Master-Thief," also in ballad form. There is nothing remarkable about the two narrative poems in this work except that her contributions were the only ones in verse (other contributors were Storm-Jameson, Basil Blackwell, Sherard Vines, Michael Sadler, and Doreen Wallace). Both poems were assigned to the Priest, one of the touring members in the group whose stories compose *The New Decameron.*[54]

Not all her postgraduate days in Oxford were devoted strictly to poetry. In the *Oxford Outlook* for June 1919 appeared an essay by Dorothy entitled "Eros in Academe." The title is more provocative than the text. The article opens with a certain amount of fustian suggestive of the *Heptameron* and reminiscent of the beginning of Dryden's *Essay of Dramatick Poesie.* The gist of the work is that Academe, strong on idealism and weak on pragmatism, is devoid of counsel in the prepossessing matters of the heart. This theme surely arose from Dorothy's own amorous needs.

It must be obvious that Dorothy in 1918-19 was struggling to serve two masters. Despite a religiously oriented background and education, she had nonetheless realized the promises of physical sensuality. Her conflict between love for the Son of man and love of a man, however, remained unresolved. In 1939, on the eve of World War II, it was still vivid in her memory when she wrote:

It is over twenty years since I first read the words, in some forgotten book. I remember neither the name of the author, nor that of the saint from whose meditations he was quoting. Only the statement itself has survived the accident of transmission: '*Cibus sum grandium; cresce, et manducabis Me*'— "I am the food of the full-grown; become a man, and Thou shalt feed on me."

... I am glad to think, *now,* that it impressed me so forcibly *then,* when I was still comparatively young. To protest, when one has left one's youth behind, against the prevalent assumption that there is no salvation for the middle-aged is all very well; but it is apt to provoke the mocking reference to the fox who lost his tail.

Editorializing in 1939 does not hide the distant fact of crisis. Nor do the professed lapses of memory. The "accident" of transmission also conveys the same thing. She has attempted to screen out the context. She subsequently— in 1947—identified the saint as Augustine and the meditation as *The Confessions.*[55] What obviously impressed her in the saint's meditation was the challenge to grow and the promise of fulfillment.

But the challenge to grow and to be fulfilled is ambiguous. Was Dorothy Leigh Sayers as single-minded in her spirituality in 1919 as she may have been in 1939? Like Augustine, Dorothy procrastinated. *Nondum amabam, et amare amabam.*

The insulation of the first nineteen years of her life had inevitably produced introspection. Personal relationships, outside her family center, had been largely filtered through her absorption in literature. She had succeeded in molding a mask of romanticism which mocked her in its ineffectiveness. The Oxford years—and even the year at Hull—did not wholly disenchant her. She resorted to the prudential power of Oxford women, maintaining "modest manners and watchful tact." She had learned, also, to preserve reticence about personal affairs.

There were surface diversions. She shared with friends like Eleonora Geach, Enid Starkie, Doreen Wallace, Philip Baillie-Reynolds, and Martin Carré an interest in amateur dramatics. There was the Rhyme Club: one member offered a line of verse, another was given "one minute to produce the rhyming line, no matter whether sense or nonsense," and Doreen Wallace would illustrate the result as quickly. (Visitors to the Rhyme Club included, on at least one occasion, Siegfried Sassoon, and, on another, Osbert and Sacheverel Sitwell, in uniform: "but they were silent and aloof, having then no heart for nonsense.") There were parties in which each person had, in turn, to add details to an original situation, thus building a story. (In February 1934, Dorothy told a *Daily Express* reporter that her first novel, *Whose Body?,* grew out of such a party-game: "It was Miss Sayers who suggested the finding of a naked unknown corpse in a bath.") There were also "coffee parties." Eric Whelpton enjoyed them with her, the Sitwells, Aldous Huxley, Doreen Wallace, T. W. Earp, Vera Brittain, Winifred Holtby, and Margaret Irwin as prominent conversationalists.[56]

Not all the young men whom she met in Oxford during the last years of the war were, to be sure, like Sassoon and the Sitwells—"silent and aloof," having "no heart for nonsense." Probably after reading Dorothy's article "Eros in Academe," Leonard Green, himself an Oxford alumnus and author, was prompted in summer 1919 to write to her requesting a contribution to his projected volume on assorted friendships. She certainly knew about *his* attitudes; Blackwell had published Green's *Dream Comrades and Other Prose Sketches* (1916) and *The Youthful Lover and Other Prose Studies* (1919). From Christchurch, in the Fen district, she was to note in a postscript to Green on the eve of her departure for France in the autumn of 1919:

> Dr. Bradford, who wrote "Passing the Love of Women" & "The New Chivalry", is a sort of neighbour of ours, & says he knows your books & has corresponded with you. He's an entertaining little crank—& rather a dear—but he can't write poetry, can he? I had an awful time trying to tell polite lies— I can't lie about verse![57]

During 1917, Dorothy's father had been assigned to another parish. The new parish was Christchurch, near Upwell on the Nene, in the diocese of Cambridge. Although the church and vicarage were smaller than those of the former parish, both were commodious. The actual distance between the two parishes was only seventeen miles, Christchurch lying to the northeast of Bluntisham.

It was to the vicarage in Christchurch that Eric Whelpton came during the summer of 1919 to be inspected by Dorothy's parents. Whelpton had been given authority by M. Berthier, headmaster of the Ecole des Roches, to engage a bilingual secretary in England in order to assist in founding "an office for educational exchanges of school children, students, and teachers between different countries." Whelpton immediately thought of Dorothy and decided to ask her to join him "in creating a suitable organisation." But first there had to be a visit to the vicarage.[58]

Encouraged by the reminiscences of Doreen Wallace (who had also been attracted to Whelpton), Janet Hitchman characterizes Dorothy at this time as "the plain, intense woman throwing herself at an uninterested man." She asserts that Dorothy was even "blatant and persistent" in pursuing Whelpton, carrying him out of Doreen's orbit.[59] Intense Dorothy may have been, but a portrait photograph taken in 1915 belies any plainness. And uninterested Eric Whelpton may have been, although there is room for doubt. "I did not know," he wrote much later, "that she was in love with me when I engaged her to work for me." Are there implications, however, in what he writes about his visit to Christchurch?

> Needless to say, we dressed for an excellent dinner of five courses and Dorothy wore an evening frock to display her bare arms which were slim and well-shaped. Mr. Sayers looked at me with suspicion at first, but calmed down when I told him that his daughter would not be in the same house as myself, and that we were not likely to meet very often out of office hours, and that anyway my affections were engaged already.[60]

Also needless to say, Dorothy was ready to accept the appointment.

She was twenty-six in 1919. Whatever may have been the reactions to her exuberant personality among people she had come to know in Oxford, she had a first-class mind, a commendable independence of spirit, and an ability to use words discreetly. She wrote to Leonard Green from Christchurch on 29 August 1919:

> I have just received your prospectus & appealing letter—being at home for the moment, just before starting for France to be Secretary to the enclosed, which, in your Schoolmastering capacity (you are one, now, aren't you?) may interest you.
> As regards "Friendship", I must confess to being one of those cynically-minded people who consider that the least said on the subject the soonest mended. Few friendships among women will stand the strain of being romantically considered—all those I've ever watched have ended in dead-sea apples (the romantic ones, I mean), & I avoid them like the plague. Men manage better, I think, because most of them spend half their lives in

> Cloud-cuckooland in any case! Of course there is the amusing cock-a-hen
> friendship—but it is so very like a game of chess, & one can't make
> literature out of KB to QR4—at least, not the sort of literature you would
> care about! This is to explain why I'm very unlikely to write much about
> the subject. If I ever do, of course, I will send it to you with pleasure, but it
> would probably be in the strain of my contribution to this year's Oxford
> Poetry (q.v. when published)—
> > Now scold me for blasphemies!
> > I shall look out for your first number, anyhow—[61]

Apart from the fact that she is bursting with excitement
over her imminent departure for France, Dorothy reveals other
things in this letter. She is discreet. She is curious about sexual
relationships. She is sophisticated. She enjoys the self-image
of a cool observer. She has a heart of iron as well as of fire.
Was she even then conceiving and appropriating for herself
the life style of her Denis Cathcart in *Clouds of Witness* (surely
modeled in part on Whelpton): "complete devotion, complete
discretion"?[62]

Interestingly enough, a book entitled *How to See the Battlefields,* written by Captain Atherton Fleming (to whom Dorothy would be married in 1926), was also published at the end of
summer 1919. He rather innocently offered his book as a guide
to those who had lost relatives in the war and wished to make
pathetic pilgrimage.

Dorothy embarked for France that autumn of 1919 on a
different sort of pilgrimage. Her study of the language, literature, and culture of France gave her an additionally compel-
ling reason for undertaking the new assignment beyond being
the associate of Eric Whelpton at the Ecole des Roches.

"Les Roches," Whelpton writes, "is one of the best schools in
Europe with a board of governors chosen from the élite of the
universities, the army, and men of letters." It had been
founded around the turn of the century by the writer Edmond
de Moleyns at a site some three kilometers from Verneuil in
Normandy: "he decided that France required an élite created
by copying the English system of education, but employing
the advanced methods practiced at Abbotsholme, St. George's
Harpenden, and Bedales."

Dorothy was not primarily involved with the instruction of
the students at Les Roches. She was secretary to the scholastic
agency and spent six hours a day in the office with Whelpton.
He recalls:

> She ran the office with great efficiency and she did a great deal to
> complete my literary education, for the correspondence was not heavy, and
> so in our spare time we read the more obscure 17th-century poets and we
> discoursed about French literature where I could hold my own.

Spare time was not limited to choice literary discussion.[63]

> When I came upon her unexpectedly I would find her reading the cheap
> crime books which were known as penny dreadfuls, the novels of Maurice
> Le Blanc and Barbey d' Aurevillers' *Les Diaboliques*. One day, when I
> teased her for reading such rubbish, she told me that she was part of a team
> consisting of the Coles, Michael Sadler and one or two others who were
> deliberately preparing to create a vogue in detective novels; she suggested
> that I should join them. I replied rather sourly that I did not imagine for a
> moment that the public would fall for such rubbish and that I would have
> nothing to do with it.

Dorothy often questioned Whelpton about his "London
haunts," the men whom he "encountered in Prince's bar,
Jules," and other places where he met his friends. He confesses to a good knowledge of wines and food and casually
notes that "some of her friends" have declared that he is the
original of Lord Peter Wimsey. He also offers the suggestion
that from two of his colleagues, both men of connections, she
may have elicited details of personal experience which eventually found their way into her novels.

The winter of 1919-20 was severe in Normandy. An epidemic
of mumps laid low a third of the boys at Les Roches, and
Dorothy undoubtedly re-lived some of her own bad days at
Godolphin. But "spring came early, so early in fact that the
apples were in full bloom by the middle of March and the
woods were full of lilies-of-the-valley two or three weeks later;
daffodils carpeted the woods with gold in between whiles."[64]

If ever the heart of iron in Dorothy Sayers yielded to the
heart of fire, it must have been in such a spring. Their almost
daily proximity in the office, their literary discussions, their
common backgrounds should have gone far to draw Dorothy
and Eric together. But it was not to be, as far as he was
concerned. By the end of term, Whelpton had decided to leave
France, and Dorothy's work at Les Roches was over.

What matter the excursions she may have made during the
year? The other people whom she met? There is no armor
against fate. It was all very well for her to write in 1935 a cool,
distant prose generalization—"Many otherwise intelligent
men have, in their haste, set the passions above intellect; but if

they live long enough, their lives will give the lie to their theories."[65] But this was 1920, and Dorothy Sayers was still unfulfilled.

chapter two

As My Whimsy Takes Me

On her twenty-seventh birthday in June 1920, Dorothy Sayers was still in France, and she was still officially a spinster. She returned to England by the end of summer and on 14 October she was once more in Oxford. She was among the 549 women who, after the principals of the five women's colleges, were the first women to receive Oxford degrees.

The weather cooperated auspiciously. "The air scintillated with sunshine; from walls and quadrangles hung the vivid ampelopsis which seemed to reflect the deep crimson of the M.A. hoods." In the Sheldonian Theatre "unrehearsed applause" greeted the principals, but when the graduating women stood before the vice-chancellor cheers burst out. It was high achievement to be among the first in a new day and age. Professor Gilbert Murray presented the Somerville graduates for their degrees, and Dorothy retired from the ceremony with both a bachelor's and a master's degree.[1]

She recognized the continuing need of productive independence. Although her aging parents occupied an ample rectory and enjoyed a comfortable income in Christchurch, she knew she could not just settle down in a country parish. That decision was accepted by her parents who, nevertheless, had some doubts about the nature of her independence. On 12 November 1920 Henry Sayers changed his will, making his "dear wife" his sole legatee.[2]

Dorothy tried to place in words her awareness of this turning point. For her, there could be no turning back.

> "Dead Past, go forth, bury thy carrion dead
> Because they do offend me grievously."
> Full sternly thus I said,
> And my dead Past obediently
> Rose up to bury its dead.

The entire poem, "Obsequies for Music," was written during 1920. The camouflage of a universal theme and of an ingeniously orchestrated setting do not wholly conceal the personal testament of repentance. Obsequies were conducted for the poet's dead loves, dead hopes, dead griefs, dead hatreds, dead follies, and disbelief and doubt. "All had died slowly," she wrote, "struggling dreadfully." Dorothy had reached a decision about the direction of her life, but she was premature in considering obsequies.[3]

One consequence of her resolve was that Dorothy decided to live in London. She described the interim as a time in which she "did a number of odd jobs." Miss D. I. Beaumanoir Hart, who first became acquainted with Dorothy in 1933, reports that she taught modern languages at Clapham High School in southern metropolitan London in 1920. She certainly did not want to continue in teaching, so she looked for other opportunities.[4]

She did continue to write. A poem much briefer than "Obsequies" but nonetheless personal was written in 1921. It is simply entitled "The Poem." It is an ironic comment on the thin line of distinction between literature and life. The immediate area of imagination and of literary creation is passion, but defying the stereotyped tradition of the inexhaustibility and endless torture of love, the poet discovers that she can experience normal fatigue, self-satisfaction, and even imperturbability after writing most feelingly about passion.

> Kiss me! It cannot be that I
> Who wove such songs of pain and fire
> Last night—that fierce, desiring cry—
> It cannot be that I should tire?

> Prove to me, prove you're not grown weak,
>   Break down this citadel of sense,
> Show me myself too faint to speak,
>   Not armoured in my eloquence.
>
> I swear my singing was begun
>   Out of love's black and bitter deep—
> But oh! The work was so well done
>   I smiled, well-pleased, and fell on sleep.
>
> Now all day long I must rehearse
>   Each passionate and perfect line,
> Mine the immaculate great verse—
>   I do not know the thoughts for mine.[5]

Behind these lines, too, there beats a vital personal rhythm.

But one published poem a year was not enough to earn her living. On 22 May 1922 Dorothy started working for S. H. Benson, then Great Britain's largest advertising agency. She was to remain for nine years.[6] Whatever her successive duties at Benson's, she learned a great deal more than she already knew about the power of the word. Her education in copy writing and the psychology of advertising also ultimately provided her, as well, with materials for fiction and criticism. From a later perspective she referred to advertising as a "cardboard" world. These years at the advertising agency contributed to her cynicism about the exploitation of human foibles, but they also offered her the opportunity to develop exactitude. "Those who prefer their English sloppy have only themselves to thank if the advertisement writer uses his mastery of vocabulary and syntax to mislead their weak minds." One must "read advertisements carefully, observing both what is said and what is omitted."

Catchiness would benefit any writer. So would soundness: "advertising never sold a bad product twice." She was also aware of the legal vulnerability of advertising phrases: the advertiser "must not tell lies that draw upon him the attention of the Home Office Analyst or make statements that the purchaser can promptly disprove for himself." She knew, too, that the language standards of certain newspapers were inviolate: "If the *Morning Star* got it into their heads that an advertisement contained some lurking indelicacy that advertisement would not be printed, though the skies fell." Her experience and convictions were the basis for a conversation in a later novel:

"That reminds me. You know that idiotic thing Darling's put out the other day—the air-cushion for travellers with a doll that fits into the middle and sits up holding an 'ENGAGED' label?"

"What for?" asked Bredon.

"Well, the idea is, that you plank the cushion down in the railway carriage and the doll proclaims that the place is taken."

"But the cushion would do that without the doll."

"Of course it would, but you know how silly people are. They like superfluities. Well, anyway, they—Darling's, I mean—got out an ad. for the rubbish all by their little selves, and were fearfully pleased with it. Wanted us to put it through for them, till Armstrong burst into one of his juicy laughs and made them blush."

"What was it?"

"Picture of a nice girl bending down to put the cushion in the corner of a carriage. And the headline? 'DON'T LET THEM PINCH YOUR SEAT!' "

"The moral of all this. . .is that we have the kind of advertising we deserve; since advertisements only pander to our own proclaimed appetites, and with whatsoever measure we mete our desires they are (most lavishly and attractively) measured to us again."[7]

Dorothy had demonstrated by the time she left Oxford that she knew how to use literary language. But it is doubtful that *Catholic Tales and Christian Songs* had much appeal for typists, estate agents, pharmacists. By the time she was ready to leave Benson's she had achieved mastery of the *living* language. She came increasingly to avoid the luxury of poetic diction and esoteric imagery. Veritably, even the plowboy as well as the bishop could turn with delight to *The Nine Tailors* or *The Man Born to Be King*.

Shortly before or after she started working for Benson's, Dorothy took lodgings on the edge of Bloomsbury, at 24 Great James Street, Holborn, just opposite the opening of Northington Street, and she retained the address until her death. She was within easy walking distance of her employer's premises. She was also at no great distance from theatres and concerts. She surely did not abandon interest in theatricals or Bach, and the only deterrent to full enjoyment in the metropolis perhaps was lack of a substantial income.

A writer astutely casting about for best-seller income in the 1920s was bound to recognize the opportunities for detective fiction. It was the golden age of the detective novel. Robert Graves and Alan Hodge have described the decade:

Low-brow reading was now dominated by the detective novel. A large number of writers made comfortable incomes from this fashion, and a curious situation arose. In Great Britain, though a few score murders or acts of grand larceny took place every year, not more than two or three of these had features in the least interesting to the criminologist as regards either motive or method; nor, in any of these, did private detectives play any decisive part in bringing the culprits to justice—this was done by competent routine procedure of the C.I.D. [Criminal Investigation Department]. Yet from the middle Twenties onward some thousands of detective novels were annually published, all of them concerned with extraordinary and baffling crimes, and only a very small number gave the police the least credit for the solution. These books were designed not as realistic accounts of crime, but as puzzles to test the reader's acuteness in following up disguised clues.[8]

Graves and Hodge might have added that one of the most frequently appearing words describing crime in British newspapers in that period between the wars is *mysterious*. Reports of crimes were also sensationalized, almost always emphasizing the bizarre. Graves and Hodge are correct, nonetheless, in their market analysis.

So Dorothy, recognizing the probable way to fame and fortune, joined the detective-story writers. The step was deliberate, considering her earlier conversation with Eric Whelpton at Les Roches. And now the same "low cunning" which was satisfied by the study of Latin and the solving of crossword puzzles came to her aid.

Her first novel, *Whose Body?,* was constructed unabashedly as a puzzle. She picked up the old Oxford parlor game—given a puzzling situation, what would you do to solve it? A timid unsuspecting architect arises one morning to discover in his bathroom a naked unknown corpse wearing only nose glasses.

It was Dorothy's later judgment that

When in a light-hearted manner I set out . . . to write the first "Lord Peter" book, it was with the avowed intention of producing something "less like a conventional detective story and more like a novel." Re-reading *Whose Body?* at this distance of time I observe, with regret, that it is conventional to the last degree, and no more like a novel than I to Hercules.

She added, perhaps too critically, "This is not really surprising, because one cannot write a novel unless one has something to say about life, and I had nothing to say about it, because I knew nothing."[9]

There are great weaknesses in *Whose Body?* The author makes continual self-conscious references to Sherlock Holmes and other detective-story figures. Much of the plot—Stevensonian and Conan Doylish—is derived and formular: the author herself spoke of "lamentable lacunae . . . due to technical ignorance."[10] Present are the familiar motifs of the brilliant, mad scientist; the exhumation of a victim in extraordinary murkiness; the confession letter; the unquestioned good-conquering-evil structure. Many of the characters are at best stereotypes.

But there are strengths. The dialog occasionally moves swiftly and deftly. Suspense is maintained. The comic element is often successful. The greatest achievement in *Whose Body?*, however, is the introduction of Lord Peter Wimsey, the titled detective now so familiar to television and detective-story fans.

In answer to the question of his origin, Dorothy once wrote to her American publishers:

> I do not, as a matter of fact, remember inventing Lord Peter at all. My impression is that I was writing a detective story, and that he walked in, complete with spats, and applied in an airy don't-care-if-I-get-it way for the job of hero. . . .
>
> At this first interview, Wimsey informed me that he had a rather attractive mother, to whom he was much attached, and an immaculate "gentleman's gentleman"—Bunter by name. Later on, I gathered more details about his personal tastes and habits. I also discovered that he was two years older than myself. . . .
>
> Lord Peter's large income (the source of which, by the way, I have never investigated) was a different matter. I deliberately gave him that. After all, it cost me nothing, and at that time I was particularly hard up, and it gave me pleasure to spend his fortune for him. When I was dissatisfied with my single unfurnished room, I took a luxurious flat for him in Piccadilly. When my cheap rug got a hole in it, I ordered an Aubusson carpet. When I had no money to pay my 'busfare, I presented him with a Daimler double-six, upholstered in a style of sober magnificence, and when I felt dull I let him drive it. . . .[11]

Lord Peter stayed for fifteen years, appearing in ten more novels, three volumes of short stories, one play, and numerous articles.

He was created according to the tradition established by Edgar Allan Poe, the father of the detective story, and a tradition retained by Conan Doyle. The detective was always a gifted amateur. He excelled in ratiocination. He was always clever about detecting the culprit and the manner—however ingenious—of the crime.

Peter Wimsey came highly endowed. He was a scholar, a sportsman, a bibliophile, a musician, a connoisseur, a retired soldier, a diplomat, a man about town. His Eton-Balliol education supplied the proper training. His family connection provided nobility. Lord Peter's charm must not be overlooked; his manners and status made him a symbol of elegance. (A few years later, this aristocratic element became the target of class-conscious critics whose views made Lord Peter and his creator appear snobbish and offensive.) As each new novel came out, Lord Peter's own history was augmented and embellished. He gradually become less foppish, less of a caricature, more clearly descended, more correctly endowed. Nevertheless, the world had to wait for many of the facts and details until the arrival of that impresario, his uncle, Paul Austin Delagardie.

Whose Body? contains some precise delineations already: Lord Peter "was not very tall—in fact, he was rather a short man, but he didn't look undersized." He had hard gray eyes, a long receding forehead, blond hair brushed back, a long narrow chin, a long nose, a long, indeterminate mouth, and long fingers. He was indeed a bibliophilist (though not yet accurate), a musician (with a decided preference for early music), a connoisseur, and a multi-linguist. He wore an eyeglass which doubled as a magnifying glass, and he carried a stick which doubled as a device for measuring and for self-defense.[12]

His conversation becomes unforgettable in its tone, variety, and allusiveness. At first he sounds dismally affected. His clownish chatter can annoy the reader. His compulsion to lapse into doggerel is downright irritating. In his speech, especially, Lord Peter exhibits the appropriateness of the family motto: "As my whimsy takes me." Fortunately for the reader, the P. G. Wodehouse strain gradually waned.

Bunter is almost an attribute of Lord Peter. What else is a gentleman's gentleman? He not only cares for Wimsey, he also assists in his investigation—and his specialty is photography. There is an inevitable Jeeveslike quality in Bunter.

Lord Peter's mother, the dowager duchess, is a delightfully comic character. In the second novel she is described as coming (like Dorothy Sayers's own mother) of "good Hampshire stock." Her flutteriness and volatility belie the genuine integrity, graciousness, and good commonsense which she possesses. "The Duchess was always of the greatest assistance to his hobby of criminal investigation, though she never alluded to it, and maintained a polite fiction of its nonexistence."[13]

Whose Body? was published in England by T. Fisher Unwin in 1923, shortly after the American edition. Dorothy had begun writing the book before starting to work for Benson's and had received a round of rejection slips before Fisher Unwin's acceptance.

The dedication of *Whose Body?* was made to "M. J.," to whom in *Op. I* seven years previously Dorothy had dedicated her farewell-to-Oxford poem. M. J.—Muriel Jaeger—was addressed by an old nickname: "Dear Jim," she wrote,

> *This book is your fault. If it had not been for your brutal insistence, Lord Peter would never have staggered through to the end of this enquiry. Pray consider that he thanks you with his accustomed suavity.*

The book appeared in October, but in September 1923 Dorothy began a six-months' leave of absence from Benson's, ostensibly to complete a second novel. In actuality, she was pregnant. She went to Bournemouth at the end of the year, probably staying with a relative on her mother's side, and delivered a son in Tuckton Lodge, Ilford Lane, on 3 January 1924. She gave him the name John Anthony and openly identified herself on the birth certificate as "an Authoress of 24 Great James Street, London." No name was recorded for the father. Registry of birth was made on 28 January in Christchurch, a suburb of Bournemouth.

The child was soon placed with a cousin, Ivy Amy Shrimpton, of the Sidelings, Westcott Barton, Oxfordshire, because Dorothy had to return to Benson's in March. But from that time forth she supported her son, sending off money regularly to Miss Shrimpton. She visited him from time to time, also, but she saw to it that the relationship was kept secret all her life. In due time, John Anthony was educated at Malvern College and at Oxford. After his mother's death in 1957, John Anthony (who uses the surname Fleming) told a newspaper interviewer that he had been *adopted* in 1934.

> Miss Sayers adopted me when I was ten. At that time I was brought up by a cousin of hers, a maiden lady of small income. We lived in the Banbury area.

This lady felt for some reason that I might benefit by a good education and told her cousin so. One day I was told to regard Miss Sayers as my mother.[14]

Dorothy Sayers had been living on the edge of Bloomsbury in many ways. She did not merely observe bohemian life, she tasted it. She herself was a "specimen of the modern independent young woman" about whom she wrote in *Clouds of Witness*.[15]

Her first great love, Eric Whelpton, had made it quite clear that he was not lastingly interested in her. She had literally written him off as a "dead love." There may, nevertheless, have been a furtive affair with Whelpton in the spring of 1923. Be that as it may, Whelpton was never to acknowledge the relationship.

It is certain, moreover, that Dorothy had an affair with the Russian-born, American writer John Cournos at that time. Like Whelpton, Cournos frequented the society of writers and artists in London. He was cosmopolitan, sophisticated, and by his own admission amorous. He, too, was handsome, and an author living on a slender income. More than that, he had been only recently jilted by an American girl named Dorothy (whom he describes in his *Autobiography* in details strikingly similar to the features of Dorothy Sayers at the time). It is not surprising that two such emotionally displaced persons were attracted to one another.

Cournos, however, also made it quickly clear to Dorothy Sayers that their encounter could not last. In that same year (1924) he married Helen Kestner Satterthwaite (Sybil Norton) and became a stepfather to her two children. Dorothy sent him eleven letters during 1924 and 1925, and also a 1922 photograph (all of which Cournos kept by him until he presented them to the Houghton Library of Harvard University in 1957—the year of Dorothy's death—with the instruction that they were to be kept sealed and not consulted without permission of the librarian).[16] Undoubtedly Dorothy believed Cournos was the father of her child.

About the same time Dorothy was obliged to write off Cournos, she became acquainted with Oswald Atherton Fleming, who was divorced on 15 July 1925, after proceedings the previous year had been initiated by his wife on the charge of adultery.

Although she had become a modern young woman, Dorothy could no longer be completely independent. What prompted her thenceforth never publicly to acknowledge her maternity? Was it consideration for her aging parents, especially for her dignified Anglican clergyman father? It is hard to believe—even if one accepts as dominant the worst reputation of Victorian respectability—that her parents could have denied her their love. Once, when Dorothy Rowe asked her how she could be so assured about the hope of the resurrection, Dorothy Sayers replied (not altogether logically), "I am as sure of it as I am that my mother loves me." By the time of Mr. Sayers's death in 1928 and of Mrs. Sayers's in 1929, Dorothy was the wife of Fleming. He did not have the custody of his own two daughters, and he was unwilling to allow Dorothy to bring her son into their home. Apart from the consideration of the demands of her career, perhaps she would have found John Anthony's presence in her home too painful a reminder of her indiscretion. But it is unwise to attribute to her any lack of sensitivity in the matter—to allege, for example, some fancied aversion to children or to dismiss her as irresponsible. One must rather remember that in 1934, when the boy was ten years old, Dorothy instructed Miss Shrimpton to tell him he had been "adopted" and was thereafter to "regard" Miss Sayers as his mother.[17]

It is poignantly revealing to read what she wrote to Dr. Welch twenty years after the event:

The point made by both Taylor & Fenn is that the "story" of Crucified God appears irrelevant because people nowadays have no sense of sin. That, of course, is literally the *crux*. . . . I'm a very poor person to appreciate modern man's feelings on all this, because I can't think of any personal misfortunes that have befallen me which were not, in one way or another, my own fault. I don't mean this necessarily in the profounder & more religious sense. I mean that I know jolly well that if anything unpleasant happened in my life I had usually "asked for it." Consequently, when I talk about carrying the sins of the world, I'm going outside my experience—anything I have to put up with looks to me like the direct punishment of my *own* sins, & not to leave much margin over for redeeming other people's! But I do see that most people to-day look upon themselves as the victims of undeserved misfortunes, which they (as individuals & as a species) have done nothing to provoke. Contemporary literature & thought seem to me to be steeped in self-pity, which is the most enervating state of mind imaginable.[18]

Dorothy must herself frequently have yielded to that enervating self-pity during the two years that followed the birth of
her son. The leave of absence from Benson's did not produce
the second novel. It produced anguish more often than not.
She was over thirty years of age, an unwanted lover.

Once again she moved on the rebound. She married Ather-
ton Fleming. He was Scottish-born. His father, John William
Fleming, had been a civil servant in Chinese Customs and had
spent most of his life in China. His mother, Jane Peebles
Maconochie, had married the elder Fleming in July 1881, and
Atherton (whose name had been recorded at birth as Oswald
Arthur) was born at Kirkwall in the Orkneys on 6 November
1881. He had two sisters and six brothers.[19]

In youth, restless and daring, he ran away from home to
enter the Boer War. He keenly remembered his departure from
Shorncliffe Camp for South Africa in 1899 and the return to
England on the *Dunnottar Castle* in 1902. He subsequently
traveled widely—to the Hawaian Islands, to the Far East, and
to the Continent. Before World War I he started the weekly
magazine *Land and Water*, which was taken over and continued by G. K. Chesterton. Fleming was avidly interested in auto
racing, especially with Daimlers. "In the days before the Great
War," he wrote, "I used to go to Caerphilly and try to climb the
hill there at a faster rate than any other of the assembled
speed-hogs." He never won the climb, but he always returned
"with a couple of Caerphilly cheeses," for he was interested in
good food even then. On 8 September 1911 he married Winifred
Ellen Meyrick, a daughter of a vicar, in the parish church of
Littlehampton, Sussex, giving his address as Coventry and
his profession as journalist. The elder Fleming was then still
alive and still serving Customs.[20]

Atherton and his first wife went to live in Kenilworth until
World War I seemed imminent. One daughter, Kathleen Mary,
was born there. Then the family moved to the Meyrick home,
Ashdowns, in Hartfield, Sussex. There in 1914 a second daughter, Ann, was born. Ann remembers visiting her paternal
grandparents: they were "finely featured"; "Grandma was
graceful and slightly theatrical; Grandpa was good-natured,
and had clear blue eyes and a Scots accent."

When Atherton went into the army, the family lived for a
while in London. Soon, however, arrangements were made for

Winifred to move with the children and their nurse to Ashurst in Sussex.[21]

Within a few months of Britain's entry into World War I, Atherton was in Flanders, reporting on the war for the *Daily Chronicle*. On 17 May 1915 he was made Temporary Second Lieutenant in the Army Service Corps and attained a captaincy by 15 May 1918. Demobilized at the end of hostilities, he returned to journalism and published at the end of summer 1919 his book *How to See the Battlefields*. He had been badly gassed during the war. His book makes clear that bombardment, rats, wretched weather, life in the trenches behind barbed wire, privations, no man's land, reports of the orgies of the huns (including their deportation of young children to be slave laborers), and the loss of a brother at the Battle of the Somme had mutilated his spirit. Actually, two of his brothers—Edmund and Edward—died in France.[22]

After the war, Fleming did not rejoin his family, although he visited them occasionally. Ann believes that he worked for an advertising agency in London and that he had lodgings in Grey's Inn. "Mother found him very changed," she writes, "and believed that the war had affected him psychologically." By 1924 he no longer sent any support for his family. Winifred Fleming reluctantly sued for divorce, and although an alimony arrangement had been agreed upon Atherton hardly ever met it.[23]

Although Fleming was forty-four when he married Dorothy and bore the evidence of life's battering, he retained some measure of his handsome appearance and sensitive personality. Like Eric Whelpton, he had been a former army officer. Like John Cournos, he was a writer. He, too, had been in France. He had been an adventurer. He was at home in the Roaring Twenties.

His first marriage dissolved on 15 May 1925, and he married Dorothy on 13 April 1926 at the Register Office in the District of Holborn, not too distant from her lodgings in Great James Street. It was two months to the day before her thirty-third birthday. There can be no surprise that the marriage was not performed by her father; Anglican clergy were forbidden to marry in the church even the "innocent party" in a divorce. "Mac," as Fleming was called, and his bride resided for a time in the flat on Great James Street.

That same year, just eight days after the marriage of Atherton and Dorothy, the duke and duchess of York announced the birth of a first child, a daughter whom they named Elizabeth. On 23 August 1926 the silent screen's great lover Rudolph Valentino died; thousands mourned. In the same year, George Bernard Shaw won the Nobel Prize for literature. It was also the year of the General Strike.

The year 1926 also saw the publication of Dorothy's second novel. *Clouds of Witness* is a continuation novel. Ample reference is made to the preceding case of investigation. The public interest in Lord Peter Wimsey led to the exploitation of the entire Wimsey family circle. The older brother, Gerald, duke of Denver, is a wrongly suspected man who easily falls under suspicion by virtue of obtuseness and a sense of personal honor. He prefers the notoriety and risk of a trial by his peers in the House of Lords to an easy exculpation by the testimony of his paramour. His wife the duchess, whom Peter cannot endure, is "a long-necked, long-backed woman, who disciplined her hair and her children." Lady Mary, the duke's sister, is five years younger than Peter, a "specimen of the modern independent young woman." Her situation is similar to that of Rachel Verinder in Wilkie Collins's *The Moonstone*—she assumes (incorrectly) that the man with whom she is infatuated is responsible for the crime, and that she must protect him at all costs. In this second novel the acquaintance of Lady Mary and Detective Inspector Charles Parker begins to develop into something more than friendship.

The dowager duchess, Peter's mother, was too good to leave out of the story. Short, plump, brisk, black-eyed, white-haired—she takes on real identity. Her talk is still apt to be disconnected and marked by an occasional malapropism, but she lands a few sharp satires on modern society. Her slyest dig is directed at George Goyles, Lady Mary's weak-kneed Romeo.

> "But, my dear, I could hardly insult Mr. Goyles by suggesting that he should live on his mother-in-law," said the Dowager.
>
> "Why not?" said Mary. "George doesn't believe in those old-fashioned ideas about property. Besides, if you'd given it to me, it would be *my* money. We believe in men and women being equal. Why should the one always be the bread-winner more than the other?"
>
> "I can't imagine, dear," said the Dowager. "Still, I could hardly expect Mr. Goyles to live on unearned increment when he didn't believe in inherited property."

She ironically maintains that

> The worse you express yourself these days the more profound people think you—though that's nothing new. Like Browning and those quaint metaphysical people, when you never know whether they really mean their mistresses or the Established Church, so bridegroomy and biblical. . . .

The character of Lord Peter has been given additional depth in *Clouds of Witness*. True, he has lost none of his banter, retains some of his affectation, still declaims verse or parody at the slightest provocation, and talks at a pace which intimidates. The details of his past career are yet only peripheral, but they are being explored. To Parker, for example, early in the story Peter confides that after the war, "I was ill, you know, and after I got the chuck from Barbara I didn't feel much like botherin' about other people's heart-to-hearts. . . ."

Sayers's sense of climax has improved in *Clouds of Witness*. Lord Peter is flown back from America to England (pre-Lindbergh) in a two-seater plane through a dreadful storm, just in time to present conclusive evidence of the innocence of the duke at the trial in the House of Lords. The trial itself, of course, has a built-in dramaturgy: pomp, the tense conflict of counterargument, the array of witnesses. Even after the acquittal there is an attempted assassination.

It should also be noted that the second novel resounds with Gallic overtones, even though some are only stereotypes. Denis Cathcart, the "victim," is deliberately modeled on the Abbé Prévost's Chevalier des Grieux. Simone Vonderaa, his unfaithful mistress, owes much to Manon Lescaut. Sayers brings in French connections by having Parker spend several days in France checking up on Cathcart's conduct there. Usually given to the reading of Bible commentaries, Parker here divulges meretricious interests in French fiction; he says to Peter, "Like one of those odd French novels, you know, Peter; frightfully hot stuff, but absolutely impersonal." Moreover, the Honorable Freddy Arbuthnot quotes Cathcart on the eve of his death as saying: "I'm goin' to ask Mary for a date tomorrow, an' then we'll go live in Paris, where they understand sex."[24]

After the publication of *Clouds of Witness* and her marriage to Fleming, Sayers turned zestfully to the business of writing. Over the next decade she was to average one novel a year, not to mention short stories, articles, collaborations, radio scripts, and reviews. Although the circumstances of life did not bring to Dorothy her ideal lover, she deployed her imaginative energies seeking for him in her own fiction.

The third Wimsey novel appeared in 1927. It was *Unnatural Death*. T. Fisher Unwin, publisher of the first two Sayers novels, became incorporated with Ernest Benn in February of that year, and *Unnatural Death* bore the name of Benn as publisher. Advertising claims and reviewers' opinions were favorable.

This novel again exploits the ingenious puzzle format—the question connected with the crime being not Who? but How? This work may well be considered a woman's story. The culprit is a woman; the three victims are all women; and a woman is the conspicuous sleuth in its pages. Inspector Parker offers a chauvinistic opinion appropriate to the situation: "When a woman is wicked and unscrupulous, . . . she is the most ruthless criminal in the world—fifty times worse than a man, because she is always so much more single-minded about it."

With a certain amount of pardonable bombast, Wimsey characterizes the conspicuous female sleuth for Parker:

> Miss Climpson . . . is a manifestation of the wasteful way in which this country is run. . . . Thousands of old maids, simply bursting with useful energy, forced by our own stupid social system into hydros and hotels and communities and hostels and posts as companions, where their magnificent gossip-powers and units of inquisitiveness are allowed to dissipate themselves or even become harmful to the community, while the rate-payers' money is spent on getting work for which those women are providentially fitted, inefficiently carried out by ill-equipped policemen like you. . . .

Thin, gray-haired and middle-aged, "with a sharp sallow face and very vigorous manner," and possessed with a natural proclivity for investigation, this spinster reveals speaking and writing patterns which represent one of Sayers's finest creative achievements. In style, she is the crisp counterpart to the sometimes-diffuse dowager. She is also genuinely religious: "Miss Climpson is a nice lady," says the boarding-house proprietress, "and that I must say, even if she is a Roaming Catholic or next to one."

Little is added to the characterization of Lord Peter. He is becoming a little more human: he evidences genuine misgivings about some of his timing, if not his judgment. He is no longer just a fashion plate—he even answers a telephone while he is dripping wet in a bath towel. He knows what it is like to wear squeaky shoes in a quiet church.

Sayers shows concern in this book for moral causes and effects. From a clergyman with the delightfully Chaucerian name of Tredgold, Lord Peter seeks advice on whether or not he should pursue his investigations because to do so might lead to an additional murder. Mr. Tredgold admits that very often one murder leads to another, or at any rate to a "readiness" to commit another. Says Peter: "It has. That's the trouble. But it wouldn't have if I hadn't started trying to find things out. Ought I to have left it alone?" Mr. Tredgold's advice to Peter is:

> do what you think is right, according to the laws which we have been brought up to respect. Leave the consequences to God. And try to think charitably even of wicked people. You know what I mean. Bring the offender to justice, but remember that if we all got justice, you and I wouldn't escape either.

Why did Sayers bring a clergyman into her story, and why, especially, did she devote a passage to such a case of conscience? Was it not likely that she was attempting—however obliquely—to make peace with her family? Mr. Tredgold is the first of several admirable clergymen who come into Sayers's stories, and surely they are modeled on her father. It is even possible that Miss Climpson was drawn in part from Aunt Mabel Leigh.

Unnatural Death is the first Wimsey novel published after Sayers's marriage. Wimsey's observation to Parker, illustrating the fallacy of attempting proof on the basis of published records alone, is perhaps relevant:

> Read any newspaper to-day. . . . read the divorce court lists. Wouldn't they give you the idea that marriage is a failure? Isn't the sillier sort of journalism packed with articles to the same effect? And yet, looking round among the marriages you know of personally, aren't the majority of them a success, in a hum-drum, undemonstrative sort of way? Only you don't hear of them. People don't bother to come into court and explain that they dodder along very comfortably on the whole, thank you. . . .

The book contains some revealing comments on sex, as well. When Lord Peter faces an attempted seduction, he is at first baffled because the lady seems to him "essentially sexless," even epicene. Being Wimsey, he "pulled her suddenly and violently to him, and kissed her mouth with a practiced exaggeration of passion"; and then he knew. "No one who has ever encountered it can ever again mistake that awful shrinking, that uncontrollable revulsion of the flesh against a caress that is nauseous." It needed not Fleming, of course, for Dorothy to write that out of conviction.

Miss Climpson's observations on lesbianism are also apropos. Her first assessment of the criminal was that "This was no passionate nature, cramped by association with an old woman and eager to be free to mate before youth should depart." Miss Climpson also contemplates the need of the young friend of the criminal: "It would be a mercy for that girl . . . if she could form a genuine attachment to a young man. It is natural for a school-girl to be schwärmerisch—in a young woman of twenty-two it is thoroughly undesirable."

For Miss Climpson, "men were intended to be masterful, even though wicked or foolish." Haltingly, she tries to explain to the young woman herself about ideal love between the sexes:

> "Love is always good, when it's the right kind . . . I don't think it ought to be too *possessive*. One has to train oneself—"she hesitated, and went on courageously—"and in any case, my dear, I cannot help feeling that it is more natural—more proper, in a sense—for a man and a woman to be all in all to one another than for two persons of the same sex. Er—after all, it is a—a fruitful affection," said Miss Climpson, boggling a trifle at the idea, "and—and all that, you know. . . ."

The young woman, described as speaking "with the air of a disillusioned rake who has sucked life's orange and found it dead sea fruit," uses the phrases of the young Sayers when she wrote to Leonard Green on the eve of her departure for France with Whelpton. Miss Climpson also touches on the subject when she writes to Lord Peter:

> However, Miss Findlater has evidently quite a 'pash' (as we used to call it at school) for Miss Whitaker, and I am afraid none of us are above being *flattered* by such outspoken admiration. I must say, I think it rather *unhealthy*— you may remember Miss Clemence Dane's *very clever book* on the subject?—I have seen so *much* of that kind of thing in my rather WOMAN-RIDDEN existence! It has a bad effect, as a rule, upon the *weaker character* of the two—But I must not take up your time with my TWADDLE!!

Unnatural Death looks both to the past and to the future in other ways. Here, at a safe distance from Godolphin and

Somerville, Dorothy decks out Miss Whitaker (in the seduction scene) in a wig and turban. There is also a glancing blow at the manipulative power of advertising. Again, there is an anticipatory remark about Lord Peter's going to the British Museum in order "to collate a 12th century manuscript of Tristan." Finally, there is a pointed characterization of London:

> To the person who has anything to conceal—to the person who wants to lose his identity as one leaf among the leaves of a forest—to the person who asks no more than to pass by and be forgotten, there is one name above others which promises a haven of safety and oblivion. London. Where no one knows his neighbour . . . London, whose rather untidy and grubby bosom is the repository of so many odd secrets. Discreet, incurious and all-enfolding London.[25]

Once she was in stride writing detection fiction, Sayers—with typical insatiability—set about discovering (and then reporting) all she could find on the subject of detective stories. On 28 June 1928, for example, she addressed a letter to the editor of the *Times Literary Supplement:*

> Sir,—I have for some time had it in mind to attempt a critical and biographical study of William Wilkie Collins, and am now engaged in collecting the necessary material. May I, through your valuable columns, ask all those who would be willing to permit access to manuscripts, letters, or papers in their possession kindly to communicate with me? I need not add that all communications would be treated as confidential.

She kept the project alive for a number of years, and although the biography was never completed, she did supply a good bibliography for the *Cambridge Bibliography of English Literature* in 1941 and the introduction to the Everyman Library edition of *The Moonstone* in 1944.[26]

She was more than willing, also, to listen to Anthony Berkeley in 1928 when he approached some twenty writers of detective fiction, proposing that they should meet for dinner at regular intervals to discuss their craft. In this manner the London Detection Club originated. The first president of the club was G. K. Chesterton. New members were added by election to the original score and submitted to an initiation ceremony which involved a skull (curiously named Eric by Sayers) and an oath. The oath required members facetiously to forswear, on behalf of their detectives, reliance in their stories on "Divine Revelation, Feminine Intuition, Mumbo Jumbo,

Jiggery-Pokery, Coincidence or Act of God." They had also to promise to observe "a seemly moderation in the use of Gangs, Conspiracies, Death-Rays, Ghosts, Hypnotism, Trap-Doors, Chinamen, Super-Criminals and Lunatics," and forever to avoid using "Mysterious Poisons unknown to Science." One last prerequisite was a willingness to honor the king's English.

The club established a fund by contributing, not cash, but the products of their pens. (Sayers contributed to five volumes during her lifetime.) The members soon acquired premises in Gerrard Street in which they maintained an extensive detection library and upon occasion heard invited speakers. R. A. Knox has recorded that, on the night after all the members had received their keys, "the premises were burglariously entered; who or by whom is still a mystery, but it was a good joke that it should happen to the Detection Club."[27]

Still another evidence of Sayers's intense pursuit of her genre appeared in 1928, although she had been at work upon it for a long time previously. In September, the First Series of *Great Short Stories of Detection, Mystery and Horror* was published by Gollancz (whose imaginative and daring advertising increased her reputation and her sales). The sixty tales in the anthology are classics, and so is Sayers's introduction. No less a critic than Howard Haycraft calls it "Authoritative without being didactic, concise but comprehensive," containing "in its relative brief compass virtually all that was to be said about the detective story up to the date of its composition." The Second Series (with a new introduction) appeared in 1931, the Third Series in 1934. A similar volume was prepared for the Everyman Library in 1936.[28]

It is with almost incredible speed that in the same year—1928—the fourth Wimsey novel was published. *The Unpleasantness at the Bellona Club* develops "That old thing in *Punch,* you know—'Waiter, take away Lord Whatsisname, he's been dead two days.' "

More significant than the plot—which is still only a sample of clever puzzle-making— is the implication of various bits of characterization which undoubtedly owe something to Sayers's husband. One of the major characters, a war veteran, complains:

A man goes and fights for his country, gets his inside gassed out, and loses his job, and all they give him is the privilege of marching past the

Cenotaph once a year and paying four shillings in the pound income-tax
. . . . It's pretty damnable for a man to have to live on his wife's earnings,
isn't it?

The war veteran's experience is similar to that of Fleming,
who had had the misfortune of having two "packets" of gas
handed him in the war. Like Fleming, the same fictional war
veteran seeks a job selling cars because he knows them and
can handle them well. He, too, suffers from memories of the
trenches, particularly of the ghastly rats. (All of this is a
variation of Wimsey's own affliction, intimated in the earlier
novels under the ambiguous term *neurasthenia.)*

Peter's comments, triggered by a married couple's bickering
in the book, may also indicate something more personal.

"It always gives me the pip," said Wimsey, "to see how rude people are
when they're married. I suppose it's inevitable. Women are funny. They
don't seem to care half so much about a man's being honest and faithful—
and I'm sure your brother's all that—as for their opening doors and saying
"thank you". . . . I've asked people, you know—my usual inquisitiveness—
and they generally just grunt and say that *their* wives are sensible and
take their affection for granted. But I don't believe women ever get
sensible, not even through prolonged association with their husbands."

Sayers exposes to critical comment certain additional subjects in *The Unpleasantness,* such as avant-garde artists,
Chelsea bohemianism, loan-sharking, an authority on glands.
In this fourth novel, Lord Peter is a little more subdued, less
affected, establishing his growing reputation as a gourmet. He
has lost some of his cardboard and paste.[29]

Late in the year still another Lord Peter book appeared. It
was a collection of twelve short stories entitled *Lord Peter
Views the Body.* It had great popularity. Gollancz announced
the "5th thousand two days after publication" and a "2d
impression by the end of the year." All of these stories are
teasers and not equally good ones. One, "The Adventurous
Exploit of the Cave of Ali-Baba," however, is as suspenseful as
anything Sayers ever wrote.[30]

At thirty-five Dorothy experienced the loss of a close family
member for the first time. On Thursday afternoon, 20 September, at the age of seventy-four, her father died in Christchurch.
Though unwell, he had attended to parish duties on Tuesday
and Wednesday. On Thursday morning, the doctor was sum-
moned and found the rector suffering from pneumonia. The

disease moved swiftly, and at 2:30 in the afternoon he died. Dorothy had been called urgently and was at his bedside.[31]

She had written about death many times, but only as a fictional necessity. Now death came close to her in reality. She loved her father. If there were no other proof, one need only look at the kindly vicars who march through her pages. The bereavement, of course, invited memories. How many grateful memories she had of the tall, gentle man who so very long ago had taken her in his arms to teach her Latin! Surely there were also memories of sternness and standards, but not without the further rejoinder, "Bring the offender to justice, but remember that if we all got justice, you and I wouldn't escape either."

Mrs. Sayers and her sister Mabel could continue to reside in the Christchurch rectory for only a limited time. The two sisters moved in March 1929 to Essex and took up residence at 24 Newland Street, Witham, in a home purchased by Dorothy, next door to her own home. Mrs. Sayers outlived her husband less than a year. On 27 July 1929 she died at the age of seventy-three. She had entered the hospital for an operation on a strangulated femoral hernia, but her heart could not sustain the ordeal. A few days after death she was interred next to her husband in the quiet churchyard at Christchurch. There is no marker on the graves. The parishioners themselves, however, erected a memorial tablet on the west wall inside the church, expressing thanks to God for the memory of the Reverend and Mrs. Henry Sayers. Aunt Mabel continued to live in the Witham home with the Flemings until her own death. Evelyn Compline (now Bedford), who had served Mrs. Sayers, stayed on with the Flemings.

The property in Witham consists of two fifteenth-century cottages, with an eighteenth-century facade, which had been combined into one living unit. Far more commodious than the flat on Great James Street in London, the Newland Street home in Witham had large back gardens with a cobble yard and a greenhouse largely given over to varieties of cactus. A cat named Adalbert and a parrot named Joey completed the establishment. After her parents died, Captain (in courtesy often elevated to *Major)* and Mrs. Fleming spent most of their time in the Essex home, keeping the London residence only for convenience.[32]

For an additional eight years Sayers continued to serve as one of the daughters of Sherlock, devoting herself to the fortunes and destiny of Lord Peter Wimsey, and writing and speaking on varied aspects of detective fiction. Then, wearied like Conan Doyle before her, she resolutely turned to other interests.

A newspaper interviewer reported in February 1934 that Dorothy Sayers said of herself, "I am a scholar gone wrong." She did manage to interrupt the flow of detective fiction briefly in 1929 by publishing a translation of Thomas the Anglo-Norman's *Tristan in Brittany,* a collection of twelfth-century romantic fragments. Two excerpts and an introduction to Thomas had been published by Sayers nine years earlier in *Modern Languages.* She had sought to publish the entire translation in *London Mercury* but was courteously refused by Sir John Squire, the editor. Finally Ernest Benn agreed to publish the *Tristan.* Sayers was fortunate in getting Professor George Saintsbury to write the introduction. But after *Tristan* she was obliged to defer medieval scholarship for a score of years.[33]

Some part-Wimsey and non-Wimsey pieces of fiction were produced in this period. *Hangman's Holiday* in 1933 introduced Montague Egg, who divides with Lord Peter the investigations chronicled in the twelve short stories it contains. Sayers also contributed her stories or chapters to five volumes by the Detective Club: *The Floating Admiral* (1931), *Ask a Policeman* (1933), *Six against the Yard* (1936), *Double Death* (1939), and *Detection Medley* (1939).[34]

The one really excellent non-Wimsey novel written and published at this time was *Documents in the Case* (1930). It is an epistolary novel composed in the tradition of Wilkie Collins's *The Moonstone* and inspired in part by the notorious Bywater case. "Robert Eustace" (the name used by Dr. Eustace R. Barton) collaborated with Sayers in this work.[35] The characterizations are splendidly drawn, and the plot is that of a novel of manners rather than an ingenious puzzle. It was Sayers's later point of view that *Documents* was nearer to her ideal than any of the earlier novels had been. It approached a serious criticism of life. The book had good sales. It was chosen as the Book Guild detective story for July 1930 and received the enthusiastic approval of Ralph Strauss and

Frank Swinnerton, among others. Miss Rowe was visiting Sayers in London when the Book Guild announcement was made, and she heard her hostess exclaim over the news: "I am rich. I am famous." As a result, the Flemings used some of the earnings for a trip to America in May 1931, sailing on the *Mauretania*.[36]

Sayers managed to turn out a number of articles dealing with detective fiction at the end of this decade. "A Sport of Noble Minds," a brief version of the introduction to her First Series of *Great Short Stories of Detection, Mystery, and Horror,* appeared in *Saturday Review of Literature* on 3 August 1929 and in *Life and Letters Today* in January 1930. "The Present Status of the Mystery Story," published in *London Mercury* in November 1930, expressed the fear that the mystery story was "in great danger of losing touch with the common man" and was becoming "a caviare banquet for the cultured." Twice she contributed analyses and comments on the same celebrated murder case: "The Murder of Julia Wallace" appeared in *Great Unsolved Crimes* in 1935 and in *The Anatomy of Murder* in 1936. Several articles devoted to the game of applying the methods of the "Higher Criticism" to the Sherlock Holmes canon also made their appearance: "The Dates in *The Red-Headed League*" in the *Colophon* in June 1934; "Holmes' College Career" in *Baker Street Studies* in 1934; "Dr. Watson's Christian Name" in *Queen Mary's Book for India* in 1943 and *Profile by Gaslight* in 1944; "Dr. Watson, Widower" before 1946. On 27 October 1936 Sayers spoke to the Sesame Imperial Club on "The Modern Detective Story." In 1939, she was persuaded to write "Other People's Great Detectives" for *Illustrated*.[37]

It was in 1930 that Sayers began association with the British Broadcasting Corporation. Practically every genre she touched was represented over the years on radio or television broadcast, from detective stories at first, to drama, to wartime talks, to Dante. Any number of her stories, novels, and plays were broadcast, and not only in the English versions. The BBC used Sayers's work in programs in Czech, French, German, Italian, Persian, Portuguese, Spanish, and Welsh. She also knew how to collect royalties regularly, taking care that all financial arrangements were handled in a businesslike manner by her agents.

Relationships with her were not always maintained easily by BBC personnel. From the first she did battle with the announcing of her name. On 28 March 1934, for example, she wrote brusquely: "will you please take steps to see that my name is removed from any further programme announcements, particularly as the 'Director of Talks' is apparently unable to give it correctly as instructed." Her pique centered in the omission of her middle initial. This was not mindless vanity, however. In a letter to Antony Brown as late in Sayers's life as 19 May 1954 (and because the problem persisted through the years), she wrote stingingly:

> N.B. If anybody gives my name as "Dorothy Sayers" I will kill them with my hands. The B.B.C. ought to know by this time, since Miss Dorothy Sayers is one of their own "artistes"; she plays the ukelele, or the balalaika or something, in music-hall programmes.[38]

Older hands thus circulated memos reminding tyros to be sure to distinguish the author by inserting the *L* in Miss Sayers's name during announcements.

She knew what she wanted, but her demands were not inspired by an unforgivable hauteur. During the preparation and broadcast of her wartime plays on the life of Christ, she was most adamant on a number of items. When it was all over, those who worked with her had to admit that everything she had required was right.

She knew her pace for talks expertly. It was exactly one and a half minutes to a page of typescript. To go less than her natural pace, she said, would make her "squeak." She also knew her limitations. To Rev. Eric Fenn, Religious Broadcasting Department, she wrote on 4 April 1941:

> I'm *not good* at the direct personal appeal—"Has it ever struck you—?" "How about your own children?" "I want you to think about—" It always makes me embarrassed, and I can *feel* my voice getting that awful, wheedling, children's-hour intonation—very bright and encouraging, like somebody trying to screw rational answers out of an idiot school. Flat statement and argument is my natural line, and I shall make a ghastly mess of the other if I try it.

Two years later she repeated her conviction to Mr. Fenn:

> I have always very definitely dug my toes in when it came to the personal touch—the "Why I—" & the "What so-&-so means to me." Not only about religion, but about everything: Why I write detective fiction—how I think of my plots—what patriotism means to me—all the rest of it. I can't tell you

why, but it afflicts me with a faint nausea. Probably it's a form of spiritual pride—but also, genuinely I think, it is a revolt against that beastly habit of the modern mind which prompts it to ask, of any proposition, not: "Is it true?" but only, "Who says it."

It is not surprising, then, that she turned down several invitations to appear on broadcasts. She especially avoided interview programs. It was a clear *No* to *Women's Magazine, A New Outlook, Woman's Hour, Talks by Eminent Women in Britain, I Speak for Myself,* and *This I Believe.* After she had made radio appearances repeatedly for her Christian convictions, she even wrote to Dr. James Welch, Director of Religious Broadcasts,

> I am becoming increasingly reluctant to go on blowing the religious trumpet. I feel as if I was getting insincere about it and being pushed into the position of saying more than my experience warrants, or at any rate saying it in ways which are not natural to me, and are therefore essentially false.

Much the same sentiment was expressed at the same time to Mr. Fenn:

> I have just been passionately writing to Dr. Welch that I think it is rather a mistake for me to go on with this business of direct exhortation or instruction in the Christian faith. I am so obviously getting to be considered one of the old gang, whose voice can be heard bleating from every missionary platform; and when that happens the surprise value of the amateur theologian has pretty well disappeared and it is time to make way for the professionals.

Sayers's first personal appearance on a BBC program was on 23 July 1930, when she discussed from 9:25 to 10:15 P.M. with Anthony Berkeley the topic "Plotting a Detective Story." Already the month before, beginning on 14 June 1930, a collaborative endeavor entitled "Behind the Screen" had been broadcast. Sayers wrote to BBC's Mr. Lambert about the collaboration: "In 'Behind the Screen' . . . the first three authors carried the story along according to their own several fancies; while the last three authors used their wits in consultation to unravel the clues presented to them by the first three." And she ventured to comment on a procedure which was even then being followed by members of the Detection Club in the composition of *The Floating Admiral* (which was to be published before the end of the year):

> There is no reason why a perfectly "correct" detective story should not be produced even where the plot is not planned in collaboration at all. If each writer writes with a definite solution in mind & lays his clues properly, those clues can be picked up & worked to a satisfactory conclusion by a subsequent writer.

Ever watchful over the fortunes of the Detection Club, she urged Mr. Lambert to include some reference to the club book. "A little mutual advertisement is always helpful."[39]

A detective serial *The Scoop* began on the last day of 1930. Like the Detection Club collaborations, six well-known detection-fiction authors each contributed two installments and read his own contributions over the air. Anthony Berkeley, E. C. Bentley, Agatha Christie, Freeman Wills Crofts, Clemence Dane, as well as Dorothy L. Sayers participated. She also spoke of the composition of *The Scoop* in her letter to Mr. Lambert:

> the plot of "The Scoop" was planned in rough outline by all the authors in committee before the broadcasting of Chapter I. After this, each writer worked to a sketch-outline of what his instalment was to contain, and points of detail which arose in the course of working the chapter out being decided in consultation with myself & his other fellow-authors.
>
> As regards the actual writing, each author was left free to develop his own style & method. Generally speaking, the writer who first introduces a new character is responsible for laying down that character's general appearance, method of speech, & other writers dealing subsequently with that character are, of course, expected to carry it along in the same lines.

Thereafter, Sayers contributed to BBC programs on detective fiction at fairly regular intervals. Several of her own short stories were adapted for radio broadcasting, as well. There were also adaptations or readings of the play *Busman's Honeymoon* and some of her novels. In December 1931 she suggested that her husband, also, might be considered for a talk—a talk on cookery. (Fleming had already written articles on food and drink for both the London *Evening News* and the *Sunday Chronicle*. His *Gourmet's Book of Food and Drink* was to be published in 1933.)[40]

In the meantime, the chronicles of Lord Peter continued. *Strong Poison* appeared in October 1930. Seven years later Sayers was to declare that *Strong Poison* "rather timidly introduced the 'love-element' into the Peter Wimsey story." This timidity was matched by the temerity of a deadly intent: "Let me confess that when I undertook *Strong Poison* it was with the infanticidal intention of doing away with Peter; that is, of marrying him off and getting rid of him—for a lingering instinct of self-preservation, and the deterrent object-lesson of Mr. Holmes's rather scrambling return from the Reichenbach Falls, prevented me from actually killing and burying the nuisance."

It is true that by the end of 1930 or early in 1931 Sayers was rich enough to leave Benson's. More than that, like Conan Doyle's exasperation with the necessity of satisfying public demands for more Holmes, Sayers's weariness of forcing all her talents into one mold distressed her. She saw her reading public as "rolling up and hanging hopefully about along the route, uttering cheers and convinced that the show was billed to continue." Every good writer—let alone one who writes one thing in order ultimately to be free to write another—is always in competition with himself.

Actually, in *Strong Poison* Sayers was frustrated in accomplishing her ulterior motive because she discovered she could not coerce her characters, especially Harriet Vane.

> I could not marry Peter off to the young woman he had (in the conventional Perseus manner) rescued from death and infamy, because I could find no form of words in which she could accept him without loss of self-respect. I had landed my two chief puppets in a situation where, according to all the conventional rules of detective fiction, they should have had nothing to do but fall into one another's arms; *but they would not do it,* and that for a very good reason. When I looked at the situation I saw that it was in every respect false and degrading; and the puppets had somehow got just so much flesh and blood in them that I could not force them to accept it without shocking myself.

Wimsey himself originally arose as a compensatory device— money, lots of money, Aubussons, Daimlers. The character Harriet Vane is also a writer of detective stories. She is a graduate of an Oxford women's college. She had cohabited with Philip Boyes (at his insistence) in a trial marriage. He had also been a writer. Such details clearly parallel Sayers's own life.

What is amazing in this encounter is that Lord Peter—so brainy, so devoted to fact-finding, so ratiocinative— simply *intuits* that Harriet Vane could not have done the murder of which she is charged. Moreover, Peter abruptly proposes during his first interview with the prisoner in Holloway Gaol. A second interview "collapses in banter." The third injected the possibility, so Harriet thought, that, if they married, Peter would always be jealous of Boyes. (He assures her that that eventuality would not arise and even offers to discuss his own "hideous past.") Upon yet another occasion Harriet refuses because a marriage would, in her eyes, bring reproach upon Wimsey's family. She offers, out of mingled obligation and gratitude, simply to live with him. They do not fall into one another's arms, however, and the book is better for it. Sayers's intentions are defeated for the time being.[41]

The next Wimsey book proceeded as if Harriet Vane had never existed. It was *The Five Red Herrings,* published in March 1931. The Flemings's summer holidays in Galloway inspired both setting and plot.

Atherton Fleming for health reasons had retired from journalism and was developing various hobbies. He turned to photography. He turned to cookery. He turned to painting. He preferred pseudonymity, signing his paintings and drawings "Pigalle." Kirkcudbright and Gatehouse of Fleet in Galloway became an appropriate holiday spot for an artist-husband who was also a Scot. The foreword to *The Five Red Herrings,* in the form of a letter to Mr. Joe Dignam, indicates a past visit—in the summer of 1930—and promises a subsequent visit to the southern Scotland holiday area. Fleming could easily blend into the patterns of the art colony while Dorothy, always demanding the facts, could scout the land, interview the stationmaster or the booking clerks about railway schedules (so important to the novel), ask endless questions about the old mines at Creetown, observe the parade of characters, intently memorize Scottish idiom, and plunge Wimsey into still another situation.

Not only is Harriet Vane shelved, the Wimsey family is not at all conspicuous. Bunter and Parker, moreover, are brought into the story only when it is well advanced. Miss Climpson and the "Cattery," the Wimsey-organized staff of women investigators, of *Strong Poison* do not appear. Later, with her customary inerrancy of self-judgment, Sayers acknowledged *The Five Red Herrings* as "a cast back towards the 'time-table' puzzle-problem." All the same, it helped to satisfy a public clamorous for more Wimsey.[42]

The Wimsey novels, which regularly greeted readers each year, included *Have His Carcase* in the spring of 1932. Harriet

Vane is back. It is she who discovers the corpse, and she is promptly placed by the police among the suspects. Again, when she requires defense, Wimsey's appearance is not unexpected—except perhaps to Harriet:

> "Then why did you come?"
> "So that you might not have to send for me."
> *"Oh!"*
> . . . .
> He said nothing, but watched the wreck of his fortune in Harriet's stormy eyes.

Harriet is actually allowed to do a considerable amount of her own investigation in this story. Wimsey, of course, joins in. Harriet's position when the book opens is clear enough:

> The best remedy for a bruised heart is not, as so many people seem to think, repose upon a manly bosom. Much more efficacious are hard work, physical activity, and the sudden acquisition of wealth. After being acquitted of murdering her lover, and indeed, in consequence of that acquittal, Harriet Vane found all three specifics abundantly at her disposal; and although Lord Peter, with a touching faith in tradition, persisted day in and day out in presenting the bosom for her approval, she showed no inclination to recline upon it.

The course of the sleuths' love runs smoother as the story advances, and by the end of the book there is a measured accord between them.

> "Let's clear out of this," he said. "Get your things packed and leave your address with the police and come up to Town. I'm fed to the back teeth."
> "Yes, let's go. . . . It's all frightening and disgusting. We'll go home."
> "Right-ho! We'll go home. . . ."[43]

In 1933 *Murder Must Advertise* oscillated back to the Wimsey-minus-Vane novel. As *Five Red Herrings* derived from summer-holiday excursions, *Murder Must Advertise* derived from Sayers's years with S. H. Benson. She had the prudence to insert a prefatory "Author's Note":

> I do not suppose that there is a more harmless and law-abiding set of people in the world than the Advertising Experts of Great Britain. The idea that any crime could possibly be perpetrated on Advertising premises is one that could only occur to the ill-regulated fancy of a detective novelist, trained to fasten the guilt upon the Most Unlikely Person. If, in the course of this fantasy, I have unintentionally used a name or slogan suggestive of any existing person, firm or commodity, it is by sheer accident, and is not intended to cast the slightest reflection upon any actual commodity, firm or person.

This form of insurance exempting the author was cancelled magnanimously in 1950 when Sayers was asked to unveil a plaque in the reception area of the offices of Benson. It reads:

DOWN THIS STAIRCASE

was precipitated to his death with malice
aforethought and for the gratification of all
who appreciate the fine art of murder

VICTOR DEAN of PYM'S PUBLICITY
25 May   MCMXXXIII
THIS TABLET WAS UNVEILED   A.D. 1950 By
Dorothy L. Sayers, M.A.

A few years later, Sayers expressed the critical opinion that although this was the first Wimsey novel in which she had attempted fusing the detective puzzle-problem with the novel of manners, it was not quite successful.

> The idea of symbolically opposing two cardboard worlds—that of the advertiser and the drug-taker—was all right; and it was suitable that Peter, who stands for reality, should never appear in either except disguised; but the working-out was a little too melodramatic, and the handling rather uneven.

The unevenness developed because she "knew and cared much more about advertising" than about the world of the drug-taker, or "Bright Young People," as she sardonically equated them.

Reviewers and the reading public were not as critical of *Murder Must Advertise* as was its author. One important reason for its wide reception was the easy vicarious transition readers could make. Few, very few, indeed, have ever found nude corpses (unintentionally) in their bathtubs. Still fewer have approached the public ducal difficulties of *Clouds of Witness*. Clubrooms filled with the superannuated were equally uncommon. The incidence of direct involvement with death by the injection of a bubble of air into an important vein, or with death by synthetic or arsenic poisoning, or with manslaughter in an art colony, or with throat-slashed hemophiliacs must be limited—very limited. Contrariwise, the largest percentage of urban dwellers must have had some familiarity with office life—its petty feuds, its clock-watching, its hierarchy, its tea (or coffee) breaks, its gossip—even if not strictly in advertising agencies.

Wimsey, too, is not the same aloof outsider in this novel. He signs on as a copywriter, entering routines, becoming familiar with typists, office boys, charwomen, and even playing his way through a cricket match. Wimsey's varied experiences afford Sayers opportunity for humor, satire, poignancy, criticism.[44]

In 1933, Fleming also published. His *Gourmet's Book of Food and Drink,* appearing under the pseudonym *Hendy,* was dedicated to his wife, "who can make an Omelette." This ambiguous culinary distinction was matched by another comment slipped into the book: Dorothy, according to Hendy, also knew how to prepare tripe and onions to his taste.

The next Wimsey novel, *The Nine Tailors,* published in January 1934, is similar to *Murder Must Advertise* insofar as the inspiration arises from personal experience. Sayers turns to the Fen backgrounds: the rains and floods, rector and rectory, churches and church people. The subtitle of *The Nine Tailors* is "Changes Rung on an Old Theme in Two Short Touches and Two Full Peals." Campanological overtones sound through the book. "Nine Tailors make a man" is an expression used in many English churches to indicate the tolling of a bell for the passing of a man. In her story Sayers deliberately named the eighth bell in the full ring of bells in the tower of Fenchurch St. Paul "Tailor Paul."

"From time to time," says the foreword,

> complaints are made about the ringing of church bells. It seems strange that a generation which tolerates the uproar of the internal combustion engine and the wailing of the jazz band should be so sensitive to the one loud noise that is made to the glory of God. England, alone in the world, has perfected the art of change-ringing and the true ringing of bells by ropes and wheel, and will not lightly surrender her unique heritage.

Change ringing is, as Sayers notes, peculiarly English. For the English, "the proper use of bells is to work out mathematical permutations and combinations." The novel draws upon campanological lore not only for setting but also for details of plot.

The technical preparation for the writing of the novel took Sayers over two years, "during which," she observed, "I had to write *Murder Must Advertise* to keep the wolf from the door." It was hard work, including "incalculable hours spent in writing out sheets and sheets of changes," until she could do any method accurately in her head. It meant visualizing "from the pages of instructions to ringers, both what it looked like and what it felt like to handle a bell and to acquire 'rope-sight'." She also diligently studied "a good deal of technical stuff about bell cages, bell inscriptions, upkeep of bells and so on." When it was all completed, "the experts could discern only (I think) three small technical errors which betrayed the lack of practical experience." She confessed that this achievement made her sinfully proud. As a consequence of the successful writing of the novel, Sayers was made an honorary member of bell-ringers' groups and a vice-president of the Campanological Society of Great Britain. It must be pointed out, however, that all her research would have been inadequate for the production of a successful novel if she had not also made her home in the Fen lands for twenty years.

In some respects, Lord Peter Wimsey is eclipsed in *The Nine Tailors* by the Reverend Theodore Venables, the rector of Fenchurch St. Paul, who was surely patterned on Sayers's father—kindly, scholarly, dutiful, unworldly. Sayers's own perspicacity later caught the correct stance: "Peter himself remained, as it were, extraneous to the story and untouched by its spiritual conflicts." Needless to say, Harriet Vane was not even a consideration this time.

There is a clear sense in which God himself is a partner in exposing crimes and punishing the criminal in this story. Besides the providential arrival of Lord Peter, the novel's use of the rector as a prominent character, and of the tower, sanctuary, festivals, and cemetery of Fenchurch St. Paul, as the main locus of the crime and punishment and the scene of grace, supports this interpretation. Indeed, the overarching providence at work in the story creates much of its real mystery.

The novel contains a self-image of the author in Hilary Thorpe, at fifteen "tall and thin and rather gawky, though with the promise of becoming someday a striking-looking woman." Hilary idolizes her English mistress of the moment; she is slated to study at Oxford; and she is determined to be a writer of bestsellers (precociously aware of the fact that poetry doesn't pay very well).[45]

On the last day of February 1934 the *Daily Express* published an interview conducted with Sayers the previous day.

She is described as the "best seller" in detective fiction on the basis of the sales of *The Nine Tailors*. It immediately ran into three impressions, nearly 100,000 copies being sold in seven weeks in the United Kingdom alone. "Most of her books," went the report, "have been translated into six European languages." The interviewer found the author "in her comfortable, book-lined flat in Bloomsbury—hard at work." She was businesslike; she smoked innumerable cigarettes through a long holder; she talked freely about her life at Oxford and her early writings. " 'I am a scholar gone wrong,' she said gravely." "I had leanings towards poetry, but it didn't pay." Her acquaintance with detective fiction had led her to the idea of writing such fiction herself. "My novels were to be novels with a mystery as a plot—not just a mystery hung around some unlikely characters."[46]

For all her later hostility to the press—occasioned wholly by injured vanity over inaccuracies in reporting her precisely—Sayers enjoyed being lionized. On the day preceding the *Daily Express* interview she had accepted an invitation to lunch at the fashionable Boulestin's with Mrs. Marie Adelaide Belloc Lowndes, one of whose stories she had included in the First Series of *Great Short Stories of Detection, Mystery and Horror* in 1928. Sales were important to her, but so was her social standing—and Mrs. Belloc Lowndes had written a congratulatory note on *The Nine Tailors*. The same spirit appears in her correspondence with Hugh Walpole when she was secretary of the Detection Club. About the same time, the newly founded Sherlock Holmes Society in London invited Sayers to become a charter member. She must have been gratified by Christopher Morley's report of the first meeting on 6 June 1934 in which he stated expansively that "Miss Dorothy Sayers, . . . to the Sherlock Holmes Society, will always be *The* Woman." Also, beginning on 3 March 1934, the BBC program *Seven Days Hard* included Sayers as the only woman among such speakers as Winston Churchill, Bernard Shaw, Harold Nicholson, Lloyd George, Hilaire Belloc, J. B. Priestley, and Sir Thomas Beecham.[47]

On 13 June 1934, her birthday, Sayers attended the Somerville College Gaudy dinner, having been invited to "propose the toast of the University." She was thus a spokesman—in this case, for "the band of Somervillian novelists"; and upon asking herself "what it was for which one had to thank a university education," she concluded that "it was, before everything, that habit of intellectual integrity which is at once the foundation and the result of scholarship." The substance of her remarks was one year later embodied in "What Is Right with Oxford?" in the official organ of the Oxford Society for the alumni of the university. However rewarding (after so much effort) her reception by established fellow writers, recognition by her own college must have indeed provided an even stronger sense of worth.[48]

The neglected Harriet Vane's connection with Lord Peter Wimsey was given proper attention in Sayers's next novel. After all, as Carolyn Heilbrun has written, "by the time Miss Sayers returned to her hero's love life, she was to discover that he had been loving one woman for five years without even having kissed her, a remarkable record for a man so carefully trained in the *métier d'amant* by the proper French mistresses." This is to say nothing about the possible impairment of Lord Peter at forty-five "by so extended an orgy of continence."[49]

Sayers's dilemma was clearly recognized and as clearly dealt with: "any character that remains static except for a repertory of tricks and attitudes is bound to become a monstrous weariness to his maker in the course of nine or ten volumes."

> So there were only two things to do: one was to leave the thing there, with the problem unresolved; the other, far more delicate and dangerous, was to take Peter away and perform a major operation on him. If the story was to go on, Peter had got to become a complete human being, with a past and a future, with a consistent family and social history, with a complicated psychology and even the rudiments of a religious outlook. And all of this would have to be squared somehow or other with such random attributes as I had bestowed upon him over a series of years in accordance with the requirements of various detective plots.[50]

At this point, Uncle Paul Austin Delagardie appeared. His entrance conveniently coincided with Victor Gollancz's securing of publication rights in midsummer 1935 to the first four Wimsey novels *(Whose Body?, Clouds of Witness, Unnatural Death, The Unpleasantness at the Bellona Club)* and *The Documents in the Case.* Thus Gollancz became the publisher of all the Sayers detective books to date. In all reprints of the first volume thereafter appeared a "Biographical Note," communicated by Uncle Paul. Following the directory-type entry (already in use) which gives lineage, education, club affiliations, and arms of Peter Death Bredon Wimsey, D.S.O., the note is *"a short biography"* of Lord Peter, "brought up to date (May 1935)."[51]

This biographical preface complemented the "Wimsey industry" (a sort of parallel to the Holmes Society) which involved Sayers and her friends for the next few years. Not only did Wimsey spoof-pamphlets appear, some of them for private distribution only, but also she and her friends gave Wimsey lectures in various places.[52]

C. W. Scott-Giles, Fitzalan Pursuivant of Arms Extraordinary, entered into a fascinating correspondence with Sayers at this time. In the spirit of the interplay of wisdom and wit which marked the Wimsey industry, he wrote on 16 February 1936, referring to the arms of Lord Peter—*"Arms:* Sable, three mice courant argent; *Crest:* A domestic cat couched as to spring, proper." He pointed out that it was curious that Lord Peter should have inherited heraldic emblems so appropriate to his own activities of watching at the mouseholes of the criminal world. "What," he inquired, "was the origin and antiquity of the arms and crest?"

Nothing daunted, Sayers supplied a "history," moving with ease and heraldic accuracy through this playful project. She creates an "extract" from Froissart which is superb. Out of the correspondence came also the inspiration for the eccentric Mortimer Wimsey (whose fuller story appeared in one of the pamphlets) and the cousin Matthew Wimsey and the contents of Bredon Hall (later appearing in the novel *Busman's Honeymoon).* Through all of this her sense of humor is absolutely delightful. One passage from her letter to Scott-Giles on 1 April 1936 is especially hilarious; she introduced the family ghosts at Bredon Hall.

> The present Dowager (a woman of taste) was always trying to get rid of the accumulation of Victorian atrocities, while her husband (fox-hunting and violent tempered) was constantly adjuring her to "let the place alone". The present Duchess has no taste at all. (It was she, by the way, who insisted recently on establishing a new "guests" bathroom exactly in the place where "Uncle Roger," a Jacobean Wimsey, is accustomed to "walk" of an evening; this is highly disconcerting for female guests, who are not pleased to see a gentleman walk suddenly out of the hot-towel cupboard when they are in no state either to receive him or to retreat into the passage. But the

71

Duchess Helen does not see ghosts, and she refuses to believe that other people do.)

It was Scott-Giles who sent to Sayers the design of the Wimsey arms which appeared on ceramic tiles surrounding a fireplace in her Witham home.[53]

With the same flair with which Sayers created Peter's marvelous mother, his silly brother, and his romantic sister, she has drawn Paul Austin Delagardie. He is an aging Casanova, full of vanities and worldly wisdom. "To appear publicly in print is every man's ambition, and by acting as a kind of running footman to my nephew's triumph I shall only be showing a modesty suitable to my advanced age."

He has unconcealed contempt for the Wimsey stock.

The only sensible thing Peter's father ever did was to ally his exhausted stock with the vigorous French-English strain of the Delagardies. Even so, my nephew Gerald (the present Duke of Denver) is nothing but a beef-witted English squire. . . . Peter, I am glad to say, takes after his mother and me. . . . He has at least inherited the Delagardie brains, by way of safeguard to the unfortunate Wimsey temperament.

Sayers has Uncle Paul lay the foundation for Peter's constitutional neurasthenia: he was "a colourless shrimp of a child, very restless and mischievous"; he "suffered badly from nightmares as a child." Peter's skill in cricket and manipulation of fast automobiles derived not from "robust physical beauty" but from "a quick eye for a ball and beautiful hands for a horse." He grew up loving books and music. Like Sayers herself, he did not find school days happy, but he possessed natural astuteness and agility. "By the time he reached the Sixth Form, Peter had contrived to become the fashion— athlete, scholar, *arbiter elegantiarum—nec pluribus impar.*" Uncle Paul takes the credit for introducing Peter, in due time, "to a good tailor, showing him the way about Town, and teaching him to distinguish good wines from bad." In fact, Peter's father seems to have relinquished his younger son entirely to Uncle Paul for tutelage in the ways of the world:

At the age of seventeen, Peter came to me of his own accord. He was old for his age and exceedingly reasonable, and I treated him as a man of the world. I established him in trustworthy hands in Paris, instructing him to keep his affairs upon a sound business footing, and to see that they terminated with goodwill on both sides and generosity on his. He fully justified my confidence. I believe that no woman has ever found cause to complain of Peter's treatment; and two at least of them have since married royalty (rather obscure royalties, I admit, but royalty of a sort). Here again, I insist upon my due share of the credit; however good the material one has to work upon it is ridiculous to leave any young man's social education to chance.

Shades of "Eros in Academe"! With such a Chesterfield for mentor, no wonder that "The Peter of this period was really charming, very frank, modest and well-mannered, with a pretty, lively wit."

Uncle Paul disfavors the university years. Peter (like Sayers) entered his college, Balliol, with a scholarship. He read history and began "to give himself airs." "He acquired affectations, an exaggerated Oxford manner and a monocle, and aired his opinions a good deal, both in and out of the Union." During Peter's second year at Balliol, his father died and Gerald succeeded to the title. Uncle Paul shares Peter's dislike of Gerald's duchess: "a scrawny, over-bred prude. . . ." In his last year at Oxford, Peter fell in love. (Here Sayers disinters and then newly fleshes the bare bones of the Barbara incident.) "He treated that girl as if she was made of gossamer," writes Uncle Paul, "and me as a hardened old monster of depravity who had made him unfit to touch her delicate purity." Barbara's parents decided she was too young to marry; "so Peter went in for his final Schools in the temper of a Sir Eglamore achieving his first dragon; laid his First-Class Honours at his lady's feet like the dragon head, and settled down to a period of virtuous probation."

Then came World War I. (This passage in Peter's life was composed, it should be noted, almost on the eve of World War II.) Most details of the war episode had been incorporated in the previous writing: France; a good officer; promotion to the rank of Major; the D.S.O.; some "good intelligence work behind the German front"; the last year of the war—"blown up and buried in a shell-hole near Caudry," leaving him with a bad nervous breakdown which lasted, on and off, for two years. Additional details concern his relationship with Barbara:

Of course the young idiot was mad to get married before he went. But his own honourable scruples made him mere wax in other people's hands. It was pointed out to him that if he came back mutilated it would be very unfair to the girl. He hadn't thought of that, and rushed off in a frenzy of self-abnegation to release her from the engagement.

When Peter returned on leave in 1916, he found Barbara married. She had not had the nerve to tell Peter beforehand. What was especially humiliating was that she had married "a hardbitten rake of a Major Somebody, whom she had nursed in the V.A.D. hospital, and whose motto with women was catch 'em quick and treat 'em rough." Barbara simply reminded Peter he himself had set her free. The brutality of the episode sent him back to France with "the fixed intention of getting killed."

After the war, Lord Peter of course set himself up in the Piccadilly flat, "with the man Bunter (who had been his sergeant and was, and is, devoted to him)." At first Uncle Paul was anxious. "He had lost all his beautiful frankness, he shut everybody out of his confidence, including his mother and me, adopted an impenetrable frivolity of manner and a dilettante pose, and became, in fact, the complete comedian." (Since Sayers was the person she knew best, she found it easy to describe Peter by terms applicable no doubt to her own postwar early London days.) Paul's last word accounts for the Bertie Wooster-Jeeves relationship in the earliest Wimsey novels. Out of his anxiety, Uncle Paul felt compelled to speak to Peter, thinking "it dangerous that a man of his ability should have no job to occupy his mind."

Thus arrived the noble sleuth, though the detective activities produced new tensions for the neurasthenic—"Peter's intellect pulled him one way and his nerves another." From *Whose Body?* to *Busman's Honeymoon* Sayers retains the effects of the old nightmares and the old shell shock. The new tensions were gradually complemented by the development of new feelings.

The arrival of Harriet Vane on the scene is acknowledged gratefully by Paul, who agrees completely with Sayers's own analysis of personality that Harriet's refusal to marry Peter immediately after *Strong Poison* was in keeping with her character. "Gratitude and a humiliating inferiority complex are no foundation for matrimony; the position was false from the start." Paul advises patience and self-discipline.[54]

Thus Sayers was ready for *Gaudy Night*. Of all her novels, *Gaudy Night* may alone be called the one toward which Sayers worked. "Taking it all in all, I think it is true," she wrote in 1937, "that each successive book of mine worked

gradually nearer to the sort of thing I had in view." She
wanted the detective story to "become once more a novel of
manners instead of a pure crossword puzzle." The Vane-
Wimsey relationship had also to be resolved creditably. She
finally knew how to handle the problem.

> On the intellectual platform, alone of all others, Harriet could stand free
> and equal with Peter, since in that sphere she had never been false to her
> own standards. By choosing a plot that should exhibit intellectual integri-
> ty as the one great permanent value in an emotionally unstable world I
> should be saying the thing that, in a confused way, I had been wanting to
> say all my life. Finally, I should have found a universal theme which could
> be made integral both to the detective plot and to the "love-interest" which
> I had, somehow or other, to unite with it.

Gaudy Night, therefore, concerned itself with academic
women and academic values. The theme was to be "that the
same intellectual honesty that is essential to scholarship is
essential also to the conduct of life." The setting was to be
Shrewsbury College at Oxford, a fictional women's college
patterned after Somerville. The malice of the criminal was to
be "the product, not of intellect starved of emotion"—although
this possible alternative would bring many of the tutors under
suspicion —"but of emotion uncontrolled by intellect." (The
malice is further refined as "emotion revenging itself upon the
intellect for some injury wrought by the intellect upon the
emotions.") When Sayers asked herself the question, "What
harm could intellectual women do, in virtue of their intellect,
to an emotional woman?" she imagined "The case of a woman
who, in her academic capacity, was obliged to expose a crime
of intellectual dishonesty committed by a man . . . , and so
deprive him of his academic status and, consequently, of his
livelihood." The situation is not implausible; regrettably it has
occurred more than once.

The theme, setting, and plot, then, had been sifted down.
Some mechanics had to be adjusted with the help of the
calendar and an architect; she rearranged some geography
and some management. She expressed apologies to Balliol
College (from whose master she had gained prior permission)
for her "monstrous impertinence in having erected Shrewsbury College upon its spacious and sacred cricket-ground."

There was some wrestling "to bring the love-problem into
line with the detective-problem, so that the same key should

unlock both at once." But where there's a Wimsey, there's a way. Harriet Vane does most of the sleuthing in this story, but Peter assists. When the investigation is all concluded, Harriet and Peter find each other on an equal footing. Appropriately enough, they stand on Magdalen Bridge in their academic gowns after attending a concert at Balliol.

> She stood still; and he stopped perforce and turned towards her. She laid both hands upon the fronts of his gown, looking into his face while she searched for the word that would carry her over the last difficult breach.
> It was he who found it for her. With a gesture of submission he bared his head and stood gravely, the square cap dangling in his hand.
> *"Placetne, magistra?"*
> *"Placet."*

All the respect and esteem and intellectual honesty and love are there. There is, also, the promise of joy, of *gaudium,* which makes the title of this book a true vanishing point in the perspective of theme and plot.

Sayers knew she had satisfied her own sense of artistic unity in *Gaudy Night.* She had some apprehension of public response. Even as she left the manuscript with her publisher, she predicted that "if it didn't strike lucky it would be a sensational flop." "The 'male reader' confounded prophecy by not merely displaying interest in academic women, but by producing a strong 'pro-Harriet' party, which asserted, in the teeth of those female readers who complained of Peter's throwing himself away on Harriet, that Harriet, on the contrary, was completely thrown away on Peter."

The book appeared on 4 November 1935. The sales were gratifying. The first edition of 17,000 copies was sold out on publication, and before the end of the year five additional impressions had been printed. Early in January 1936 Gollancz advertised in the *Sunday Times* that *Gaudy Night* had headed the Christmas sales with twenty mentions out of a possible twenty-one, "thus rivalling the record of *The Seven Pillars of Wisdom* during its best months." By April 1936 the book had gone into a sixth impression, making a total (of British printings only) of 40,000 copies.

Sayers put more of her personal life into *Gaudy Night* than she had in any previous novel, although general readers would have assumed that it was all "pure" fiction. The entire setting obviously draws upon her Somerville days: tutors, halls, libraries, chapel, porters, Second-Year play, some students sitting up late at night "over the fire with coffee and parkin," long discussions "about love and art, religion and citizenship." Her Harriet Vane thinks of her "bitter years" when she had "gone to London to write mystery fiction, to live with a man who was not married to her." She mentions "the struggle to earn a livelihood" that "had absorbed all her time and thought." She "had broken all her old ties and half the commandments." In an ancient trunk she finds a "faded tie that had belonged to her dead lover" and the academic gown "worn only once at the taking of her M.A. degree." She sees her face in a mirror—

> rather pale, with black brows fronting squarely either side of a strong nose, a little too broad for beauty. Her own eyes looked back at her—rather tired, rather defiant—eyes that had looked upon fear and were still wary. The mouth was the mouth of one who has been generous and repented of her generosity; its wide corners were tucked back to give nothing away.

Harriet Vane engages in research on Sheridan Lefanu, providing an interesting parallel to Sayers's own work on Wilkie Collins. She maintains that "If you learn how to tackle one subject—any subject—you've learnt how to tackle all subjects." A sister of one of the tutors in the novel is expecting a first baby: "It is always an anxious business to have a first baby at thirty-five." About responsibility accepted in bringing children into the world, the same tutor says, "But if the domestic responsibility is to take precedence of the public responsibility, then the work should be handed over to some one else to do." Understandably, Peter urges Harriet to write out her bitter experience therapeutically, "even if it hurt like hell." "What would that matter, if it made a good book?" "What's the use of making mistakes if you don't use them?"[55]

Peter Wimsey made one more appearance before the end of 1936, and it was on stage. More than one person had attempted (without complete success) to make a drama out of Sayers's materials. Now the author herself, with the collaboration of her friend Muriel St. Clare Byrne, was about to place Peter behind the footlights. Earlier in the year, after the success of *Gaudy Night* Sayers dropped in on Miss Byrne in London to tell her of a hilarious experience she had just had with an Essex chimney sweep. She felt like putting him on the stage, he was so rich a character.

"Why don't you, then?" retorted Miss Byrne.

Miss Byrne, with valuable experience in the teaching and criticism of drama, persuaded Dorothy to learn how drama was written. Together they would use the chimney sweep for the opening. They would use a Sayers clue, write 18,000 words, 6,000 in each of three acts, and the stage itself would show the exercise of the Fair-Play Rule. The result, of course, was *Busman's Honeymoon.*

It opened in London, after an initial production in Birmingham, at the Comedy Theatre on Wednesday, 16 December 1936, and it ran for nine months. It was produced by Amner Hall and directed by Beatrice Wilson. Dennis Arundell played the part of Peter, Veronica Turleigh played Harriet, and Norman V. Norman did Bunter. Drama critics offered the usual mix of judgment. The BBC arranged for a radio adaptation of the play on 5 February 1937.[56]

The novel version of *Busman's Honeymoon* was issued in June 1937 after the publication of the play. It is subtitled "A Love Story with Detective Interruptions." In the dedicatory note (addressed to her friends Muriel St. Clare Byrne, Helen Simpson, and Marjorie Barber), Sayers touches upon both the lineage from the play and the nature of the novel: she called it a "sentimental comedy," and "a ha' porth of detection to an intolerable deal of saccharine." The novel, understandably, indulges in freer form than can the play. *Busman's Honeymoon* was the last Wimsey novel. There were still to be published some Lord Peter short stories, and the spoof industry flickered on. Several Detection Club collaborations were to follow. There was even talk of using Lord Peter in a novel to be entitled *Thrones, Dominations,* but it was abortive. From 1938 on, BBC presented even more adaptations of, or readings from, Sayers's detective fiction, drawn both from her short stories and her novels.[57]

From 25 June 1933 through 18 August 1935, Sayers wrote a weekly column of detective-story reviews for the *Sunday Times.* She reviewed over three hundred fifty books during that period, the authors of which sound like a Sherlockian hall of fame. She laid down precept upon precept, sometimes explicitly, sometimes implicitly. She ranged through all the components of fiction. Her reviews attracted considerable interest, even stimulating a flow of correspondence to the editor. Irked especially by slothful writing, she eventually took to citing "The Week's Worst English." In her last column of 1934 she vowed, *"I will not cease from mental fight nor shall my sword sleep in my hand till I have detected and avenged all mayhems and murders done upon the English language against the peace of our Sovereign Lord the King, his Crown, and dignity."*[58]

In consequence of her writing for the *Sunday Times,* Sayers found herself billed to speak at book exhibitions sponsored by the newspaper. She was also sought after to speak before many groups on topics related to detective fiction. At Cambridge University, for example, during the winter of 1934 she discussed "whether or not it is possible to treat the detective story with any marked literary dignity." Mary Ellen Chase, who was one of her auditors, thought the talk was "matchless," "largely formed of vivid rhetorical questions." The undergraduates "listened to her, spellbound, transformed, entranced." This virtuosity seemed all the more brilliant to Miss Chase because of Sayers's unassuming appearance.

> There can be few plainer women on earth than Dorothy Sayers; and the adjective is an extremely kind one. She seemingly had no neck at all. Her head appeared to be closely joined to the regions directly between her shoulder blades in back and her collar bone in front. She had a florid complexion, very blue, near-sighted eyes, and wore glasses which quivered. Her thinning hair rarely showed evidence of care or forethought in its total lack of arrangement. Like many British women, she had small taste in dress, favouring what used to be known as "georgette," often purple by some sorry choice of colour, with too much lace in all the wrong places. She was large, rawboned, and awkward.

At forty-one Dorothy Sayers was already showing the inescapable results of aging and a sedentary life. Mary Ellen Chase, however, was aware of something more than the plain appearance of Sayers: "Just as I have never seen a less attractive woman to look upon, *I have never come across one so magnetic to listen to."* Miss Chase was reminded that Socrates was ugly beyond belief, "yet no one has noted that Ion and young Phaedo, Glaucon and Alcibiades were distressed by his flat, distended nose or his flabby, sagging jowls."[59]

Sayers spoke in Oxford, also, early in March 1935. Her subject was "Aristotle and Detective Fiction." She offered the same lecture to the English Association in London in June.

Miss Byrne presided at the meeting. (Sayers was later to consent to being a vice-president of the association in 1943.)[60]

There had, of course, been various published criticisms of her writings. It was Sayers's character to weigh these, even if they were only perfunctory. There had, also, been attempts at cleverness. In April 1933 Eustace Portugal's article "Death to the Detectives!" in the *Bookman* whimsically attacked selective twentieth-century examples of the key tradition in detective fiction. "A wag once stated that the perfect mystery story would consist of two sentences only—'A shot rang out. The great detective fell dead.' " Portugal fantasizes the destruction of Lord Peter Wimsey, among others.[61]

Noel Stock says that around this time Ezra Pound "In reading Dorothy L. Sayers . . . began to think that it would be better if she gave some of her time to the larger 'crimes' in the world of economics and government and he wrote to her accordingly. In reply she said she did not think there was enough element of mystery in what he proposed. . . . " Pound, in characteristically idiosyncratic spelling and mechanics, told her she was wrong. She, however, apparently thought that there was not a groatsworth of wit to this Pound, as far as fiction went.[62]

Before the end of 1937, Sayers received a left-handed compliment for her writing from *Scrutiny*. Q. D. Leavis, as Carolyn Heilbrun notes, "with that lack of courtesy as marked in the Leavises as their astuteness, railed at her in *Scrutiny* with such vehemence as positively to affirm Miss Sayers's importance as a literary figure." The article was entitled "The Case of Miss Dorothy Sayers." It purports to deal critically with factors in *Gaudy Night* and *Busman's Honeymoon,* but the tone of snideness eclipses everything else. Sayers, says Mrs. Leavis,

> displays knowingness about literature without any sensitiveness to it or any feeling for quality—*i.e.* she has an academic literary taste over and above having no general taste at all. . . .
>
> And Miss Sayers' fiction, when it isn't mere detective-story of an unimpressive kind, is exactly that: stale, second-hand, hollow. . . .
>
> . . . evidently Miss Sayers' spiritual nature, like Harriet Vane's, depends for its repose, refreshment and sustenance on the academic world, the ideal

> conception that is of our older universities—or let us say a rationalised nostalgia for her student days.
>
> Miss Sayers, who might evidently have been an academic herself, is probably quite sound on the philological side.

The critic betrays not only a lack of the soul-saving sense of the comic but also the pique of the thwarted lioness: her real objections to Sayers are that the Wimsey books are "respectable" "best-sellers" and that Sayers's descriptions of the academic world are "romanticizing and extravagant claims." The latter point may be well taken, but the case of Q. D. Leavis is poorly offered by virtue of a preemptive bitterness which itself makes extravagant claims.[63]

Little is to be gained by the attempt to identify the originals of each of the characters in Sayers's fiction. Every novelist draws upon his own experiences, including the persons he has known, while he projects his anxieties and ideals. It neither cheapens nor augments the quality of an author's writing to be able to say that character X was so-and-so in the flesh. Sayers obviously drew portraits from people she knew, but here she added, there she subtracted. Some characters are transparent: the vicars owe much to her father; Harriet Vane is in many respects a self-portrait; Pym's Publicity undoubtedly had counterparts in Benson's; there *was* an Essex chimney sweep; the tutors of Shrewsbury must have been evacuated from Somerville. Sayers herself, however, reminds us in *The Mind of the Maker* that Shakespeare is more than Hamlet.[64]

The reputation of Dorothy Leigh Sayers in the craft of detective fiction rests upon a number of achievements other than simply portraying characters. She put criticism of life into her stories. She worked to the model of Wilkie Collins, with the novel of manners in view. She knew how to use language. She successfully managed intrigue and suspense. She educated readers in a variety of subjects pertinent to plots and settings. She created enduring characters.

Sayers, of course, did not achieve equal distinction in her fiction. Few writers do. Sometimes—as in *Five Red Herrings* or *Have His Carcase*—intricacy of plot development may become oppressive. Some of the short stories are only puzzles. But at her best—for example, in *The Documents in the Case,* in *The Nine Tailors,* in *Gaudy Night*—she is superb on almost every count. The evidence in the last analysis chiefly lies in the constant reprinting of her works.

All of this, however, was receding. Events were leading Sayers resolutely away from the golden age of stories of sleuths. For one thing, in *Gaudy Night* she had realized her ideal in detective fiction. In it, also, she had solved the problem of what to do with that "nuisance" Peter Wimsey. All that remained was what she accomplished in *Busman's Honeymoon*—he was married off. Moreover, the pattern of "The Long Week-End," as British society knew it between the wars, was drawing to a close. The social revolution impelled by political, psychological, and technological developments, in turn, forced upon many artists and writers a crisis of personal identity.

chapter three

The Zeal of Thy House

The temperament of Dorothy Sayers consistently required hard work. That is to say, she seldom undertook an assignment without giving it her assiduous best.

Her fiction was increasingly well written: the plots were intriguingly constructed; the characters were given full dimensions; the style was efficient, witty, urbane. Her reviews and criticism attracted deserved attention. Her occasional articles on detective fiction, accuracy and effectiveness in language-use, the psychology of advertising, and the Fen district all manifested deliberate concern with facts and reasoned conviction. Her lectures fascinated audiences for the same reasons; they revealed her charm and personal magnetism as well. Her book-lined study was a witness to her habits and cast of mind.

A scholar gone wrong? Who is to say? The patterns of life, fortunately, are varied. It is quite true, as Cyril Ray has written, that "she was always grateful for the immense prestige found for her by the series of detective novels" and "for the financial security they had brought her."[1]

Her reputation among writers and would-be writers, professional societies, and university groups continued to mount.

She found herself ever more steadily sought after: interviews, critiques, lectures. With the production on stage of *Busman's Honeymoon,* she also began to gain prominence with theatre people.

Thus, Margaret Babington, acting as the emissary of the Friends of Canterbury Cathedral, called upon Dorothy Sayers shortly after *Busman's Honeymoon* was produced to ask her, as a successful West End dramatist, to write a play for the 1937 Canterbury festival. Sayers knew of the interests and work of the bishop of Chichester and former dean of Canterbury, Dr. George K. A. Bell—especially that he had initiated the Canterbury Festival and had been triumphant in securing the services of T. S. Eliot to write *Murder in the Cathedral* for the 1935 festival. Moreover, Charles Williams, with whom Sayers had begun friendship, had written *Thomas Cranmer of Canterbury* for the 1936 festival. Sayers was hesitant to accept Miss Babington's invitation: "I don't want to mug up the history of kings and archbishops."[2]

What finally persuaded her was the advance information that the 1937 festival was to be a Service of Arts and Crafts. She could avoid the kings and archbishops. Who *were* the artists and craftsmen who built the cathedral? She found the answer she needed—and her inspiration—in the medieval Latin account of the cathedral construction written by Gervase of Canterbury, who recorded the gutting by fire of the Norman Choir in the twelfth century and the building of the new Choir under William of Sens. In one passage Gervase comments on the accident which occurred to William of Sens in 1178: he fell from the scaffolding beneath the great arch. In a single query of Gervase about the source of the accident—*vel Dei vindicata, vel diaboli desaevit invidia*—Sayers got her clue.[3] Between the vindicating justice of God and the envy of Satan there is indeed margin for speculation on the cause of human accidents, and the dilemma of the artist, as well.

The theme of her play, which she entitled *The Zeal of Thy House,* is that God who endows artists with their talents will not tolerate a hubristic attitude on their part. The title of the play was borrowed from Psalm 69.9 and St. John 2.7. The words of the title, described as "a forbidding title" by the *Church Times* reviewer and "unattractive" by the *Times* reporter,[4] point to God's jealousy. Significantly enough, Sayers wrote four years later:

> I know it is no accident that *Gaudy Night,* coming towards the end of a long development in detective fiction, should be a manifestation of precisely the same theme as the play *The Zeal of Thy House,* which followed it and was the first of a series of creatures embodying a Christian theology. They are variations upon a hymn to the Master Maker. . . .[5]

After an interval of twenty years, the incredible materialized unexpectedly. Years before in Oxford she had started to write poetry evocative of medieval settings and values. At that time there had been "no money" in that direction. Now, financially secure and widely known, she was being *invited* to produce a play with a medieval focus, and she could return to verse if she chose. After all, her immediate predecessors in the festival drama had written their work in poetry.

On 15 April 1936, while *Zeal* was being written, Sayers wrote to Dorothy Rowe about staging problems in the Chapter House. "The play has had to be arranged for the peculiar stage in the Chapter-House, where all important exits & entrances have to be made through the audience." She accompanied her note with a half-page sketch of the space available to her.

When Dorothy Rowe replied, it was to commend the play (a typewritten copy of which had been sent to her). Sayers, answering on 25 April 1937, expressed her gratitude. Single-mindedly she wrote: "I do feel that if one has to write a play on a religious subject, the only way to do it is to avoid wistful emotionalism, and get as much drama as one can out of sheer hard dogma." She confessed apprehensions about the adequacy of the Chapter House for the production:

> I hope the action will arrange itself effectively on the steps and stage as they stand. Since the Chapter House was built in the 14th century, I suppose we can scarcely blame the architects for not having provided suitable back-stage accommodation. . . .
>
> Reassure yourself about the scenes; they are permanent structures of wood and canvas designed and built by Laurence Irving. On the left-hand side is a cramped space where half a dozen people can easily stand together if they are thin and hold their breaths; on the right-hand side, a narrow passage and awkward staircase lead to something I have not yet dared to investigate, but where, I believe, performers can be got on and off in sufficient numbers, and from which they can, by running very hard, escape, to appear again at the bottom of the building, after traversing most of the Cathedral and Cloisters.

She invited Dorothy Rowe to attend the first performance "together with a number of friends and sympathisers."[6]

So *The Zeal of Thy House* was written, and on the afternoon of Saturday, 12 June 1937, it was presented, opening the festival week for 1937. There were no kings or archbishops, but archangels were present—present during the entire play—to imply that everything in life is *sub specie aeternitatis*. (One reviewer, however, found them less medieval: "Their attitude to mortals suggests that of schoolmasters of the best type, Olympian and amused, but sympathetic and genuinely anxious for the true welfare of their wards."[7])

In the shadow of archangels, then, William of Sens's story unfolds. He is chosen by the Canterbury monks as their architect. He proceeds with the building of the Choir.

> Two years of toil are passed: what shall I write
> About this architect? . . .
>
> Jugglings with truth, and gross lusts of the body,
> Drink, drabbing, swearing; slothfulness in prayer;
> With a devouring, insolent ambition
> That challenges disaster. . . .
>
> Six columns, and their aisles, with covering vaults
> From wall to arcading, and from thence again
> To the centre, with the key stones locking them,
> All well and truly laid without a fault. . . .
>
> Behold, he prayeth; not with the lips alone,
> But with the hand and with the cunning brain
> Men worship the Eternal Architect. . . .
>   True as a mason's rule
> And line can make them, the shafted columns rise
> Singing like music; and by day and night
> The unsleeping arches with perpetual voice
> Proclaim in Heaven, to labour is to pray.

Here is the eternal ambiguity of the artist. He works with God because he is a creator, but he is apt to neglect God for the work; and so he faces the danger of idolatry.

The complication sets in with the coming of Lady Ursula de Warbois, an exceedingly rich widow who becomes more interested in the architect than in the architecture. William tries rather bumptiously to indicate to Lady Ursula the priority of his work: "In one man's life / Is room for one love and no more—one love; / I am in love with a dream." Women only destroy dreams! But Lady Ursula cunningly accepts Eve's role and tempts this Adam to share his dream by her fire. The archangels take temporary comfort in theology. But inevitably William mounts the scaffold. The atmosphere is full of omens—an eclipse, bad weather—and of scandalous talk. Not only workmen but monks are affected by William's conduct. William's ascent to the great arch is a visible parallel to his mounting hubris. A choir crescendos as he climbs. A great cloud of witnesses—archangels, monks, workmen, even Lady Ursula—is present at his fall. William does not die, but he is sorely maimed. The balance of the play deals with the building of the temple within the man. Lady Ursula conveniently decides to enter a convent. William finally confesses:

> A year ago
> An idle mason let the chisel slip
> Spoiling the saint he carved. I chid him for it,
> Then took the tool and in that careless stroke
> Saw a new vision, and so wrought it out
> Into a hippogriff. But yet this mason
> Was not less to blame. So works with us
> The cunning craftsman, God.

In saying this, William of course put himself on the side of the angels. The work on the Choir would be finished, but William had to bow out. The Archangel Michael works on his flinty heart to gain a last concession:

> Thus shalt thou know the Master Architect,
> Who plans so well, He may depart and leave
> The work to others. Art thou more than God?

When archangels instruct, who can fail to learn?

An hour after the first performance of *The Zeal of Thy House* (in a shortened form) in the Chapter House, a Service of Arts and Crafts was held in the cathedral.

It was intended to be a Thanksgiving to God for His gifts to mankind through artists and craftsmen: also a service of dedication, in which the artist recognised that the exercise of his art was a religious act, and asked the blessing of God on his vocation. After the entry of the Mayors of a number of Kentish boroughs, there was a procession which included eminent persons associated with architecture, painting and sculpture, literature and music.[8]

The author of *Zeal* marched in the procession.

The play continued in Canterbury from 12 through 18 June 1937. Like *Murder in the Cathedral,* it was later taken to London and then to the provinces. It had a run of one month in Westminster Theatre (29 March through 30 April 1938), then moved to the Garrick Theatre (opening 10 May 1938), and finally to the Duke of York's Theatre (where it was presented from 13 June through 2 July 1938). Harcourt Williams, who created the part of William at Canterbury, appeared in the London production. So did Frank Napier, joint director with Williams of the festival production.[9]

Reviewers of the premiere production all made reference to the author's ready transition from Wimsey to William of Sens with some surprise. Attendants at the play were also struck by the use of modern idiom in Sayers's play. To her thinking, religion had already suffered too much in the house of its friends by needless archaism of language.

> Her monks are human beings, mixtures in varying proportions of the sublime and the ridiculous, and her pilgrims, just because they express themselves in the language of the twentieth-century trippers, are sufficiently quick with life to be of Chaucer's company.
>
> She asks the audience to assume that the medieval mind was much like our own, and that not only the housewife's remark, "So I said to her, you can take your wages and go," but the mental outlook of churchmen and artists is constant through the ages. Taken on these terms the comedy of the architect's dealings with the churchmen, the workmen, and the wealthy patroness, has unfailing liveliness, and the reckoning which he is called upon to make with his soul a deeply moving reality.

Twentieth-century language and an attendant liveliness were primary concerns to Sayers in the religious drama that she was to produce over the next dozen years.[10]

One morning, just before the opening of *Zeal* at the Westminster Theatre in London, Sayers talked with an interviewer from the *Church Times*. The interview was conducted in a small room at the Westminster during rehearsal time. "Miss Sayers hurried into the little room where I awaited her, greeted me with a good humour, for which I was specially grateful, pulled her hat off her cropped head, lit a cigarette, and said, briskly, 'Well, what can I do for you?' "

Inevitably the talk began on the subject of detective fiction. After all, here was the famous creator of Lord Peter Wimsey.

"Please don't begin by saying how odd it is to find a detective novelist writing a play about Christian dogma," she said. "I am so tired of that remark."

She talked about both fiction and dogma in the course of the hour, honestly admitting that the detective stories were started because she was "hard up at the time," and wanted "to earn a little money." It had taken her "fifteen years of practice" before she was able "to hammer out the kind of novel" she wanted to write— *Gaudy Night*. She agreed that the detective was the only figure of romance left. "Life is often a hopeless muddle, to the meaning of which [people] can find no clue; and it is a great relief to get away from it for a time into a world where they can exercise their wits over a neat problem, in the assurance that there is only one answer, and that answer a satisfying one." She insisted that the detective story proper, as distinct from the "thriller," has an intellectual appeal. "And it may claim to be the one form of fiction in which the virtuous character is made more exciting and sympathetic than the sinner!"

Sayers emphasized the similarity of theme in *Gaudy Night* and *The Zeal of Thy House:* "integrity of work overriding and redeeming personal weakness." Psychologically, also, the problem of William of Sens and of Lord Peter is much the same. Wimsey and William seem odd bedfellows only because of an "unhappy and unnatural divorce between religion and life."

"You believe, do you not," asked the interviewer, "that the drama might be used to-day, as it was in the Middle Ages, as a means of getting Christianity 'across' to non-churchgoers, to people with fantastic misconceptions of the real nature of Christianity?"

Cautiously she replied. "Yes, though it is dangerous to dogmatize about it in days like these when there is no telling in what direction the next international upheaval will turn people's minds." She emphasized her belief that the Christian philosophy, nonetheless, ought to be offered as a lively option to people who are eager to be presented with some working philosophy of life in the theatre.

She distinguished between zeal and skillful knowledge. A dramatist "must understand what he is writing about, and he must try to put the Christian point of view fairly." High motives on the part of good Christian people may result only in "hopeless failures from the dramatic point of view because in playwriting piety and good intentions are not enough."

She felt dullness in Christian religious drama unforgivable:

> I am afraid that the pious themselves are partly to blame. Artists who paint pictures of our Lord in the likeness of a dismal-looking, die-away person, with his hair parted in the middle, ought to be excommunicated for blasphemy. And so many good Christians behave as if a sense of humour

were incompatible with religion; they are too easily shocked about the wrong things. When my play was acted at Canterbury, one old gentleman was terribly indignant at the notion that the builders of that beautiful Cathedral could have been otherwise than men of blameless lives.

To the representative of the *Church Times,* Sayers's "downright way of speaking" was disconcerting; the twinkle in her eyes, however, was reassuring. "She is a most exhilarating person, with a great sense of fun, and not an atom of that chilling hauteur which is commonly associated—no doubt, quite unjustly—with literary celebrity."[11]

From its first presentation in Canterbury and London, *The Zeal of Thy House* has remained in the repertory of British religious drama. It was revived in Canterbury 24-29 June 1940. Various groups over the years have produced the play, most often in churches and schools. Although the milieu of the play differs greatly from the milieus of the detective stories, there are some extensions from the latter into the former. In religious narrative God, or any one of his surrogates, does the sleuthing business. That is not to say, of course, that the archangels in *Zeal,* for example, are merely Lord Peter and Charles Parker with wings. There are, rather, similarities of function. The hounds of God are always on man's traces. Moreover, Sayers's Prior is another kindly vicar-figure. Even Lady Ursula's presence is a variation of the love-story with detective interruptions. The supernumeraries in both genres provide much the same sort of comedy of manners.

The poetry of *The Zeal of Thy House* does not approach the quality of theme and tone in *Murder in the Cathedral,* but Sayers's play has an equal intensity of action.

That November Sayers received a letter from R. A. Scott-James of the *London Mercury* expressing his pleasure with her Canterbury Festival play and with the ensemble spirit of the actors. She was gratified. She told Scott-James that she had been trying "very hard" to get *Zeal* offered in London at "a series of Christmas matinees"; but the theatre managers were not interested. "As you doubtless know, the great difficulty is the reluctance of commercial managers to take a courageous line with serious plays that need nursing and, of course, the reluctance of the public to come to anything which looks like doing them good or making them think, even though they may like it very much when they do get there."[12]

In November 1938 Sayers also wrote to Val Gielgud, to whom in October she had sent a copy of her nativity play *He That Should Come,* to say that the tour of *Zeal* was ending "(for the time being anyway) with Birmingham Dec. 6-12." She indicates that she has been "very busy rushing about the country the last week or two," and that she has been asked to do the 1939 Canterbury play: "so I'm going to be uncommonly busy."[13]

Sayers had now touched the magic string in both the novel and the drama. She was acknowledged as one of the leading writers of the day. In October 1938 she had accepted the presidency of the Modern Language Association for the ensuing year, succeeding Sir Malcolm Robertson. The editor of the journal of the association wrote for the October issue:

> We are fortunate in having in our 1939 President a lady who is not only a distinguished novelist but also a fine scholar. If any of our readers are unacquainted with her literary work, we would refer them to an account of the writer by Mr. Frank Swinnerton in his delightful book called *The Georgian Literary Scene. . . .*

(Swinnerton had offered the opinion that Sayers represented "the farthest point yet reached in the development of detective stories towards complete sophistication.") The presidential office of the Modern Language Association, of course, was honorific. It was obviously gratifying to Sayers, even though her main duty was simply to preside at the Annual General Meeting of the association in the following year and to give a speech at the dinner meeting. The attendance at the general meeting "was much smaller than usual," writes the editor of the association journal, "except at the dinner, at which there was an unusually large attendance."[14]

Sayers was becoming a very busy person. She was not able to work on the Wilkie Collins biography, but she still gathered materials. A new Wimsey novel would never again appear, but there was published a short story, a sop to Cerberus, in which Sayers announced the birth of a son to Peter and Harriet when "The Haunted Policeman" greeted readers of *Harper's Bazaar* in February 1938.[15] She composed in autumn a skeletal story, and loaned her name, for an advertising campaign in behalf of "The Perils of Night Starvation" for Horlock's in a new and special medium, "a strip cartoon entitled 'Tight-Rope.' " The

Times twitted her, and she took time to write a clever letter to
the editor:

> Sir,—My attention has been drawn to your leading article of yesterday,
> "Whither Wimsey?" You are curiously out of date in your information if
> you suppose that this is the first time that either Peter Wimsey or myself
> has been connected with the advertising profession. Peter was himself an
> advertising copy-writer for a short time with the firm of "Pym's Publicity"
> (is it not written in the book called "Murder Must Advertise"?), while I for
> nine years held a similar position with Messrs. S. H. Benson, Limited.
>
> I heartily agree that the style of advertisement in question is not up to
> Peter's standard or mine—but then the advertisers refused to make use of
> the elegant copy I prepared for them and re-wrote it according to their own
> notion of what was fitting. That is what invariably happens to copy-
> writers.
>
> It may be of interest if I add that I undertook this advertising job when a
> small amount of capital was needed to finance the provincial tour of my
> play *The Zeal of Thy House,* and I had already invested in it as much as I
> could justifiably contribute from my revenue as a writer. Since no assis-
> tance was forthcoming from the Church for a play written and performed
> to her honour, I unblushingly soaked Mammon for what I could get in that
> quarter. *Et laudavit Dominus villicum iniquitatis.*[16]

Sayers had reason to be in an expansive mood. She was
cresting another success. She had been able to escape from a
character "whose existence has to be prolonged through a long
series of books"—though ironically he had helped her to
escape. It was pleasant to be sought after, to be asked one's
opinions, to be honored.

For Passion Sunday, 3 April 1938, she had been asked to
write an editorial for the *Sunday Times.* The subject, "The
Greatest Drama Ever Staged," was probably suggested to her
by the editor, and the prominence of her name in the theatre
lay behind it. She made no nominations for an award in world
drama; rather she launched into the central dogmas of Christianity. She worked from the "bad press" for official Christianity in recent years to the nature of the perennial "good
news" of the Gospel. She outlined the plot of the incarnation,
crucifixion, and resurrection, and then stated that though
some may consider it "devastating," some, "rubbish," some,
"exhilarating," some, "revelation," it is *not dull.* "If this is
dull, then what, in Heaven's name, is worthy to be called
exciting?"

Numerous letters enthusiastic about Sayers's article reached the editor. A bishop, an admiral, an author, among others,

wrote to commend the newspaper for publishing it. One elderly reader wrote: "The article by Miss Dorothy L. Sayers is the most practical, condensed, and thorough exposition of our religion expressed in plain English which I have seen or heard during eighty years of Church membership and attendance."[17]

The burst of acclaim led the editor to request for the Easter Sunday issue another article from Sayers: "The Triumph of Easter." It can best be described as a sermon on a text from St. Augustine: "O felix culpa! O happy guilt, that did deserve such and so great a Redeemer!" It deals with the problem of sin and evil, which all religions have to face. The triumph of Easter is that Christ, through his crucifixion and resurrection, could transform evil and suffering into redemption.[18]

At some time during 1938 Sayers was invited to address a women's society. It is clear that the society considered Sayers a feminist. The secretary had suggested to Sayers in the invitational letter that she "must be interested in the feminist movement." The careers of Harriet Vane and Lady Ursula de Warbois, of course, encouraged the interpretation. No doubt also the sort of apparel in which Sayers was photographed during this period fostered the feminist-emphasis image. (On 8 September 1936 she was photographed wearing a shirt, tie, jacket, and hat which gave her the appearance of stumping for women's rights.) In any event, she was publicly defensive when she started to deliver her speech. Referring to the secretary's letter, she said:

> I replied—a little irritably, I am afraid—that I was not sure I wanted to "identify myself," as the phrase goes, with feminism, and that the time for "feminism," in the old-fashioned sense of the word, had gone past. In fact, I think I went so far as to say that, under present conditions, an aggressive feminism might do more harm than good. As a result I was, perhaps not unnaturally, invited to explain myself.

Explain herself she did. She spoke to the subject "Are Women Human?" Attention, she stated, ought not to be directed to "sex-equality," nor to slogans. "What, I feel, we ought to mean is something so obvious that it is apt to escape attention altogether, viz.: not that every woman is, in virtue of her sex, as strong, clever, artistic, level-headed, industrious and so forth as any man that can be mentioned; but, that a woman is just as much an ordinary human being as a man, with the same individual preferences, and with just as much right to the tastes and preferences of an individual." She spoke about jobs, about the home, about interests, about apparel, emphasizing the *human* priority in each. She communicated to the gathering a personal pique:

> I am occasionally desired by congenital imbeciles and the editors of magazines to say something about the writing of detective fiction "from the woman's point of view." To such demands, one can only say, "Go away and don't be silly. You might as well ask what is the female angle on an equilateral triangle."

She was to deliver another such address during the war years: "The Human-Not-Quite-Human."[19]

Sayers was also sought out by the BBC to write a radio play for broadcasting on Christmas Day, 1938. She prepared *He That Should Come,* a play with the confessed intention of showing the birth of Christ "against its crowded social and historical background." Except for the envelope structure which contains a prologue and epilogue featuring the meeting of the Magi twelve days away from Bethlehem, the play has only one scene, the Bethlehem inn "crowded with as many and various types as possible."

She was adamant that the play be presented "in an absolutely natural and realistic style." She expressly forbade the slightest touch of ecclesiastical intonation or of "religious unction." In an echo of her childhood epiphany (with respect to Cyrus the Persian), she indicated that "it is in the interests of a true reverence towards the Incarnate Godhead to show that His Manhood was a real manhood, subject to the common realities of daily life; that the men and women surrounding Him were living human beings, not just characters in a story; that, in short, He was born, not into 'The Bible,' but into the world."

Val Gielgud was the director. Harcourt Williams acted as one of the Magi. Music was composed by Robert Chignell. The play was broadcast at 6:40 P.M. that Christmas day, and the critics were kind: "a beautiful modern Nativity play"; "arresting," "a very touching human drama."[20]

Within two years Sayers had become a leading religious dramatist and a noteworthy spokesman for the Christian faith. It was not to be a temporary innovation. As a schoolboy wrote in an essay on Christian apologetics: "Miss Dorothy Sayers turned from a life of crime to join the Church of England."[21]

By the late 1930s Sayers had taken to wearing a watch in the left breast pocket of her rather mannish-looking jacket. A heavy gold chain, with fobs, was attached to the watch, securing it through a lapel buttonhole. It was a little ostentatious, but she had reached a period when utility was more important than style. She *had* to be mindful of the passing hours: there were numerous appointments, train schedules, lecture-limits. The watch and chain became a fitting symbol of her alertness, also, to the times—"days like these when there is no telling in what direction the next international upheaval . . . ." For months prior to the outbreak of war, apprehensions and alarms rode high. The news media documented many of the atrocities occurring on the Continent. Growing armaments increased anxieties. A ruthless ideological warfare preceded the outbreak of open conflict. The battle for men's minds met Sayers ready to enter the lists.

The two decades which intervened between the end of the first global war and the start of the second made a different person of Dorothy Leigh Sayers. World War I left her in an Oxford tinted with Tristan, romantic and uninvolved. World War II found her informed, pragmatically idealistic, and involved—at least in the ideological front line.

On 5 January 1939 she gave her presidential address to the Modern Language Association, talking "from notes" on the subject "The Dictatorship of Words." She began her address practically and directly by observing that "to-day the Great Powers had in their armoury four arms—Navy, Army, Air Force—and propaganda." It was propaganda which had made possible "Germany's bloodless conquest in Austria and the Sudetenland." She was militantly opposed to a "muzzled Press which disseminated nothing but propaganda, concealing or distorting facts in addition to preaching dubious doctrine."[22]

In mid-February, at a Livery luncheon given by the Company of Stationers and Newspaper Makers at Stationers Hall, Sayers referred to an "eminent Hungarian psychologist" who had said "that any country able to embrace a form of totalitarian government was not fitted for the writing and reading of detective stories"—because good detective-story writing could flourish only in nations "peculiarly good at seeing both sides of a question."[23]

It is not out of character, then, that in the editorial she wrote for the *Sunday Times,* printed one week after England declared war on Germany in September 1939, Sayers should raise the topic question "What Do We Believe?"

> When a strong man armed keepeth his palace, his goods are in peace. But when a stronger than he shall come . . . he taketh from him all his armour wherein he trusted. So to us in war-time, cut off from mental distractions by restrictions and black-outs, and cowering in a cellar with a gas-mask under threat of imminent death, comes the stronger fear and sits down beside us.
>
> "What," he demands rather disagreeably, "do you make of all this? Is there anything you value more than life, or are you making a virtue of necessity? What do you believe? Is your faith a comfort to you under the present circumstances?"

The article is not as polished a statement as "The Greatest Drama Ever Staged" of the previous year. What she writes is not in detail wholly remarkable. What is significant is the clear concern for basic principles, presented in authoritative tone.[24]

That concern and that tone had been possessing her in the meantime as she was working on the second of her Canterbury festival plays. Working almost feverishly to meet the deadline, she had turned over copy so that *The Devil to Pay* could be presented at the cathedral in June 1939.

The Devil to Pay is a new approach to the old Faust story. She knew the vulnerable situation she occupied in endeavoring to pick up after Marlowe and Goethe, but her convictions overrode her misgivings.

> All other considerations apart, I do not feel that the present generation of English people needs to be warned against the passionate pursuit of knowledge for its own sake: that is not our besetting sin. Looking with the eyes of to-day upon that legendary figure of the man who bartered away his soul, I see in him the type of the impulsive reformer, over-sensitive to suffering, impatient of the facts, eager to set the world right by a sudden overthrow, in his own strength and regardless of the ineluctable nature of things.

Sayers's Faustus may be said, among other things, to portray some aspects of the dictator figure—given to plangency, infantilism, fantasy, and as a result foisting upon the world anarchy, savage cruelty, and destruction. When a character wallowing in romanticism occupies power, his skewed doctrinaire quality may be lethal because he cuts off viable alternatives. When Sayers's Pope, having heard Faustus out, replies to him in charitable tones and recommends "The slow and stony road / To Calvary," Faustus replies: "Follow Christ? That way is too long and uncertain."

Sayers's Pope, incidentally, had an amusing provenance. While the play was being written, she corresponded with Dorothy Rowe, lamenting the indecent haste which some producers expected of dramatists—"one really ought to be able to allow 3 months for brooding & three months for hatching."

> Meanwhile, I am struggling with Acts II & III of *Faustus*. Having invented a tender, wise, unworldly & purely symbolical Pope for dramatic & theological purposes, & written him a tender, wise &c. speech, I was fool enough to consult the Encyclopaedia in an idle way to see who the contemporary Pope actually was. He turns out to have been the notorious Alexander VI—the most flagrantly vicious & corrupt Borgia that ever defiled a family or The Vatican. This seemed a little too thick—I mean, symbolism is all very well, but *nobody* could accept Alexander VI as a symbol of anything but putrefaction. I shall have to make it Julius II, & turn the Battle of Pavia into the Sack of Rome. Oh, dear!

The play has weaknesses. The theological arguments are "spun out a little too fine and too long." The poetry is not Sayer's best. The highly pertinent theme gained little from association with sixteenth-century history and stagecraft. The heavy load of the "supernatural," which Sayers felt impelled to carry in the play, smacks too much of superstition and credulity for the modern mind.

Like *Zeal*, *The Devil to Pay* had a London run. It was not enthusiastically received. James Agate criticized the play as a melange of metaphysics and mysticism equally unpalatable and unconvincing: "I suggest that this is a play for mystics who confound, and are comforted in confounding, plain-song with plain thinking." As contemporary argument, it had no validity for him. Sayers was disappointed. What may have been fairly well received in church was jostled aside in the marketplace.[25]

Perhaps the fault lay in the sheltered ignorance and arrogance of men's minds. At any event, in June she also published a pamphlet entitled *Strong Meat* (including in it a second article, "The Dogma Is the Drama"). *Strong Meat* is a plea to *grow* in grace and wisdom. The title and theme are taken from the Epistle to the Hebrews (5.13-14), sifted through a now-familiar sentence from St. Augustine's *Confessions* (vii.10). She will have no escapism. "There is no retreat here to the Paradise of primal ignorance; the new Kingdom of God is built upon the foundations of spiritual experience."[26]

"The Dogma Is the Drama," composed after the 1937 Canterbury festival, deals with those foundations. Sayers openly admits that her faith—and the faith she would inculcate—stems from the Creeds, the Gospels, and the offices of the church (as in the Uses of Sarum and York and in the *Book of Common Prayer).* Her open confession has an immediate, twofold purpose: to disavow the impression (on the part of certain young men who had been excited by *Zeal)* "that if there was anything attractive in Christian philosophy I must have put it there myself;" and to rebuke authors of "anti-Christian literature written by people who ought to have taken a little trouble to find out what they are attacking before attacking it."[27]

Before the final production of *The Devil to Pay* (on 19 August 1939), Sayers was persuaded to spend a Wednesday afternoon and evening at a garden party at a boys' school in Woburn Hill, Addlestone, Surrey. Guests, according to the advertisement, were invited to meet "Miss DOROTHY L. SAYERS (The famous Authoress and Playwright)" "from 3 p.m. onwards and until everybody's gone and *the lights are put out."*[28] Within a month the Home Secretary put into effect an order to close all places of amusement during the initial stages of hostilities, for blackouts had become a necessary pattern.

On the last day of September 1939, a Saturday, Sayers was in Coventry, speaking to a joint meeting of the Coventry Diocesan Youth Council and Friends of Coventry Cathedral on "Religious Drama and Production."[29] In a little over a year, the massive German air attack of mid-November 1940, aimed at demolishing British industry, would succeed in devastating most of the Warwickshire city. Following the trend established in her published work earlier in 1939, she must have informed her audience of the importance of basic convictions.

Doubtless the crowding uncertainties of the hour urged Sayers to draw up her will on 13 April 1939. It was the thirteenth anniversary of her marriage to Atherton Fleming, and his sensitiveness to the steady drift of the times toward war, as well as his physical condition, daily reminded Sayers within her own home of the transitoriness of life. In the will she appointed her longtime friend Muriel St. Clare Byrne literary executrix; she left the copyrights and playing rights of *The Zeal of Thy House* to Harcourt Williams and Frank Napier (both of whom were also involved in *The Devil to Pay);* she set up a trust for her husband and son and, in the event of their predeceasing her, for her cousin Ivy Amy Shrimpton, with the freehold in Witham under such circumstances going to Somerville College. She could not know then that Williams, Napier, Atherton Fleming, and Miss Shrimpton were all to predecease her.[30]

It should be obvious that Sayers knew the difference between innocent conviction and passionate intensity. She labored to make men aware. It was worth a try. It was certainly not enough to ask men in the grimness of shock what they believed. Contemplation must be accompanied by decisive action. If Faustus couldn't successfully accomplish that, could the Wimseys somehow seize the imagination?

During the late autumn she put together a series of "Wimsey Papers" which were intended to go beyond cluckish comments on blackouts and rationing to tackle policy, propaganda, and personal responsibility. Lord Peter and Harriet, the dowager duchess and Uncle Paul, the Reverend Theodore Venables and Miss Agnes Twitterton, Miss Katherine Climpson and Colonel Marchbanks, Miss Letitia Martin and Miss M. Baring of Shrewsbury College, the duke of Denver and Mr. Ingleby of Pym's Publicity are all reintroduced to readers for this purpose. Sayers delightfully preserved character in each case, but she wrote no more merely to amuse than she did merely to report on the maintenance of morale. She was concerned with the aims of war and peace, with leadership, with economics and national housing, with educational reform and cultural heritage.

The "Wimsey Papers" began to appear in the *Spectator* on 17 November 1939 and continued through the end of January 1940. Peter has the last word: he writes to Harriet in the unmistakable tones of Sayers speaking to herself.

You are a writer—there is something you must tell the people, but it is difficult to express. You must find the words.

Tell them, this is a battle of a new kind, and it is they who have to fight it, and they must do it themselves and alone. They must not continually ask for leadership—they must lead themselves. This is a war against submission to leadership, and we might easily win it in the field and yet lose it in our own country.

I have seen the eyes of the men who ask for leadership, and they are the eyes of slaves. The new kind of leaders are not like the old. . . .

It's not enough to rouse up the Government to do this and that. You must rouse the people. You must make them understand that their salvation is in themselves and in each separate man and woman among them. If it's only a local committee or amateur theatricals or the avoiding being run over in the black-out, the important thing is each man's *personal responsibility.* They must not look to the State for guidance—they must learn to guide the State. . . .

I can't very well tell you just how and why this conviction has been forced upon me, but I have never felt more certain of anything. . . .[31]

That imperiousness—must, must, must! Dorothy L. Sayers was determined that the center *should* hold, that anarchy should not reign. She seldom passed up the opportunity—from "local committee" to the prime minister.

Such a compulsion lay behind her severe attack on Mr. Henry Savage in the *Spectator* on 1 December 1939. Mr. Savage had earlier written *Spectator*'s editor objecting to concepts in both T. S. Eliot's recently published Boutwood Lectures at Corpus Christi, Cambridge, *The Idea of a Christian Society,* and also the reviewer's dogmatic interpretation. It is to be feared that Sayers displayed both conviction and passionate intensity in the encounter: "Though he himself obviously attaches none but a picturesque or mythological meaning to such expressions as 'God,' 'Son,' and 'Salvation,' it would appear to be but an elementary gesture of respect to discover what theological meaning they convey to Christians before attacking Christian doctrine—or, at the very least, to make the courteous assumption that they convey an intellectual meaning of some kind"; "It is almost impossible to refute criticism based on solid ignorance of the subject at issue, but the time has come, I think, when Christians should take the trouble to label ignorance at sight, because it is damaging and dangerous, and is rapidly becoming an intolerable nuisance."[32]

This new testiness in Sayers's mien, as well as the compulsion to "tell the people," surfaces in a book which she was also putting together during that eventful fall of 1939. The title was direct and demanding—*Begin Here: A War-Time Essay.* In the preface she apologizes for the "indecent haste" with which the book had to be written, with no time "for the careful verification of references, or for submitting the text to expert criticism." It is her hope that the book does, on the whole, express what she believes to be "the truth about our present troubles," and that "it will serve its purpose if it suggests to a few readers some creative line of action along which they, as individuals, can think and work towards the restoration of Europe."

The book is a continuation of the exposition of topics Sayers had introduced in "What Do We Believe?," *Strong Meat, The Devil to Pay,* and the "Wimsey Papers."

> War is an ugly disaster; it is not a final catastrophe. Whatever men may have said in their haste and terror, let us get that fact firmly into our heads. They are no final catastrophes. Like every other historical event, war is not an end, but a beginning.

The point of leverage in the book is cogently presented: "For good or evil, and whether we like it or not, we have to recognise that our civilisation— the civilisation whose existence is now at stake—is Western, Mediterranean, and Christian." This does not mean either that we are distinctly aware of the assertions and assumptions of our civilization or that we have always acted with consistency. We may have been living on borrowed capital, recognizing neither the auspices nor the obligation of it. Middleton-Murry's *Heaven and Earth* (1938) probably influenced Sayers in the writing of this book.

What Sayers calls for in *Begin Here* are creative attempts to put together the fragmented Western-Mediterranean-Christian principles. "We must think creatively as individuals, always remembering that we are not only individuals, but responsible to the church and state, nation and empire, continent and world of which we are living parts and which have no meaning without us." We must combat inertia. We must recognize the urgency. We may not leave the task to others: "we must do it ourselves, and we must begin now and here."

The world was no longer committed to the long weekend, with only fun and games. The new barbarism had to be conquered. The moated isle took on grim isolation. Dunkirk and the collapse of France; the coalition of the totalitarianisms of Hitler, Mussolini, Stalin, and Tojo; blitzkriegs; and foreign governments in exile established in London—all were to make graphically clear that their finest hour for the English did not arrive without shock, sacrifice, austerity, and tragedy. But *not* final catastrophe.[33]

Nothing less than the practice of her own preaching accounts for the incredible pace of Sayers's involvement during the first year of World War II. Her publishing record was amazing. She lectured widely and participated in numerous conferences and committee meetings. She spoke on radio. She traveled up and down the island. She scolded—in print—a king and a former teacher, cabinet ministers and newspapermen, a bishop and the rank and file of church members, politicians and status-quo-ers, theologians and featherbedders, literary critics and the uninformed. With a Pauline glare, she reproved, she corrected, she instructed in righteousness.

She was distinctly in the frame of mind to listen responsively to the request advanced by Dr. James Welch, Director of Religious Broadcasting, BBC, in February 1940. "I wrote to Miss Sayers asking whether she would write a series of plays on the Life of Our Lord for broadcasting in the Sunday Children's Hour." Might she introduce the character of Jesus? Might she be allowed to employ the same kind of realism she had used in *He That Should Come*? Might the plays use modern speech? Dr. Welch agreed on each point. During 1940 and 1941 Sayers worked on these plays, completing five of a total of twelve by December 1941.[34]

She had developed as early as 1939 a strong conviction about the relationship of dramatic realism to the story of Christ. At the beginning of a little essay called "Divine Comedy" she had said:

> I have heard it now twice over—from two independent producers of two separate plays—the exact same warning in almost identical words:
> "Well now, ladies and gentlemen, I think there's only one thing I have to say to you before we start reading through. Although this is a play about—er—angels and God and Christ and so on, you don't want to go extra slow, or put on a special tone of voice or anything. Just treat it as you would an ordinary play. Speak the lines quite naturally and play it straight.

This Hamlet-like observation was an attempt to combat unreality. "At the name of Jesus, every voice goes plummy, every gesture becomes pontifical, and a fearful creeping paralysis slows down the pace of the dialogue." This sanctimoniousness derives, in part, from the traditional church services:

> The Bible is appointed to be read in churches, where the voice struggles helplessly against the handicaps of an Elizabethan vocabulary, a solemn occasion and overpowering background, a mute assembly, and acoustics

with a two-second echo. The more "beautifully and impressively" it is read, the more unreal it sounds. Most unreal of all is the speech of the story's central character—every word a "familiar quotation," pulpit-dissected, sifted, weighed, burdened with a heavy accretion of prophetic and exegetical importance. In a sense never contemplated by the Evangelist, we feel it to be true that never man spoke as this man, for by this time the words have lost all likeness to the speech of a living person.

In part, also, the unreality derives from adjustment to the edict which in Britain until only within the past few years forbade the representation on the stage of the person of Christ. "If our modern theatre had anything like the freedom of Oberammergau or the mediaeval stage, I believe one could find no better road to a realistic theology than that of coaching an intelligent actor to play the Leading Part in the world's drama."[35]

The presentation of the first play was planned for the Sunday before Christmas, 21 December 1941. Ten days before the broadcast, at the request of Dr. Welch, Sayers attended a press conference "at which she read a statement outlining some of the dramatic difficulties involved in writing the plays and some of the methods she had used; she also read, at the request of a member of the Press, some excerpts from the dialogue in the plays."

Then the battle of the scripts began. A few of the journalists "used the occasion for sensational reporting," dwelling on two aspects of the plays calculated to arouse objections in Britain: the representation of Christ, and the use of modern speech. Immediately, people who had not even heard a single play began to condemn Sayers's work as "irreverent," "blasphemous," "vulgar," and "scandalous"! The lord chamberlain had had no objection to the plays being broadcast, providing an audience was not present! What, it was argued by defenders of Sayers's efforts, was the difference between airing the words of Christ over radio and a minister's reading the same words in a church? Was there any different kind of "impersonation" between that of the projected radio broadcasts and that at a performance of Bach's *St. Matthew's Passion?*

The Lord's Day Observance Society and the Protestant Truth Society seemed to think so, and they were militantly opposed. The secretary of the former launched an expensive advertising campaign against this act "of irreverence bordering on the blasphemous." Its language—"many modern slang terms"—would be "in effect a spoliation of the beautiful language of the Holy Scriptures which have been given by inspiration of the Holy Ghost." Petitions were sent to Prime Minister Winston Churchill and also to the archbishop of Canterbury urging that they ban the broadcasts.

Dr. Welch noted that much of the opposition could not be taken seriously. Some said that Singapore fell to the Japanese because the plays were broadcast, and they appealed for them to be discontinued "before a like fate came to Australia"! There was, to be sure, a supporter who claimed the plays made possible the November 1942 victories in Libya and Russia!

Letters poured in to newspaper editors' desks. One large-circulation newspaper even noted, "Seldom has a correspondence in this paper been carried on by readers with so much intensity of feeling on either side as that concerned with the religious radio-plays written for the B.B.C. by Miss Dorothy Sayers."

The Central Religious Advisory Committee of the BBC, composed of all representative Christian denominations, unanimously pledged their public support of the venture. "Why?" asked Dr. Welch. "Because they had read the plays."[36]

Even so, on 19 December 1941, Ernest Thurtle, Esq., M.P. (the parliamentary secretary to the Minister of Information, the Right Honorable Brendan Bracken, M.P.), was asked by Sir Percy Hurd, M.P., in the House of Commons whether he was "taking steps to revise the script of the series of plays on the life of Jesus, which are announced to be broadcast by the British Broadcasting Corporation from 21st December, in the Children's Hour, so as to avoid offence to Christian feeling?" (Sir Percy, it may be noted, was "supported by an ex-Lady Mayoress of London, the Council of the Church Association, and particularly by the Lord's Day Observance Society. . . .") Mr. Thurtle gave a clearly negative answer to Sir Percy and reminded him that a committee headed by the bishop of Winchester was studying the situation. Sir Percy received practically the same answer from the Minister of Information himself on 21 January 1942.[37]

There was a pleasant irony in the efforts of the opposition. Sayers herself has written of this:

> It is moreover irresistibly tempting (though is it kind or Christian?) to mention the Lord's Day Observance Society and the Protestant Truth

Society, who so obligingly did all our publicity for us at, I fear, considerable expense to themselves. Without their efforts, the plays might have slipped by with comparatively little notice, being given at an hour inconvenient for grown-up listening. These doughty opponents secured for us a large increase in our adult audience and thus enabled the political and theological issues in the most important part of the story to be treated with more breadth and pungency than might otherwise have seemed justifiable. Their beneficence is none the less real for having been unintentional.[38]

Needless to say, the radio plays *The Man Born to Be King* added to Sayers's successes.

There was a large audience—and, for the most part, a grateful one. Dr. Cyril Forster Garbett—at the time bishop of Winchester (and subsequently archbishop of York), the chairman of the Central Religious Advisory Committee of the BBC for over twenty years (until 1945)—"who drew on himself the enemy's heaviest weight of fire and the most violent barrage of abuse," came to regard *The Man Born to Be King* as "one of the greatest evangelistic appeals made in this century." The plays were also broadcast in Canada, Australia, South Africa, and New Zealand.[39]

The plays were written, of course, after ample study and with Sayers's usual careful attention to detail. She had to face several challenges: the historicity of her subject, the relationship of theology to drama, the language barrier, the particular architectonics, the demands of the radio medium, and the development of theme and structure.

Val Gielgud, at Sayers's request—not to say badgering, was chosen to be the director of the series. "I have never been paid a greater compliment, professionally speaking," he wrote, "than when she made it an absolute condition of the broadcasting of *The Man Born to Be King* that I should be the producer of the series." He also expressed the belief "that the only plays specially written for broadcasting which have rivalled adapted stage plays in listening popularity were those written by Miss Dorothy Sayers on the theme of the life of Our Lord. . . ." Both Sayers and Gielgud call attention to the incredible fact that each of these plays had to go on the air after only two days' rehearsal. This was a wartime exigency, all the more incredible because "normal" rehearsal time would have required up to three weeks, and because the casts were large and there were big crowd scenes in addition. The second play was broadcast 25 January 1942, the third on 8 February, and the remaining nine at approximately monthly intervals through 10 October 1942.[40]

Robert Speaight, the voice of Christ in the plays, was the only actor in the cast who received any publicity in the announcements or in the press. Speaight had been secretary of the Oxford University Dramatic Society while a student at Lincoln College, and his roles after becoming a professional actor in 1926 included Hibbert in *Journey's End,* Hamlet and other leading parts at the Old Vic, and Becket in T. S. Eliot's *Murder in the Cathedral.*[41]

Gielgud had made Sayers's acquaintance for the first time in connection with *He That Should Come.*

> I must admit that my first reaction was one of considerable surprise. I had somehow got into my imagination that the creator of Lord Peter Wimsey must be in some sort a feminine counterpart of that nobleman. I expected to meet a sophisticated lady, garbed probably by Paquin or Molyneux, smoking fat Egyptian cigarettes, and displaying an exotic taste in wine and first editions. I expected to encounter an intelligence, informed and lively, but tinted with the brilliance of the accomplished amateur. I could not have been more mistaken. As far as anything connected with her work is concerned Miss Sayers is professional of the professionals. She can tolerate anything but the shoddy or slapdash. Of all the authors I have known she had the clearest, and the most justifiable view of the proper respective spheres of author and producer, and of their respective limitations. She is authoritative, brisk, and positive. She is also—I hope she will forgive me—both domesticated and naive: domesticated in an intensely practical preoccupation with the running of her Essex home; naive in her charmingly child-like interest in all the details of "behind the scenes," in her pleasure at establishing a personal relationship with members of her casts.

No wonder that in the published version of the plays Sayers said that Gielgud was the kind of director who "knows our necessities before we ask, that he patiently endured many trials (myself not the least), and that—if playwrights know anything about the matter—of such is the Kingdom of Heaven."[42]

There had been other problems, quite apart from the waves made by the Lord's Day Observance Society and the Protestant Truth Society. There was some in-house indecision at the BBC as to how many plays by Sayers should be commissioned, how long each play should be, and just when the plays should be broadcast. All of this was consequential to Sayers, who wrote to specifications of medium, time-allowance, and scope.

From the beginning, moreover, Sayers wanted Gielgud to be the director of her plays. In a postscript to a letter to Dr. Welch written 23 July 1940 she said:

> I am still obstinately set upon Val Gielgud's production. Very likely it is impossible. I do not care if it is. If the cursing of the barren fig-tree means anything, it means that one must do the impossible or perish, so it is useless to tell me it is not the time of figs.

It *did* look impossible to Dr. Welch. For one thing, someone told him that Gielgud did not understand children; for another, there was some question as to Gielgud's religious sensitivity. Moreover, since the plays were being commissioned for the *Children's Hour* program, it was logical that Derek McCulloch, the director of *Children's Hour,* should be the director. Reluctantly, Sayers accepted and proceeded to correspond with Mr. McCulloch about basic concepts in her plays.

On 11 October 1940 she wrote:

> When you are writing for children of all ages it is difficult to hit on the highest common factor of their combined intelligence, but I always think it is far better to write a little over the heads of the youngest rather than insult the older ones with something they think babyish. . . .
>
> Also I gathered from [Dr. Welch] that one of the ideas is to catch adults in the net that we spread for the children, and if that is so, then we shall have to get a little above the quite simple and pretty-pretty.

McCulloch agreed and wrote: " 'Talk to the Sixth Form and let the others pick up what they can' is what an enlightened headmaster advised a preacher to his boys." He also sent to Sayers—to consider as a model—four of the *Paul of Tarsus* scripts which had been written by L. du Garde Peach for the *Children's Hour.* (She told Dr. Welch in a subsequent letter—6 November 1940—that du Garde Peach wrote good dialogue, but that there was too much shipwrecking and sermonizing for her taste.)

She also wrote McCulloch about the qualities to be sought in the voice of Christ:

> a very intelligent and sympathetic actor . . . is what we want. In addition to those qualities, I feel that the third indispensable thing is a voice which is essentially alive and flexible. Technically the most exacting feature of the part is the immense range of expression it will demand, from the fieriest denunciation to the most compassionate tenderness all telescoped into a very few minutes.
>
> The one kind of Christ I absolutely refuse to have, at any price whatsoever, is a *dull* Christ! We have far too many of these in stained-glass windows.

McCulloch, "Uncle Mac" of the *Children's Hour,* may have found these comments a bit rankling.

In November 1940, Miss May Jenkin, McCulloch's associate, wrote to Sayers to query the advisability of some interpretations of language and character in the first play, "Kings in Judaea." On 22 November Sayers wrote a fuming letter to Miss Jenkin in reply:

I am glad you like KINGS IN JUDAEA. I shall now proceed to be autocratic—as any one has a right to be, who is doing a hundred pounds' worth of work for twelve guineas.

I don't think you need trouble yourselves too much about certain passages being "over the heads of the audience". They will be over the heads of the adults, and the adults will write and complain. Pay no attention. You are supposed to be playing to children—the only audience, perhaps, in the country whose minds are still open and sensitive to the spell of poetic speech. The two passages you mention are those which I had already dealt with in my letter to Mr. McCulloch; because I knew that they would present a difficulty to adults—though not to children—and that your first impulse would be to cut them.

But you are not children. The thing *they* react to and remember is not logical argument, but mystery and the queer beauty of melodious words. To you and me, for instance, the poetry of de la Mare is both obscure and fragile, because it evades all attempts at interpretation and breaks when forced into an intellectual pigeon-hole. But that does not worry children. Nor do children feel any particular religious awe at the Sermon on the Mount; what fascinates *them* is the mysterious Trisagion of A & M 160, and the beasts and the wheels of Ezekiel. I don't suppose it would occur to you to put in a reading of the Athanasian Creed as an attraction for the Children's Hour; yet I know a small boy of seven who urgently demanded this of his mother as a special birthday treat. It is the *language* that stirs and excites: "Not three incomprehensibles and three uncreated; but one uncreated and one incomprehensible."

As regards Melchior's astrological speech: they will like the sound of the planetary names and the unusual words. The grand noise will convey its message without any need for understanding. (Read Greening-Lamburn's account of the effect on a class of elementary school-children of Homer in the original Greek). It is true that the children may not grasp the implications of the "imperial star" and the "constellation of the Virgin"— does that matter? If they hear and remember the words, one day they may suddenly light upon the meaning. Though, actually, some of the older ones may be a good deal better up in astrology than the rest of us, since the poor little wretches have to do Chaucer's *Prologue,* with notes, as a set book for Matric., besides coping with Spenser and God knows what. But the important thing is the magical sound of the words, not what their brains make of it.

The same thing goes for the "Mortal-Immortal". I will swear that no child has ever heard unmoved, "When this corruptible shall have put on incorruption, and this mortal shall have put on immortality". What does he know of corruption? Nothing. But it is moving to him precisely because his mind and ear are *not* corrupted like those of people who read the penny papers.

I knew how *you* would react to those passages; it is my business to know. It is also my business to know how my real audience will react; and yours to trust me to know it.

Nothing will induce me to let you put in explanations and bright bits of information at the beginning. If you do it here, you will want to do it at every change of scene. . . .

And so on, stridently discussing Joseph's idiom and modern idiom in the play in general, with an aside on how to handle Harcourt (Billy) Williams. Then—

It takes about two months, generally speaking, to write a play of this kind. So I can hardly promise to produce them at the rate of one a fortnight, though I will try to get ahead as quickly as possible, so as to have something in hand.

I was *asked* for twelve plays. That was *your* arrangement. But if there is any doubt about it, you had better let me know. And quickly. I cannot possibly select incidents and arrange their place in the series, unless I know *for certain* how long the series is to be, and what proportion each is to bear to the whole.

On 26 November 1940, McCulloch wrote to Sayers supporting all of the points in Miss Jenkin's letter and suggesting the time-honored procedure for calming the storm—let Miss Sayers come to Bristol for a committee meeting! She wrote back on 28 November to "Uncle Mac":

O, no, you don't, my poppet! You won't get me to do three days of exhausting travel to Bristol in order to argue about my plays with a committee. What goes into the play, and the language in which it is written, is the author's business. If the Management don't like it, they reject the play, and there is an end of the contract. . . .

I must also make it plain to you that I am concerned with you as a producer for my play. In that capacity, you are not called upon to mirror other aspects of your work at the B.B.C.; you are called upon to mirror *me*. If you prefer to act as the director of a committee of management, well and good; but in that case, you cannot also exercise the functions of a producer. You can reject the play, in which case the matter is closed; or you can accept it, in which case you must offer me another producer with whom I can deal on the usual terms, which are perfectly well understood among all people with proper theatrical experience. I am sorry to speak so bluntly; but I am a professional playwright, and I must deal with professional people who understand where their appropriate spheres of action begin and end.

In a letter to Dr. Welch on that same date, Sayers describes the impasse, insisting that the "details of this controversy" are not his affair. The BBC had called in a professional playwright, and it must now give her a professional director "who knows where a producer's job begins and ends." "In his own sphere the producer is God—but he is not God in the author's sphere."

> I knew at the beginning that this kind of trouble was likely to arise. That is why I made strong representations about getting Val Gielgud, who *is* a professional, and *does* know his job. I have never had any kind of impertinence or stupidity from him, nor (I think he would tell you) he from me. . . .
>
> Theatre, you see, is theatre. It is because these little committees of the Children's Hour have no experience of the theatre that they never succeed in producing theatre, but only school lessons in dialogue. And I cannot do with it. Get me Val, and I will go to Bristol or Manchester or anywhere and work twenty hours a day, with the actors. But I must have a producer who is a professional producer and nothing else, and who can talk the language of the theatre.
>
> If there is any more nonsense, there is an end of the plays and of the contract. I have stopped work on the series, and shall do no more till this business is put on a proper professional footing.
>
> I am sorry for all this, which is in no way your fault. You see now why I am disliked at the B.B.C., and why Gielgud enjoys (or so I am told) an extraordinary reputation as a Sayers-tamer! He knows his job; that is the secret of that, as of many other remarkable reputations.

Thus Dr. Welch found himself obliged either to toss the entire project out or to create by his own great conciliatory powers a relative calm so that *The Man Born to Be King* could be realized. McCulloch in December offered Dr. Welch eleven reasons for not wishing to meet Sayers, as Dr. Welch had suggested, or to produce her plays in the *Children's Hour*. Dr. Welch promptly informed Sayers of McCulloch's "generosity." On 31 December 1940 Dr. Welch initiated an Internal Circulation Memo among BBC officials showing both his convictions and his peace-making ability: "But I know Miss Sayers fairly well: she is an artist who writes out of great artistic travail when inspiration visits her, and in such periods of creation she is admittedly difficult."

It is significant that no one had written to Sayers saying, in effect, "Don't you know there's a war on?" To her credit, she had written to Dr. Welch on 7 December 1940:

> It's distressing that all this should have boiled up just when Hitler was making all other considerations seem so petty. But things do happen like that. He dropped a beautiful stick of incendiaries across Witham on Wednesday night, and I prepared to make a dash to safety, clutching a MS on the Creative Mind under one arm and John the Baptist (half-finished)

Reverend Henry Sayers

Mrs. Henry Sayers

Dorothy Leigh Sayers, aged 8

Panache

Whither goest thou, knight with the shining crest,
  "And the golden, gay habergeon?"
I am riding into the wondrous West,
  To the land where honour is sought + won.

. . . .

'Whence comest thou, knight with the bloody crest,
  "And the stained-shattered habergeon?"
Oh! I am returned from the weary West,
  Now that the battle is over + done.

'What were thy deeds in the far-off West,
  "Of derring-do + of chivalry"?"
I fought all day, nor at night had rest,
  'gainst foes so many I could not see.

"What didst thou win in the wondrous West,
  'In the land of honour + high renown?"
  Only the scars on my brow + breast,
  And the thought of those that my 'lance
                    struck down.

Dorothy Leigh Sayers. 1911.

Written in the album of Ivy Phillips at Godolphin School, 1911

1915, after gradua-
tion from Oxford

DR. ALLEN · PUTS HIS BACH IN.

DLS in the Going-Down Play,
Oxford, 1915

A contemporary cartoon of
Dr. Hugh Allen

Right: Eric Whelpton in Venice

Below right:
Dorothy H. Rowe, 1915

Below left: Atherton Fleming,
aged 19 (*Courtesy of
Mrs. Ann Fleming Schreurs*)

The public figure, 1936
(*Popperfoto*)

The photograph DLS
gave her friends

The church, Bluntisham-cum-Earith

The rectory, Bluntisham-cum-Earith

The home in Witham, Essex (*Courtesy of Mrs. Eileen Bushell*)

Winter of 1949-50, a photograph by Atherton Fleming

DLS, Robert Speaight, and Val Gielgud working on *The Man Born to Be King* (*From Gielgud's* Years of the Locust, *by permission, and courtesy of the British Museum*)

New Year's greeting,
1942, drawn by
Atherton Fleming

Sketch by DLS of her ten-weeks-
old pig in a letter to her friend
Norah Lambourne, 14 March 1949.
"We call her Fatima, after Blue-
beard's wife because she is sure to
go poking that long nose of hers in
where she should not."

DLS and her "adopted" porcupines
in the London Zoo, 1940. Photo by
Wolf Suschitsky

under the other. Fortunately, the A.F.S. got the things put out before the heavy stuff could follow them up.

For the rest of the story, the completed plays and the broadcasts are evidence enough. Appreciation mounted. Rev. Eric Fenn wrote to Miss M. T. Candler, Copyright Arrangements, BBC, on 21 January 1941: "The plays are much too good to be lost." In March Dr. Welch wrote to Miss Candler to make clear that the plays would be forty-five minutes in length, that they would not be produced by Children's Hour but by Val Gielgud's department, and to say that Sayers "certainly put in about two months' work on the first play, which is an admirable piece of work." Gielgud assumed command. Dr. Welch had earlier reported that "Miss Sayers can be very difficult on matters of interpretation and production, but Val tells me, from his experience of producing her Nativity Play, that if she sees eye to eye with the producer she is a tower of strength." He added: "She is not prepared merely to write and hand the stuff over to a producer; and for that who can blame her?"[43]

Sayers was regularly in touch with Gielgud, once he was appointed director of *Man Born to Be King*. On 13 January 1942 she wrote to him:

> How right Christ was about bringing not peace but a sword. One has only to mention His name & everybody is up in arms. I wish it didn't make me so self-conscious about the job. I wish one didn't see Mr. Kensit [of the Protestant Truth Society] behind every page of the A[uthorized]. V[ersion]. I wish we hadn't had to fight desperate rear-guard actions with the Press, trying to shut them up, & yet not to alienate them so hopelessly that they would start a fresh campaign of hate against the next play. When we go to Heaven, all I ask is that we shall be given some interesting job & allowed to get on with it. No management; no box-office; no dramatic critics; & an audience of cheerful angels who don't mind laughing.

She reported local reception of the plays. Concerning the second play in the series, she wrote on 27 January 1942:

> My husband said it was a "good show", & added that we'd "got a good Christ." That's retired-army opinion—he's not strong on religion & is a severe critic of radio plays.

On 9 February 1942, concerning the third, she wrote:

> This is just to say, fluffs or no fluffs, my husband thought this the best show of the three, & says he astonished himself by ending up very much moved—giving, indeed, a touching impersonation of the "gruff warrior with tears in his eyes", familiar to sentimental fiction!—a thing, according

to him, which hasn't happened to him for years. He says that anything which moves *him* would move anybody!—Personally, I think gruff warriors tend to overestimate their own insensibility; still, there's no doubt about it, the thing *did* get across to him, especially the ending.

After the eleventh play, she wrote to Gielgud on 22 September 1942 that she had had a nice letter from "the poor dear Archbishop of York," thanking her for writing the plays. He was especially moved by the Crucifixion play. She considered his comment a tribute to Gielgud and the company because "he didn't much like the script when he read it." She summed up her gratitude by saying of the archbishop: "He's not a bad old stick, really."[44]

When it was all over, Mr. B. E. Nichols, Controller of Programs for the BBC, wrote on 16 October 1942 to thank Sayers for the plays and to offer a complete set of processed recordings of the twelve plays. This meant seventy-five double-sided records. She accepted with pleasure. She was equally interested in collecting photographs of all who had participated in the broadcasts; for this she had the assistance of Miss Ethel Eaves of the BBC.

A little over six months after the last play, Mr. Nichols wrote again to say that the BBC was already talking of doing the plays live again and to tell her that copies of her book were to be presented to all the members of the Central Religious Advisory Committee, to the archbishop of Canterbury, and also to the king, "who had taken a great interest in the recent broadcasts and asked for particulars of the casts."[45]

In retrospect, Sayers's work on *The Man Born to Be King* seems so preemptive that it comes as a surprise to learn that she divided her time on several occasions while engaged in writing the plays.

Early in January 1940 she received a request from Sir Hugh Walpole, a fellow member of the Detection Club, to join a committee he was heading on books and manuscripts. She consented, though she bluntly said she could not contribute money. She spoke of the national scene.

How do you find yourself in the midst of all this shemozzle? I am trying to do a little mild propaganda in the way of articles and lectures, but I can't say I think the official people give us a very inspiring lead. If you are in town, perhaps you would lunch with me one day when I am up. I am there fairly often, though less often now that I am not doing anything in the theatre.[46]

A little mild propaganda, indeed! A review in *Spectator*'s first February issue. An article on "The Contempt of Learning in 20th Century England" in *Fortnightly* in April. An address in Derby on 4 May 1940 at the Biennial Festival of the Church Tutorial Classes Association, "Creed or Chaos?" (which was also presented in two radio broadcasts on 11 and 18 August 1940). Two articles, "Notes on the Way," in *Time and Tide,* 15 and 22 June 1940. In early August: "Vox Populi" for *Spectator.* Contributions also in August to *Time and Tide:* "Pot *versus* Kettle." She ranged from the marks of good pulpiteering, through the necessity for an intelligent and informed faith, to acclaim for Winston Churchill, to economics, to an abortive governmental scheme for censorship, to the privileged position of the press, on to sensible means of conducting social surveys![47]

Somehow Sayers also found time during the early weeks of 1940 to produce still another play. Considering that only a few weeks previously, in *Begin Here,* she had censured with vehemence what she unhesitatingly labeled the low level of dramatic fare in London's West End, it is disturbing to see that she herself this time turned out a very slight entertainment. Perhaps it was an effort accomplished earlier, say at the time of *Busman's Honeymoon.* She called the play *Love All* in production; the title in manuscript is *Cat's Cradle.* It was presented in Torch Theatre (a private place of entertainment), Knightsbridge. It opened Tuesday, 9 April 1940, and closed 28 April. It was never published.[48]

It may have been a symbolic gesture in keeping with the title of this play that led Sayers in that same April 1940 to "adopt" the African brush-tailed porcupines in the London Zoo. The Zoological Society, like all other organizations dependent on the public, was in financial difficulties because of the war effort and started a scheme by which private citizens could provide the upkeep of various animals of their choice. Mr. Wolf Suschitzky, the eminent photographer of animals, took pictures of Sayers with her charges.[49]

A little over a week after her address in Derby, Sayers learned with the rest of the world of the German invasion of the Netherlands, Belgium, and Luxembourg. On the same day—10 May 1940—Winston Churchill replaced Neville Chamberlain as prime minister. The next day, the British and the French sent expeditionary forces into Belgium to join the Belgian army in its resistance. The Nazi blitzkrieg, with devastating swiftness, reduced Rotterdam to rubble in a matter of hours, drove across the Meuse at Sedan, and raced down the Somme valley to Abbéville at the Channel. The British and French forces were cut off with the Belgian army, and the fall of Brussels within a few days obliged them to move back to Ostend and Dunkirk. By unmatched heroic efforts, on 4 June 1940, 215,000 British troops and 100,000 French troops were evacuated from the beaches at Dunkirk. They had to leave behind them thousands of men to be taken prisoners and almost all their equipment. By 17 June 1940 three fifths of France had surrendered to Nazi control. Queen Wilhelmina and the Dutch government had fled to London. General Charles de Gaulle, heading the French National Committee, was also in London and supported by the British government.

In *Begin Here,* Sayers had already singled out Winston Churchill from other government leaders as a man of letters who had made "the one really stirring and inspiring speech on the progress of the present war." She added to her acclamation in the first of the two articles she wrote in June for *Time and Tide.* She also referred to the evacuation at Dunkirk: a "colossal military disaster," true; yet "Not success but heroic failure stirs the pulses of free men in free countries."

> There are few songs of victory, and no songs of unopposed victory. I doubt whether even a Nazi poet could make an epic out of the massacre of Poland. Agincourt and the Armada are celebrated as the exploits of the outnumbered; . . . The most moving war-poems are made about valiant rear-guard actions—Corunna, Thermopylae, Roncevaux. . . . It has been our privilege to witness a stranger thing than ever poet sang—the epic of the little ships.[50]

This passage in "Notes on the Way" in *Time and Tide* is indicative of the direction Sayers was to take in two immediate patriotic expressions: she was again writing poetry. The first poem, "For Albert, Late King of the Belgians," appeared in July in *Life and Letters To-day.* Why, within a fortnight of the arrival of the British and French expeditionary forces in Belgium to assist the Belgian army, should the Belgian King Leopold III have ordered his soldiers on 26 May 1940 to capitulate to the Nazis? It was a betrayal. In contrast, Albert, Leopold's father, who succeeded to the Belgian throne in 1909, had lived through the atrocities of World War I and become a symbol of true royalty.

> A dead man walking
>> In the Low Country
> Came on a weeping woman
>> With her son laid on her knee.
>
> "Why do thy tears fall down so fast?
>> For whom dost thou complain?"
> "Behold the body of my son
>> Broken and slain."
>
> "His flesh and blood were squandered
>> For a false traitor's kiss—
> In all the world was ever
>> Sorrow like this?"
>
> "O pity me, proud mother,
>> How happy is thy lot!
> I am the father
>> Of Iscariot."[51]

The second poem was "The English War." In the customary style of her earlier poems, Sayers used an epigraph before her verse, a sentence of Philip Jordan's given in a radio broadcast: "What other race on earth, well aware of its danger, isolated to fight, would utter a great sigh of relief that all had abandoned it, and say to itself: 'Well, thank goodness for that; now we know where we are'?" The epigraph states the theme of the poem. She heeded her own judgment that the "most moving war-poems are made about valiant rear-guard actions," and she started her poem with bulldog courage:

> Praise God, now, for an English war—
>> The grey tide and the sullen coast,
> The menace of the urgent hour,
> The single island, like a tower,
>> Ringed with an angry host.
>
> This is the war that England knows. . . .

The poem was published in the first week of September 1940, very near the first anniversary of Britain's entry into World War II. It is a truly patriotic poem, full of a sense of history and destiny—more a solemn oath than a prayer.[52]

A short time later, Sayers gave a speech in London entitled "The Mysterious English." Like "The English War," it is clearly patriotic. Indeed, there are verbal echoes resounding between the two works, and there are recurrent images. There are reasons why André Maurois's epithet "mysterious" is accurately applied to the English. Linguistically, the English are mongrels and thus not a race but a nation. English law has been spared abstraction; it is concerned not with Right but with rights, not Liberty but liberties, not Man but individual men. The English are not only mongrels, they are also magpies: the sea has been to the English a "moat defensive, and also the high-road to adventure," enabling them to collect, among other things, an empire! Many contradictions have been built into the English national character: arrogance and courtesy; criticism and tolerance of criticism. Sayers excludes only "the semi-intellectuals," "that curious little cosmopolitan crowd" who have recently "lost their English roots and wish to persuade us that Englishry is the last infirmity of Blimpish mind."[53]

Out of such a discriminating mind, her response to an appeal from the Ministry of Information in July 1940 can easily be understood. Sir Richard Maconachie, acting on behalf of the ministry, had written to Sayers soliciting her aid in the government's anti-rumor campaign. She wrote to Sir Richard sharply and at length. She acknowledged the dangers of rumor. "But," she wrote, "to be frank with you, I am rather disturbed by the form which this anti-rumour campaign appears to be taking." She felt it had a "rude and contemptuous tone" about it. Sensibly, she stated: "I do not know of any body of people who can be put in good heart by being treated with contempt, or encouraged to despise one another."

She had some suggestions. "Chatterbug" (Maconachie's term) was an unfortunate word to employ: "it reminds one of 'jitterbug', which was the word applied to those who said that trouble would come and find us unready, and whom events proved to be right." Such terms implied a "terrible archness" which she personally disliked.

> Tell us, if you like, that we are gods, heroes, buccaneers, bulwarks of liberty, trustees of the nation, discreet, sober, vigilant, and all the rest of it—for men become what they themselves believe themselves to be; or rather, don't say it, but imply it. (The Prime Minister is a master of this kind of implication; I don't know, come to think of it, that he has ever said in so many words that I am a marvellous person, but his public speeches do contrive to leave me with that exhilarating impression of myself). But so far, the announcements of the anti-rumour campaign leave me with the feeling that I am a scoundrel and a treacherous coward, though perhaps slightly less so then the greengrocer and the woman next door, of whom the very worst may be expected.

She also told Sir Richard what she thought about the double standard on rumor. Why should newspapers have immunity and ordinary citizens none in reporting rumors? "I have already drawn the attention of Mr. Harold Nicholson to one typical, though particularly vicious, example of flesh-creepery in a Sunday paper gossip-column—a tale offered on no better authority than that of 'an old friend whom I met in an air-raid shelter', exactly, in fact, the kind of story on which we are expected to pour scorn and contempt if told us by the milkman." She staunchly upheld the view that any argument advanced for freedom of the press is also an argument for freedom of speech. "We shouldn't mind your pillorying us if you pilloried the gossip-columnist as well." She realized she was being "a destructive critic" and proposed some angles of positive approach. She concluded her letter by saying:

> I'm perfectly certain that one has to encourage, encourage, encourage, and *never* give a man a bad opinion of himself. It's fatal to egg people on to suspect and abuse and sneer at one another and dance on each other's faces. Also, we have had a good many shocks lately, and are easily startled, and I know by experience—being a timid person myself—what is apt to happen. One says uneasily, "I see in the paper that—" or, "George has got hold of a story that—"; whereupon the strong-minded person leaps on one, crying: "Shut up! You ought to be ashamed to spread such a story". To which, believe it or not, one's instant reaction is: "He knows it's true, and doesn't want to admit it". The psychology of the thing is far more subtle than it looks at first sight, believe me.[54]

Sir Richard wrote to thank her and to ask her permission to submit her ideas to the Ministry of Information. Perhaps, therefore, her statement was read in the right places and helped to show how abortive the government scheme for censorship really was.

In mid-October 1940, the author Helen de Guerry Simpson, one of Sayers's close friends, died at her home in England. Although Helen Simpson had been a student at Somerville during part of Sayers's time in Oxford, the two had not become friends until 1930. Sayers visited Helen Simpson on the Isle of Wight in June 1940 in the week France fell to the Nazis. They were both troubled for France and for the future. When Sayers asked Simpson's opinions about the chances, she did so with the belief that the Australian-born writer "could look at England in perspective from half a world away," and she was reassured to hear Simpson say, "It's bad. But I think it will be all right, because when something like this happens, the English are rather a wonderful people." The testament of this friendship led Sayers to write an article for the January 1941 *Fortnightly,* commemorating the character of the writer. To her, Miss Simpson touched nothing which she did not adorn. In casual conversation with strangers, in club work, in her writing, in standing for Parliament, Helen Simpson was marked by "brilliant vitality and vigorous mental drive." Sayers added: "I do not think I have ever met a person so vividly and unfeignedly interested in his fellow-men and their affairs."[55]

During the remainder of the war years, the bulk of Sayers's work was devoted primarily to religious matters. She attended conferences, spoke on the radio, addressed various groups, published additional items. She accepted many challenges to offer her critical judgments: the nature of the church; the Judeo-Christian heritage; forgiveness and the enemy; the seven deadly sins; vocation and work; Christian esthetics; the idea of the devil. To her reputation as a writer of detective fiction and of drama she added a new reputation as a spokesman for the church.

Sayers was the only woman invited to speak in the sessions of the Archbishop of York's Conference held at Malvern College in Worcestershire early in January 1941. Originally planned for London in the autumn of 1940, the conference had had to be postponed because of air raids. Mr. H. C. A. Gaunt, headmaster of Malvern, offered the school premises to the more than two hundred participants during the winter-term holidays. Twenty bishops, six deans, and scores of clergy were among the members of the conference. "The aim of that Conference was to consider how far the Christian faith and principles based upon it afford guidance for action in the world of to-day." Dr. William Temple, archbishop of York, had consented to act as chairman and convener of the conference.

It is understandable why the author of *Begin Here* and *Creed or Chaos?* was invited to become not only a participant but one of the ten speakers. (Other speakers included Sir Richard Acland, Bt., M.P.; Rev. V. A. Demant; T. S. Eliot; Professor H. A. Hodges; Kenneth Ingram; D. M. Mackinnon; J. Middleton Murry; Rev. W. G. Peck; and Maurice B. Reckitt.

The paper by Mr. Reckitt was read by the archbishop because the speaker was ill and unable to attend the conference.) Preparations for the conference included the study of two "Documents," composed in each case of a statement and implicatory questions on the general aim, and circulated beforehand among the participants as a basis for the discussions.

There was a diversity of thought "in doctrine, philosophical and practical outlook" represented by those in attendance. The discussions were marked by "clash of opinion"; "animated debate"; and challenge upon challenge to the status quo, to threats of increased bureaucracy, to setting one's own house in order, to creeping totalitarianism. There were also calls to action.

Sayers had been requested to speak to two questions from "Document A":

1. Is the Church's witness concerned with the possibility of a breakdown of civilization, and with the economic and political causes of such a breakdown? If so, upon what grounds?

2. Does the present situation derive in any degree from the fact that the modern church has been more concerned to raise the moral level of social effort rather than to discover and correct falsity in the dominant purposes of corporate life?

The church's concern with the cause of a possible breakdown of civilization, and the concern for the root as well as for the fruit of human behavior, had already occupied Sayers's attention. Opening the second session of the conference in the afternoon of Wednesday, 8 January 1941, she spoke on the subject "The Church's Responsibility."

With acumen she lucidly pointed out that there are "two bodies of opinion within Christian society," "one feeling that Christians should live like actors; the other, that they should live like Nazis." That is: "There are people who think the Church of Christ should live within the world as a self-contained community, practising its peculiar loyalty, and offering neither particular approval of, nor opposition to, those departments of human activity which are vaguely summed up in the words 'civilization' and 'the state.' " Although actors and Nazis are surely unlike, they nonetheless exhibit the same basic attitude, each toward its own identity. This view held by Christian society is fallacious in its assumption. Christians are men, subject to man's nature, and one law of man's nature is that "he tends to be a civilized being." All human activity—spiritual, mental, physical—is potentially good: "not negatively, by repressions, but positively, and as an act of worship."

As to the second question: Sayers's basic conviction was that there are two ways for man to go—either the way of the Gospel (which means to meet redemptively the mingled pattern of good and evil in life) or the way of the Law (which means either yielding to inertia or yielding to evil). Christ himself, Sayers reminded her audience, came not to administer the Law but to fulfill it. The plain, blunt truth is that "The Kingdom of Heaven is not of this world; and the attempt to yoke it to any form of secular constitution is treason."

Earnest though she was in delivering them, Sayers's definitions and distinctions did not greatly advance beyond her previously published statements. One passage in her address was seized upon by the press and sensationalized:

> Suppose, during the last century, the Churches had devoted to sweetening intellectual corruption one quarter of the energy they spent on nosing out fornication—or denounced legalized cheating with one quarter the vehemence with which they denounced adultery. But the one was easy and the other was not. The Law cares little for sacraments; but it is reluctant to alter marriage laws because the alterations upset the orderly devolution of property. And of fornication it takes little cognizance, unless it leads to riot and disturbance. But to upset legalized cheating, the Church must tackle government in its very strong-hold; while to cope with intellectual corruption, she will have to affront all those who exploit it—the politicians, the press, and the more influential part of her own congregations. Therefore she will acquiesce in a definition of morality so one-sided that it has deformed the very meaning of the word by restricting it to sexual offences. And yet if every man living were to sleep in his neighbour's bed, it could not bring the world so near shipwreck as that pride, that avarice, and that intellectual sloth which the Church has forgotten in the tale of the capital sins.

Bernard Causton, in his prefatory account of "The Scene of the Conference" which appears in the published proceedings, wrote:

> It was not an easy conference to report quite apart from the diminished space available in small war-time newspapers. The complexity of the subjects discussed did not lend itself to brief reports. Miss Sayers' paper, which summed up so much that people have waited for years to hear stated from a Christian standpoint, suffered in this fashion. Needless to say, that

passage in her paper was singled out by sub-editors which rebuked the Church for having so long overlooked economic and cultural atheism while delivering homilies which enabled the self-righteous to

> Compound for sins they were inclined to
> By damning those they had no mind to . . .

It is extremely irritating for a speaker, who shuns stunt appeals, to have such an extract torn from its context, but, on the balance, perhaps even this publicity does more good than harm. It may cause a slight shock to a few deaf adders over their breakfast-table reading. But there is also in England a purely secular community which hears and understands as little of the Church's contributions to modern thought as it does of the teaching of Confucius. Reading such an arresting passage in the newspaper it may well prick up its ears and remark "Why, that is what I have been saying for years." Once curiosity has been aroused, readers may turn to the Speaker's books and find that the complacent optimism of the pagan philistine also comes in for astringent treatment.

Sayers anticipated in the Malvern Conference address some areas of special emphasis in speeches and articles she would prepare in the succeeding months: religion *and* theology; the nature of work and vocation; integrity in every work of the intellect; the neglect of the arts by the church. "Still less than in the matter of intellectual truth is [the Church] able to realise that the Divine Beauty is sovereign within His own dominion; and that if a statue is ill-carved or a play ill-written, the artist's corruption is deeper than if the statue were obscene and the play blasphemous."[56]

Whatever may have been the failures or the successes of the Malvern Conference itself in the long perspective, there can be no question concerning either the consequent increasing esteem for Sayers's opinions in church circles or the number of occasions in which her opinions were sought.

In February she had a violent bout with influenza, but 24 February 1941 she wrote to Val Gielgud, acknowledging gratefully his consent to direct *The Man Born to Be King,* and saying that she had to be in London on 5 March 1941 "to do a bit of religious twaddle on the air."[57]

On that date, Sayers participated in a series of broadcast talks under the general topic *The Church Looks Ahead.* She was fourth in the program, having been preceded by J. H. Oldham, D.D., Maurice B. Reckitt, and Philip Mairet. (Those who followed her were M. C. D' Arcy, S.J., V. A. Demant, and T. S. Eliot.) Sayers's contribution was "The Religions behind the Nation."

The perspective and conviction of her opening statement are impressive:

> It is comparatively easy to say that we want to defend our civilisation and our culture. But what *is* our culture? How did we come by it? What is it based on? What distinguishes it from the thing we call barbarism? And—perhaps the most disquieting question of all—is that culture really something in the power of which we live and die, or is it merely a slogan which we repeat in order to persuade ourselves that there is something in this country worth living and dying for?

She immediately answers these questions by asserting that "what determines the culture of a people is its religious outlook." While she admits that such a view is disputed by a number of people ("especially those who imagine that the cultural progress consists in gradually getting rid of religion in favour of scientific enlightenment and a realistic interpretation of history"), she defends her own position by explaining that *"the kind of culture we make for ourselves depends upon the assumptions we hold in common about what is GOOD."* She is quick to underscore *assumptions:* "Not the doctrines we preach, not the things we seek to establish by argument, but the things we take so much for granted, that we never argue about them at all." The war, of necessity, brings these things imperiously to attention. What is more, the postulate nature of our thinking about *good* (and, for that matter, *reason)* demands an exercise of faith: "the enlightened human reason ... cannot *prove* that goodness is not an illusion, and I cannot *prove* that reason itself is not an illusion." A nation neither vigorously Christian nor boldly anti-Christian, and unwilling to give up Christian ethics (though unable to assert them positively), is living on borrowed capital.[58]

On 8 March 1941, Sayers gave an address by invitation at The Dome, Brighton, on the subject "Vocation in Work." The subject is one of the topics in her Canterbury Festival play *The Zeal of Thy House.* It is dealt with in *Begin Here* and in *Creed or Chaos?* It was to become a basic subject in *The Mind of the Maker,* which appeared in mid-summer 1941.

An abridgement of the Brighton address appeared in *A Christian Basis for the Post-War World,* published in 1942. This entire work was the outgrowth of ten peace points presented by leaders of churches in Britain to the *Times* on 21 December 1940. The first five points came from Pope Pius XII. All ten peace points emphasized personal responsibility and integrity. Subsequently, in the June 1941 sessions of the Convocation of York, unanimous approval was given to the peace points, and a committee of bishops and clergy authorized the publication of a book in which "competent writers" would set forth comments, respectively, on the peace points "to make clear what measures must be taken" and "the difficulties to be overcome, if the policy they represent is to be successfully fulfilled." Herbert Williams, the bishop of Carlisle, was appointed editor, and he secured the contribution of Sayers on Point IX: Vocation in Work. She used the Brighton address for this purpose.

She discusses the creative and the sacramental nature of work. Man, made in the image of God the Creator, is *homo faber.* Some measure of the distance twentieth century thought had departed from the concept (and conviction) of vocation in work is to be found in the term *employment,* a substitution for *work,* and in the way the present has "set a strange value on leisure for its own sake—not the leisure which enables a man to get on properly with his job, but the leisure which is a polite word for idleness." With her usual clearheadedness, Sayers brings her address to a close by observing that "It is strange that whereas this age is beginning to look like the age in which the working class will become the ruling class there was never perhaps an age in which work was less loved or less reverenced for its own sake." She ventured to hope that whatever the period after World War II brought, it would somehow be "a period of eager, and honest, and dedicated work."[59]

In March 1941 Sayers published "The Church in the New Age" in *World Review:* it was reprinted in July in the American periodical the *Living Age* under the title "The Church in War's Aftermath." Her terse and emphatic theme was that the duty of the church in the world in war's aftermath will be the same it has been in every age, "namely, to bear resolute and incorruptible witness against it"![60]

In April 1941, *Fortnightly* published her article "Forgiveness and the Enemy." Five years afterward, Sayers noted that this essay was first commissioned and then suppressed by "the Editor of a respectable newspaper," who "wanted (and got) . . . Christian sanction for undying hatred against the enemy." The newspaper editor had something sulfurous in mind, but Sayers would not approach Christian sanction irresponsibly. She knew she was wrestling with a case of conscience.[61]

Within days, the bishop of Chichester wrote to the *Times,* citing the Pope's Easter 1941 appeal to all belligerent nations to spare on both sides the noncombatant population, especially women and children. The plea came immediately after the destruction of Belgrade. The bishop concentrated on the issue of night-bombing and asked the British government to make a solemn declaration to refrain from night-bombing of "towns with a civilian population," provided that the German government would do the same. The editor of *Fortnightly* reprinted the bishop's letter in the June 1941 issue along with the invited responses "from a number of men and women whose opinions would be valued" on such an important issue "for the Christian conscience." Sayers was one whose opinion the editor had sought. Her opinion was consistent with her point of view in *Begin Here* and the Malvern Conference address:

> An agreement by "civilized man" to accept limitations to the horrors of war seems workable only when the two parties accept also a common Theology—that is, acknowledge the same sanctions for conduct. How does one treat with a party who looks upon treaty-breaking as a major instrument of policy? Nor is Hitler likely to acknowledge a deadlock or to admit the necessity of a common consent of opinion, since this would be a denial of his whole "ideology."
>
> Also (from the practical point of view), I do not know what is meant by "towns with a civilian population." All towns contain some civilians. If we mean towns with a *wholly* civilian population, that may or may not include towns where war-industries are carried on, but it *must* mean towns where there are no anti-aircraft defences. To publish to the Germans that a town is undefended is immediately to invite its annihilation by day as well as by night; the town of Belgrade, which the Bishop of Chichester cites, is a case very much in point.

Bishops should have high and holy motivations, but they may sometimes be naive. If one is to premise Christian principles, then how does one justify war to begin with, let alone the patterns of bombing?[62]

During June 1941 Sayers gave six talks over BBC radio on *God the Son.* Each talk was a ten-minute program. One might think this exercise an easy offshoot on her work *The Man Born to Be King.* It is unlikely, however, that she changed the principle which she set down to Mr. Ackerley at the BBC ten years earlier: "anything one says about Religion demands so much care & planning beforehand, for fear of tumbling inadvertently into some foolish heresy or saying something one doesn't exactly mean." In addition, during the period of their acquaintanceship, Sayers had often discussed theology precisely with Dr. Welch. Prior to her two broadcasts on "Creed or Chaos?" in August 1940, Dr. Welch had written to her: "don't spare the dynamite!" After he had heard her that summer, he wrote again: "Thank you for the two Sunday afternoon talks; I am rather hard-boiled, but your last talk did really get under my skin." To him she had sent a criticism of the January *Broadcast Minds* program offered by a religious leader: "I am sorry to speak so strongly; last night's performance was more than usually sickening. My husband, who is no great lover of learning, was quite revolted." Having continuously thus put herself in a spot of vulnerability, she no doubt carefully spent the sixty minutes devoted to God the Son. At that very time, moreover, she was pursuing diligently the whole doctrine of the Trinity.[63]

The intensity with which Sayers performed during the second and third years of the war is, manifestly, nothing short of amazing. There must have been many evenings when, with blackout shades drawn and the growing restrictions on food and fuel requiring austerity, she prolonged into the night hours her reading, study, and writing. She was to intimate this cheerfully in "Lord, I Thank Thee" within a few months. For herself, Sayers set few limitations, for she was not "employed"; she was a worker, a creator, to whom the work mattered far more than all the inconveniences attending it.

She had said to herself during the winter and spring of 1941, "I have often uttered a few brief statements about divine vocation in work: why don't I give sustained thought to my *own* vocation—give thought and personal illustration to the sacramental and creative aspects of the work of the writer?" In such fashion, *The Mind of the Maker,* one of her greatest works, came into being. It was published in July 1941.

What gives structure to *The Mind of the Maker* is the Christian doctrine of the Trinity as it is reflected in the artist's process of making. Father, Son, and Holy Ghost are related to the artist's trinity of Idea, Energy, and Power. Here, once again, is *homo faber:* man made in the image of God the Creator.

Beyond the lesson in semantics given in the first chapter of *The Mind of the Maker* ("The 'Laws' of Nature and Opinion"), Sayers discusses "The Image of God," and asserts that it is first necessary to understand that all language about God is analogical. Of course God is mysterious, but so is everything else in degree, yet not to the extent that the resources of analogical language utterly fail. And so to the Trinity.

"I suppose that of all Christian dogmas," she says,

> the doctrine of the Trinity enjoys the greatest reputation for obscurity and remoteness from common experience. Whether the theologian extols it as the splendour of light invisible or the sceptic derides it as a horror of great darkness, there is a general conspiracy to assume that its effect upon those who contemplate it is blindness, either by absence or excess of light.

The first "Person" of the writer's trinity is *the Idea:*

> The ordinary man is apt to say: "I thought you first began by collecting material and working out the plot." The confusion here is not merely over the words "first" and "begin". In fact the "Idea"—or rather the writer's realization of his own idea—does precede any mental or physical work upon the materials or on the course of the story within a time-series. But apart from this, the very formulation of the Idea in the writer's mind is not the Idea itself, but its self-awareness in the Energy. Everything that is conscious, everything that has to do with form and time, and everything that has to do with process, belongs to the working of the Energy or Activity or "Word." The Idea, that is, cannot be said to precede the Energy in time, because (so far as the act of creation is concerned) it is the Energy that creates the time-process. This is the analogy of the theological expressions that "the Word was in the beginning with God" and was "eternally begotten of the Father." If, that is, the act has a beginning at all, it is because of the presence of the Energy or Activity. The writer cannot even be conscious of his Idea except by the working of the Energy which formulates it to himself.

To answer the query, "That being so, how can we know that the Idea itself has any real existence apart from the Energy?" Sayers writes: "Very strangely; by the fact that the Energy itself is conscious of referring all its acts to an existing and complete whole." Every choice of episode, phrase, or word "is made to conform to a pattern of the entire book, which is revealed by that choice already existing." The judgment by a writer "That is, or is not, the right phrase" means that "it is a phrase which does or does not correspond to the reality of the Idea." All of this (and more) is present when a writer says, "I have an idea for a book."

The book is then the manifestation of an Idea. Here enters the second "Person" of the writer's trinity. "The Energy . . . is the thing of which the writer is conscious and which the reader can see when it is manifest in material form." It is dynamic in a temporal and spatial existence. Energy "is something distinct from the Idea itself, though it is the only thing that can make the Idea known to itself or to others, and yet it is (in the ideal creative act which we are considering) essentially identical with the Idea—'consubstantial with the Father.' "

The third "Person" of the writer's trinity is Creative Power.

> It is not the same thing as the Energy (which for greater clearness I ought perhaps to have called "The Activity"), though it proceeds from the Idea and the Energy together. It is the thing which flows back to the writer from his own activity and makes him, as it were, the reader of his own book. It is also, of course, the means by which the Activity is communicated to other readers and which produces a corresponding response in them. In fact, from the reader's point of view, it *is* the book. By it, they perceive the book, both as a process in time and as an eternal whole, and react to it dynamically.

There is then in the artist's making a trinity in unity. By an act of the intellect, each part of the trinity is separately distinguishable, but the substance is in actuality indivisible. "These things are not confined to the material manifestation: they exist in—they *are*—the creative mind itself." Thus a writer may say with perfect accuracy: "My book is finished—I have only to write it."

In addition to developing the basic structure of the artist's trinity in creating, in *The Mind of the Maker* Sayers also treats such topics as the immanence and transcendence of the author in his works, the free will of an author's characters, autobiography, and the relationship of the trinitarian concept to literary criticism.

Unquestionably, *The Mind of the Maker* is one of Sayers's most important works. She had insisted in her preface that the book was a commentary "on a particular set of statements made in the Christian creeds," and that it was neither an apology for Christianity nor "an expression of personal religious belief." But the work pulsates with vital, personal convictions. It is a synthesis of the sort she prescribes for the creative artist. It reflects a wide range of reading and represents sustained thought. It is one of the rare treatises in Christian esthetics.

Times Literary Supplement considered the book "an essay of great penetration and acumen, which will be much valued in theological circles, and which incidentally throws no little light on the process of creative writing." Theological circles, to judge from two samples, agreed. The *Church Times* considered the book "a brilliant success" and observed that "Theology in Miss Sayers's hand is more exciting than crime." C. S. Lewis, reviewing *The Mind of the Maker* in *Theology,* found it "full of illumination both on the theological and the literary side." He added, "This is the first 'little book on religion' I have read for a long time in which every sentence is intelligible and every page advances the argument."

There is an indication that Sayers thought of *The Mind of the Maker,* during or after its composition, as a part of a necessary effort for guiding a generation obliged to reassess social and spiritual values, directions, and goals. The page preceding the title page of the British first edition of the work announces that a series entitled "Bridgeheads" will be edited by Dorothy L. Sayers and M. St. Clare Byrne. Besides *The Mind of the Maker,* four volumes are listed as "In preparation."[64]

Whatever Sayers did in the first years of the war, she seemed to do in the midst of something else. Sometimes she confessed to exasperation, but most of the time she bustled with gusto. To Dr. Welch she wrote in the middle of 1940:

> Life has been full of complications, including, among other things, a wistful magazine editor, anxious to know, instantly, briefly, and at the shortest possible notice, what place Hitlers and such have in the Divine scheme of things, and why;—one of those easy little questions to which anybody may be expected to rattle off a reply on the type-writer without thinking twice about it.

To Val Gielgud in April 1941: "I seem to be spending all my time haranguing Baptist Ministers and the Royal Air Force about the Christian Religion, with bursts of Welfare workers and other well-meaning and importunate bodies; but I am trying to get rid of the whole lot within the next few weeks, and shall then perhaps be able to gird myself to dealing properly with drama." She was overly confident, apparently, because on 22 July 1941 she wrote to Gielgud again, outlining her varied pursuits:

In the intervals, I've had to cope with 1) the six talks on God the Son, 2) getting out *The Mind of the Maker,* with personal letters to various bishops and persons of importance, 3) the Woman Question, now boiling up in various places, 4) the Purification-of-the-Press anti-vested-interest campaign, which I am conducting guerrilla-fashion all over the shop, 5) speeches on this and that for Bishops-who-want-a Christian England, with much ancillary correspondence, 6) the P. G. Wodehouse uproar in all its branches, 7) trying to get a housemaid.[65]

It should be noted that Sayers did not succumb to the masterful invective of William Connor, the columnist "Cassandra" of the *Daily Mirror,* on 15 July 1941 in which P. G. Wodehouse was attacked for treason. Wodehouse was taken prisoner by the Nazis with the occupation of France; after being shunted from interment camp to interment camp until he reached sixty years of age, he was finally placed under house arrest in Berlin. Whether it was naiveté or stupidity, Wodehouse agreed to do a broadcast to America "from a script written and prepared by Henry W. Flannery, an American correspondent with the Columbia Broadcasting System," and he was then asked by the German Foreign Office "if he would like to do a series of broadcasts over the short-wave radio to America, for which he would be permitted to write his own scripts." He did not avoid telling what had happened to him: "How to Be an Internee in Your Spare Time without Previous Experience." His subtle humor not only passed over the Germans but apparently also exceeded general British sensibilities at the time. He appeared simply to be another Lord Haw-Haw broadcasting Nazi propaganda. Feelings ran high in Britain, and Connor's vehement attack despoiled the Wodehouse name.

Dorothy Sayers was astute enough to rise to Wodehouse's defense. Nobody seemed to know just exactly what it was that Wodehouse had *said* in the radio broadcasts. It was simply *assumed* that he was giving comfort to the enemy. What about the time-honored principle that a man was to be *assumed* innocent until *proven* guilty? She was quite sure that Wodehouse, politically naive, was unconscious of the propaganda value to the Nazis in his action.[66]

The weary prolongation and exhaustion of the war caught many people off guard. Sayers, however, seemed to maintain an unflagging zeal for her conviction of the right. To her, it was more than a matter of making virtue a necessity.

Very little in official religious matters of the time escaped her notice or attention. On Friday, 15 August 1941, Mr. R. A. Butler, the new president of the Board of Education, received an anxious deputation desiring him to make religious education a reality to every child in British schools. He indicated to the deputation his desire "to postpone legislation on Christian teaching in the schools till after the war." Letters began to flow into the newspapers, outlining various proposals in the entire range of subjects related to the teaching of religion in the schools. Among them, Sir Francis Freemantle expressed his opinion that the whole matter could be handled easily by having "a plain, simple, and apposite teaching of religion, as Our Lord taught it." He felt strongly that students should not be obliged to accept the application of Christ's teaching in the contexts of early Christianity; he especially rejected the need to instill in the young any extensive theological training. Imagine the reaction of Sayers, who followed this issue closely, when she read Sir Francis's letter. She wrote to the editor of the *Times:*

> I do not know what is the alternative to the "compressed" theology of which Sir Francis Freemantle complains, but I strongly suspect it to be precisely that diluted theology which is responsible for the chaos in which religious education finds itself to-day. We have been trying for some time now to teach "religion" without theology, and the result is scarcely encouraging.
>
> Unfortunately, the teaching of Christ appears "plain and simple" only so long as we do not attempt to make it "apposite" to the complex nature of man and society. The disciples, who, after all, were well placed to hear it "as Our Lord taught it," did not find it plain sailing by any means; and one Gospel at least is solid theology from cover to cover. In the face of Christ's own words, we can scarcely ignore the relations of Christian doctrine with the Jewish law, nor can we, without abandoning our whole cultural heritage, ignore its relations with the philosophers of Greece and Rome, or even of Alexandria, since these condition our Western and modern way of thinking. A religion without theology and without relation to secular thought is apt to become a spiritual chimaera bombinating in a mental vacuum. And that is exactly what our "religious education" looks like to a good many people.[67]

The subject of religious education was still uppermost in Sayers's mind when she accepted an invitation to speak to the Public Morality Council at Caxton Hall, Westminster, on 23 October 1941. Her talk, an augmentation of remarks delivered at the Malvern Conference in January, was "The Other Six Deadly Sins." Her opening statement displayed her awareness of the difficulty of religious education, her customary clear thinking, and her courage.

> Perhaps the bitterest commentary on the way in which Christian doctrine has been taught in the last few centuries is the fact that to the majority of people the word "immorality" has come to mean one thing and one thing only. The name of an association like yours is generally held to imply that you are concerned to correct only one sin out of those seven which the Church recognises as capital. By a hideous irony, our shrinking reprobation of that sin has made us too delicate so much as to name it, so that we have come to use for it the words which were made to cover the whole range of human corruption. A man may be greedy and selfish; spiteful, cruel, jealous and unjust; violent and brutal; grasping, unscrupulous and a liar; stubborn and arrogant; stupid, morose, and dead to every noble instinct—and still we are ready to say of him that he is not an immoral man.

This should be sufficient to show Sayers's perspective and intent.[68]

About this same time Sayers prepared a little essay entitled "Christian Morality," which she says in *Unpopular Opinions* was suppressed before it appeared "because American readers would be shocked by what they understood of it." Actually, the essay is only a brief and harmless restatement of ideas which she had already expressed frequently: "Setting aside the scandal caused by His Messianic claims and His reputation as a political firebrand, only two accusations of personal depravity seem to have been brought against Jesus of Nazareth." First, he was a Sabbath-breaker. Secondly,

> He was "a gluttonous man and a winebibber, a friend of publicans and sinners"—or (to draw aside the veil of Elizabethan English which makes it all sound so much more respectable) . . . He ate too heartily, drank too freely, and kept very disreputable company, including grafters of the lowest type and ladies who were no better than they should be.

It was Sayers's opinion that the churches had labored for nineteen and a half centuries "to remove this unfortunate impression made by their Lord and Master."

> They have hustled the Magdalens from the Communion-table, founded Total Abstinence Societies in the name of Him who made the water wine, and added improvements of their own, such as various bans and anathemas upon dancing and theatre-going. They . . . , feeling that the original commandment "Thou shalt not work" was rather half-hearted, have added to it a new commandment, "Thou shalt not play."[69]

She scored not only against self-styled defenders of morality; she also scored against the self-styled defenders of freedom. During 1941 she wrote a scathing article against irresponsibilities of journalists, "How Free Is the Press?" (Points she had already made in "Pot *versus* Kettle" are reiterated: no one will dispute the *principle* of freedom of the press; what she disputes is abuse of the *practice*—subservience to advertisers and proprietors, manufacturing of opinion.) She itemizes a catalogue of abuses: sensational headline; false emphasis; suppression of context; garbling; inaccuracy; reversal of facts; random and gratuitous invention; deliberate miracle-mongering; flat suppression. She illustrates her opinions by what she calls "quite trivial examples drawn from personal experience." Thus she cites the journalistic distortion of the focus of her remarks in the Malvern Conference. She berates the newspaper that deliberately postdated an attempted burglary of her flat because the news otherwise would be "cold"; further, because the article inaccurately credited *her* with disturbing the thieves because of the greater snob-value that would attach to a famous writer. She angrily takes issue with the telephone-interviewer who fictionalized his report by claiming that Sayers's eyes glittered over one remark. And so on. Deliberate inaccuracy especially vexed her.[70]

All of this activity was concurrent with her efforts to complete the radio plays *The Man Born to Be King*. There was a large amount of letter writing connected with the reception of the plays. Her letter to the editor of *Daily Telegraph and Morning Post*, written at the beginning of 1942, responded to certain excesses in the utterances of one of the chief opponents to the broadcast, Mr. Kensit of the Protestant Truth Society:

Sir,—Mr. Kensit is not content to say that dramatic presentations of Christ are wicked, or that I am blasphemous and incompetent. He affirms categorically that—for anybody, apparently, or in any context—"to place imaginary words on His lips is perilously near sacrilege."

This is hard hearing for Protestants, who have hitherto supposed that John Milton was a not wholly irreverent or irreligious poet. Yet, in "Paradise Regained," the Son of God is made to conduct, at great length, and in a style singularly unlike that of His recorded utterances, an argument with Satan which bears little relation to the brief report of the Evangelists.

Worse still, "Paradise Lost" presents us with a good deal of conversation between the Father and the Son in Heaven, to which we should find some difficulty in assigning a word-for-word origin in Scripture.

When Mr. Kensit makes a public holocaust of the mediaeval Mystery plays, together with the works of all the mystics, Catholic and Protestant, who have recorded the dialogue of Christ with the soul, he must not forget to heat the furnace seven times hotter for the great Puritan—or at least, since this is war-time, send him to be pulped with the rest.

It is not my place to defend my own work; but when it is a question of religious tyranny and the suppression of the written and spoken word, I am ready to write my "Areopagitica."[71]

Sayers also managed to deliver two major addresses during 1942. In Reading on 13 February she spoke to the Humanities Club at the university on "Creative Mind." The university's magazine *Tamesis* for spring 1942 reported that "Miss Sayers . . . set before us the way in which the creative mind uses language to express poetic truth, a way which science, with its need for a measurable medium of expression, often fails to anticipate." This address was the first codicil to *The Mind of the Maker*. Sayers's concluding paragraph offers a sharper perspective on her remarks than the university magazine's brief statement:

It is right that the scientists should come to terms with the humanities; for in daily life scientists are common men, and the flight from language will never avail to carry them out of its field of power. They must learn to handle that instrument, as they handle other instruments, with a full comprehension of what it is, and what it does, and in so doing they will come to recognize it as a source of delight as well as of danger. The language of the imagination can never be inert: as with every other living force, you must learn to handle it or it will handle you. "The question is," said Humpty Dumpty, "which is to master—that's all."

She returned from Reading ill and took to her bed. On 16 February she wrote to Val Gielgud:

I missed the first instalment of your new serial! So stupid. I went to bed with a cold, and could have heard it quite comfortably, but fell instead into an uneasy slumber, haunted by Mary Magdalen and other feverish apparitions.[72]

On 23 April 1942 Sayers spoke to a group of churchmen in Eastbourne on the topic "Why Work?" The real question she discussed was "What is the Christian understanding of work?" She attempted to answer this question by setting forth three propositions: (1) "Work is not, primarily, a thing one does to live, but the thing one lives to do"; (2) "It is the business of the Church to recognise that the secular vocation, as such, is sacred"; (3) "The worker's first duty is to serve the work."

The Church's approach to an intelligent carpenter is usually confined to exhorting him not to be drunk and disorderly in his leisure hours, and to come to church on Sundays. What the Church *should* be telling him is this: that the very first demand that his religion makes upon him is that he should make good tables. Church by all means, and decent forms of amusement, certainly—but what use is all that if in the very center of his life and occupation he is insulting God with bad carpentry? . . . The only Christian work is good work well done.

On Sunday, 13 January 1943, the "Platform" page of *Sunday Pictorial* carried portions of the Eastbourne address along with an editorial remark: "World famous as a detective story writer, Dorothy Sayers at 49 has now established herself as a leading writer on religion."[73]

A touch of humor carried Sayers through many of the dreary hours of the war period. Her morale seems to have remained high. One can almost see the set of her jaw, the squaring of her shoulders, the determination in her eye. Her training had not only equipped her to enjoy cultural niceties and to assume thought and expression with sustained integrity; it had also provided her with self-reliance and fortitude and hope.

In "Lord, I Thank Thee," a poem published in November 1942, there is a tone of serendipity which belies neither the austerity of life in Britain at the time nor the earnestness of Sayers's convictions, let alone her sensitivity to the havoc of war. She was trying to be lighthearted for the sake of morale.

One notes the same measured self-control in a passage of a letter she wrote to Derek McCulloch on 5 November 1940:

> The local warden has just come in to say that there is a time-bomb across the street, which "looks as though it might go off any minute". He adds that "the police and the military are surrounding it"—as though it were a truculent parachutist. It's a mild one, I gather—about 250 lb. But I had better retire from the window and put the MS of the play in the air-raid shelter. . . . Weds. morning. The bomb has not "gone off"—it has grown to 500 lb. It will be a land-mine to-morrow.[74]

Necessity had taught her many things, to be sure. During the war years Dorothy Sayers raised pigs in her back yard. She fed them unneeded scraps and fruit. One pig was named Fatima and became the subject of a Christmas poem:

> This is our yard, and in it stands
> Our Mistress (on hind-legs, with hands);
> The other one (the quadruped)
> Was Fatima—but now she's dead.
>
> When our establishment took charge
> Of Fatima, she was not large;
> But lord, how she did feed and feed,

A very prodigy of greed!
She was, in short, a perfect Pig;
And, when she got very big,
A lorry came, and she was taken
To where Pigs vanish into bacon.

Hear Pussius Catus moralize:—
To be a Pig is most unwise;
Better by far to be a Cat,
Who, if he likes, can put on fat
And grow majestic and immense
Regardless of the consequence,
Since, though he bulge with fish and meat,
He never will be fit to eat.

So, because Pussies and Mankind
Are so enlightened as to find
Each other quite uneatable,
Puss can afford to wish you well,
Hoping your Christmas may be good,
And beautiful with glorious food.[75]

Fatima, of course, is viewed through the eyes of Sayers's cats. The poem is entitled "From the Catalects of Pussius Catus," and it represents the sort of thing she did privately for friends. Dorothy Rowe received a printed greeting with a linocut designed by Sayers depicting a cat reclining on a brick wall and containing another sample of the "Catalects." For Christmas 1945 Sayers sent to friends a privately printed mock epic on a cat: "Aeneas at the Court of Dido." The next year's greeting card had linocuts made by Norah Lambourne with Sayers's verses entitled "A Cat's Christmas Carol." The BBC used her "War-Cat" poem more than once. Still another cat poem appeared which showed the influence of the thought of Charles Williams: "For Timothy in the Coinherence." (Timothy, Muriel St. Clare Byrne's velvety white cat, stalks through Sayers's poem in seriocomic manner as an "affirmative image" of grace and affection.)

Like T. S. Eliot, Sayers was fascinated by the magisterial and the mysterious in cats. They were useful creatures, but after their kittenish and sociable stage they could become maddeningly dictatorial and indifferent creatures. Once Sayers gave a tabby to Val Gielgud, swearing "that his mother was a genuine witch's cat" and pronouncing "with her usual decision, that the only possible name for him was Merlin." Gielgud asserted that "Away from the studio floor one did not argue with Dorothy, and certainly Merlin was no ordinary cat"! After a visit with Charis Frankenburg in July 1948, Sayers wrote this note to her hostess and her daughter:

> Blitz my cat sends greeting to you & to Ursula, whom he has met—though he cannot *wholly*, he says, approve of a household whose sacred hearth is ministered to by two dogs & no cat at all; there must, he feels, be a lack of that quiet dignity & velvet solemnity which only feline ministrants attain in perfection. Nevertheless, he wishes you well, & will dedicate his next mouse to you.[76]

Granted her steady involvement in numerous activities and her good morale, Dorothy Sayers may well have awakened on 13 June 1943, her fiftieth birthday, "with the same forward-looking excitement and interest in life" that she had enjoyed when she was five. (This had been her personal manifesto in *Strong Meat.*) She had become famous through her books and her broadcasts on five continents. Her opinions were being sought by many groups and individuals. She carried on a far-flung correspondence with distinguished people. Her creative mind was still at work.

For example, to Robert Speaight in late July she was bubbling with enthusiasm, indicating to him that she was "trying to think out a new, & refreshingly ungodly" play on an episode from Froissart, "full of swords & treason." The same idea was still strong when she wrote in mid-August to Val Gielgud:

> I have at last got an idea for *your* play—if it works! An episode from Froissart—"Mechanism of Treason" with (most suitably) an Italian villain and (less fortunately) a mediaeval battle (please prepare effects of horses neighing and assorted ironmongery)—On the other hand, not a very big cast—about 6 important men and one woman with S. A.

The Froissart play, however, never appeared. Perhaps an earlier apprehension about the timeliness of the play won out over her enthusiasm: "The only idea which is at present nagging to be written is one which probably couldn't be performed anywhere till twenty years after the War, when it had ceased to be topical or interesting!"[77]

At the 1943 annual General Meeting of the English Association, held in the Alliance Hall, Westminster, on Saturday, 29 May, she was elected a vice-president of the association. Dr. F. S. Boas was elected president.[78] She was still generating respect among the professionals.

In the October *Fortnightly* she published another poem. Entitled "Aerial Reconnaissance," it is a dramatic monologue in a folksy style, suggesting some East Anglian who had known, as she herself knew from youth, what an area looks like when icy floods devastate the land. The tone of the poem is significantly unemotional. There is no apparent involvement with people. The bomb damage is presented only matter-of-factly. A powerhouse, ships, dikes, railroad, and flooded fields, bridge, and piers—all destroyed—are described with detachment.[79]

Three brief essays were also produced by Sayers in 1943: "The Gulf Stream and the Channel," "They Tried to Be Good," and "The Human-Not-Quite-Human."

The first of these is a companion piece to "The Mysterious English," and it is essentially an exposition of this text: "By these two geographical jokes—the Gulf Stream and the Channel—everything that appears remarkable in the temperament and history of the British can be sensibly and satisfactorily accounted for." The second essay was also devoted to the British character, but it is not playful like the former—rather, it is highly satirical. Her central theme is that what had influenced Britain in the twenty years between the wars was progressive humanism, which built upon the assumption that there were "no sinful men," only "fundamentally good and perfectible men thwarted by oppressive circumstances." This "voice of Enlightenment" scolded and wagged a finger about the naughtiness of war, power, navies, empire, possessions, self-interest, armament, frontiers: England, like a nursery child, had "tried to be good." Such an attitude, Sayers maintains, underlies the failure to recognize "evils" such as the appeasement policy and unilateral reduction of armaments.

The third essay was written several months after its complement "Are Women Human?" It is also satirical.

> The first thing that strikes the careless observer is that women are unlike men. They are "the opposite sex"—(though why "opposite" I do not know; what is the "neighbouring sex"?). But the fundamental thing is that women are more like men than anything else in the world. They are human beings. *Vir* is male and *Femina* is female; but *Homo* is male and female.

Yet for all this uncompromising philology, males tend to treat females as not quite human. Suppose, she suggests, that the male were subjected to all of the sniggering dishonesty—she does not once use the term *chauvinism*—to which the female is subjected.

> Probably no man ever troubled to imagine how strange his life would appear to himself if it were unrelentingly assessed in terms of his maleness; if everything he wore, said, or did had to be justified by reference to female approval; if he were compelled to regard himself, day in day out, not as a member of society, but merely (salvâ reverentiâ) as a virile member of society. If the centre of his dress-consciousness were the codpiece, his education directed to making him a spirited lover and meek paterfamilias; his interests held to be natural only in so far as they were sexual. If from school and lecture-room, Press and pulpit, he heard the persistent outpouring of a shrill and scolding voice, bidding him remember his biological function, if he were vexed by continual advice how to add a rough male touch to his typing, how to be learned without losing his masculine appeal, how to combine chemical research with seduction, how to play bridge without incurring the suspicion of impotence.

Sayers carries this kind of attack into the fields of journalism, haberdashery, economics, work. No, women are not human! "Blessed be God," says the Jew (and even Cournos had repeated it in his *Autobiography!*), "that hath not made me a woman." To be sure, she told her audience, Jesus was a prophet and teacher who "never nagged" at women, "never flattered or coaxed or patronised, . . . never made arch jokes about them, never treated them either as 'The women, God help us!' or 'The ladies, God bless them!' "[80]

Christmas 1943 was a time of mingled blessing for Sayers. On Christmas Day she tried unsuccessfully to reach Val Gielgud by telephone, desirous not only of wishing him a Merry Christmas but probably also of sharing some part of the day with someone for whom she had unbounded admiration. (He was to write of her in 1965, "We both loved Oxford. We were both extremely positive in the expression of our opinions. We both hated humbug, waste of time, and bad cooking.") Unable to reach him, she finally wrote to him on 4 January 1944:

> I concluded that you were radiating peace & goodwill from some studio or other. I then devoted myself to the Festive Season, including the cooking of 2 ducklings, sage & onion stuffing, apple sauce, 2 veg., Christmas Pudding in rum (which burns better than brandy, I find, & is more mollifying in the sauce)—with a background feeling that I had a cold coming on (due to the arctic temperature of a railway-compartment on the 2.15 returning from London, me containing only a Welsh Rabbit at the time). On Boxing Day I

cooked some more things & felt worse, & on Monday I went to bed in a dissolved state, cursing Hitler for having put handkerchiefs on coupons, & lost interest in my surroundings.—All of which doesn't explain why I have put off writing so long—except that what one doesn't do at once one doesn't do at all, if one is like me.[81]

During 1944 Sayers continued to publish. In March, her poem "Target Area" was published simultaneously in England in *Fortnightly* and in America in *Atlantic Monthly*. The poem clearly displays the author's awareness of the intricacies of human relationships. No one lives to himself. What shall be said of the complexities of the special relationship between teacher and student, between friend and friend, between artist and artist? Or the effect upon these relationships posed by divergent loyalties or divergent ideologies? And when open conflict further widens the distance?

The poem recalls Fräulein Fehmer, Dorothy's piano teacher at Godolphin, who had returned to her home in Germany before World War I. Dorothy had not forgotten her. She had sent her some of the books she published. She could never hear Chopin played without remembering Fräulein Fehmer's strong hands and the controlled performance in Hall. Then she learned that her former teacher had become a Nazi. The last she heard was that Fräulein Fehmer had retired in Frankfurt, the target area of the poem. The news report of the bombing run on Frankfurt caused Sayers to pinpoint her thoughts and memories of her former teacher and the life she had chosen. Was a Nazi able to enjoy Chopin after the ravishing of Poland? Was friendship easily foregone for Nazism? Was a Nazi piano teacher—a member of the civilian population—to be spared in night-bombing? Much of what Dorothy Sayers wrote in "Target Area," of course, applied to herself as well as to Fräulein Fehmer. She, too, lived in daily and nightly apprehension of bombings. She, too, was getting on in years. She was herself visited with thoughts of "the personal assault, the particular outrage."[82]

That same March there appeared in *John o' London's Weekly* an article by Frederick Laws entitled "Tolerance the Essence of Criticism," which Sayers noted and responded to. Laws's chief target was Alfred Noyes, but he also lashed out at Norman Nicholson, Lord Elton, Hamilton Fyfe, C. S. Lewis, Sir Richard Livingston, and Sayers for imposing what he considered moralistic criticism. "If these critics . . . would say simply that they judge books according as they appear likely to aid or hinder the cause of Christianity, we should know where we were." Sayers drew her sights and fired off a letter to the editor:

Sir,—I fear that, even with the object of assisting Mr. Frederick Laws to know where he is, I cannot very well "say simply" that I "judge books according as they appear likely to aid or hinder the cause of Christianity."

For one thing, it would not be true. For another, it would be inconsistent, since I have repeatedly warned people against judging works of art in this "simple," not to say naive, manner.

In the third place, I should not use such a phrase as "the cause of Christianity," since Christianity is not, in that sense, a "cause" at all; it is a statement of fact about the nature of the universe, or it is nothing.

To be sure, it is of no disadvantage to a book that its underlying assumptions should be in accordance with the facts; but neither correctness of data nor piety of intention will suffice to make a good work of art out of a bad one.

Every such work must be judged primarily by the standard of its proper technique; if it is not true to that standard it is true to nothing, and good for nothing. The relation between this "proper truth" and "absolute truth" is, however, by no means "simple." The *locus classicus* on the subject is Jacques Maritain's *Art and Scholasticism;* in my own less scholarly way I have made some observations about it in my Introduction to *The Man Born to Be King,* pp. 19-20, in my pamphlet *Why Work?* pp. 15-18, and (rather less directly) in *The Mind of the Maker,* pp. 77-78, as well as in various public addresses.

If, on the other hand, it is a question of criticizing, not the work of art itself, but the philosophy which (implicitly or explicitly) it expresses, then it is surely not improper for the critic to say whether, in his opinion, that philosophy is true or false.

There is a famous equation which purports to show that 2=3; while I greatly admire its elegance and ingenuity as a work of art, my "tolerance" does not, I admit, stretch so far as to oblige me to admit the conclusion.

This may be pure bigotry on my part; nevertheless, I do certainly feel that the affairs of daily life are more satisfactorily conducted on the assumption that 2=2. But to "say simply that I judge books as they appear likely to aid or hinder the cause of" simple addition, would be to oversimplify my attitude.[83]

Fantasy rather than forensics was the feature of a new type of work from Sayers's hand which appeared in September 1944. It was a juvenile entitled *Even the Parrot: Exemplary Conversations for Enlightened Children.* Two brief contradictory epigraphs precede the initial statement of the book: one is Wordsworth's "Let Nature be your teacher," and the other is Whistler's "Nature is usually wrong." The initial statement indicates the source of the title and imparts Sayers's own particular philosophy:

> *"Even the Parrot," said my Nurse, severely, "knows better than to eat the peel."*
> *I might have retorted that in this matter Man showed himself superior to the brutes. But I knew very well she would only have told me not to be pert. When she was not looking, however, I continued to eat my apples with the skin on, and have persevered in that course to this day (except, naturally, at dinner-parties). Nevertheless, I have lately begun to wonder whether my Nurse was not in principle right, and my Enlightened Humanism wrong, however much in harmony with the spirit of my young age. Accordingly, I venture to present a few Exemplary Conversations in the traditional manner, based upon my Nurse's hypothesis that God has given wisdom to the animal creation.*

There are five stories: "The Canary or Healthful Slumbers"; "The Cat or Family Affection"; "The Bee-Hive or the Perfect Society"; "The Boa-Constrictor or the Rules of Diet"; and "The Rabbit or Town-Planning."

The conditions of wartime England are present on almost every page. A fine for blackout offense, air-raid wardens, sirens, munitions factories, Herr Hitler, German attacks, evacuation of children, aerial bombardment, War Effort, calling up of women, airplanes and tanks, Home Guards, defenses—all are presented casually in the conversations.

Most of the characters are transparent personifications: Nurse Nature; Doctor Draught; Dr. Quickstep; The Livelys; Mr. Thatchett, the farmer; Mr. Secondhand, the village schoolmaster; Uncle Peregrine, a great traveler; Angela Wishwell, the daughter of a banker; Mr. Ramrod; and Mr. Meek, the curate.

The exemplary conversations about the animal creation manage to inculcate many subjects besides those indicated in the titles. The book could be considered a tantalizer to help children learn about Double Summer Time and Greenwich Mean Time, the constellations, birds of many a feather, the Zoological Gardens, the pharmacopeia, carbon dioxide, civilization, Queen Elizabeth's Golden Age, decline in birthrate, domestic economy, clinical apparatus, Karl Marx, G. D. H. Cole, work, service to the community, lethal chambers, the Mercantile Marine, reptiles, *cholera morbus,* castles and fortifications—a very mixed bag. It is obvious that Sayers did not write *Even the Parrot* merely for a lark, but the Poll-parody is entertaining.[84]

Before the year 1944 was over, Sayers also provided introductions for two different books. The first, published in October, was the introduction to the Everyman Library edition of Wilkie Collins's *The Moonstone,* and her words constitute the last major comment she made in print on Collins. For all of its relative brevity, Sayers's introduction suggests the major areas (other than the sheer impedimenta of biography) she would undoubtedly have developed in her long-projected critical biography of Collins. She discusses the nature of a "classic"; the "perfections" of Collins—the Fair-Play Rule ("no vital clue . . . concealed"), the Most-Unlikely-Person ploy, his picture of mid-Victorian society, his portrayal of the passion of love—;Collins's characterizations; and his style.

The quality in which Collins surpasses almost all of his contemporaries is that he "evaded the falsification of character and situation which was almost forced on novelists by the early Victorian taboos on sex." As a result, "he is one of the very few male writers who can write realistically about women without prejudice and about sex without exaggeration." All his characters, Sayers says as her final verdict, "do not exist simply and solely in order to make their moves on the chequerboard of intrigue; they have a full and lasting existence outside the story through which they pass; they are solid characters living in a real world."[85]

The second introduction by Sayers in 1944 appeared in Garet Garrett's *A Time Is Born,* published in November. It is extremely slight by comparison to the work she had done on Collins.[86]

During the last, trying winter of the war, Sayers gave two important addresses. The first, delivered at Dulwich College, was "Towards a Christian Aesthetic." This address is an important corollary to *The Mind of the Maker* and the Reading address "Creative Mind." Sayers's lecture was one in a series organized by Dr. V.A. Demant at the request of the Rev. C.W. Dugmore, then chaplain of Dulwich College, to be given on the Edward Alleyn Foundation. Each lecture was scheduled for one Friday a month during the winter. The lectures were given during the period of the flying-bomb attacks upon London in which Dulwich suffered heavily. Dr. Demant noted that

One or two lectures were interrupted by near-by explosions while speaker and audience took refuge under the seats. Before the course was completed the Chaplain lost his house and the College was so seriously damaged that the later lectures had to be postponed for six months.

Under such circumstances, Sayers's lecture on Christian esthetics appears at the very least ironic, and she herself as admirably stalwart. In the midst of physical crisis and devastation, she began her remarks with these words: "I am to speak to you to-night about the Arts in this country—their roots in Christianity, their present condition, and the means by which (if we find that they are not flourishing as they should) their mutilated limbs and withering branches may be restored by re-grafting into the main trunk of Christian tradition."[87]

The second of the two addresses Sayers gave in that last winter of the war was delivered under circumstances similar to those of Dulwich College. On 22 February 1945 she spoke to the English Goethe Society on "The Faust Legend and the Idea of the Devil." The lecture, says the editor of the society's publication, was "punctuated most appropriately by the sound of the rocket bombs then falling on London." Her lecture looks back to *The Devil to Pay* and *The Mind of the Maker,* among her own writings, and forward to the Dante studies.[88]

At fifty-two years of age, and after six years of war, Dorothy Leigh Sayers had passed through the most amazing development in her life. She had forcibly rearranged her priorities and forthrightly uttered her strengthened convictions. For her, the fundamental question remained "What do we believe?"

chapter four

Affirmations

The poetry of Dante Alighieri the Florentine was the last great love in the life of Dorothy Leigh Sayers. She discovered Dante in her fiftieth year, two years before the end of the war, and with the suddenness of an epiphany she recognized that here was a mind who could command all her energy, absorb all her conviction, and finally focus all her interests.

Her mentor—as she openly acknowledged—was Charles Williams, a brilliant Oxford University Press editor who was virtually self-taught. Demanding as were his duties, he had nonetheless been able to author a remarkable corpus of writings in poetry, drama, fiction, theological studies, and literary criticism. Williams enjoyed reading detective stories and had reviewed many of them in the old *Daily News* and, later, in the *News Chronicle*. He was at home in the world of medieval romance, especially in the Arthurian cycle. The interests and ideas of Sayers coincided at several points. It will be remembered that Williams's play *Thomas Cranmer of Canterbury* had been produced for the Canterbury Festival in 1936, the year preceding the production of Sayers's *The Zeal of Thy House*. Their acquaintance began at about that time.[1]

Williams introduced Sayers to the poetry of Dante. "While I still knew Dante chiefly by repute," she wrote, "*The Figure of Beatrice* was published [1943], and I read it—not because it was about Dante, but because it was by Charles Williams." She conceded that Williams convinced her in this work of the validity of the Florentine poet's reputation as a "Great" poet.

> But it was still some time before I made up my mind to tackle Dante in person; after all, fourteen thousand lines are fourteen thousand lines, especially if they are full of Guelphs and Ghibellines and Thomas Aquinas. A friendly critic can often give the impression that a poem is more colourful and exciting than it really is by picking out the jolly bits and passing over the rest, and I knew well enough the rambling and disjointed habits of the average mediaeval writer. Besides, the world always hinted that Dante, besides being great, grim, religious, and intellectual, was also "obscure".

When, by her assessment, "only a sense of shame and a series of accidents" made her "blow off the dust" from the three volumes of the Temple *Divine Comedy* (which had originally belonged to her Grandmother Sayers), and she at last sat down to read *Inferno,* canto I, she was "resolute" but inwardly convinced that she would read perhaps ten cantos "with conscientious and self-conscious interest and attention, and then—in the way these things happen—one day forget to go on."

The impact of Dante upon her "unprepared" mind was not in the least what she had expected.

> I can remember nothing like it since I first read *The Three Musketeers* at the age of thirteen. Neither the world, nor the theologians, nor even Charles Williams had told me the one great, obvious, glaring fact about Dante Alighieri of Florence—that he was simply the most incomparable story-teller who ever set pen to paper. However foolish it may sound, the plain fact is that I bolted my meals, neglected my sleep, work, and correspondence, drove my friends crazy, and paid only a distracted attention to the doodle-bugs which happened to be infesting the neighbourhood at the time, until I had panted my way through the Three Realms of the Dead from top to bottom and from bottom to top; and that, having finished, I found the rest of the world's literature so lacking in pep and incident that I pushed it all peevishly aside and started out from the Dark Wood all over again.

The reference to "doodle-bugs"—the flying-bombs used by the Nazis against the British in the last days of World War II— indicates when this rapture over Dante occurred in Sayers's life. It was not, however, a first fine careless rapture; it was to persist to her last day.

Sayers noted that in her first serious efforts at reading Dante—encountered "for the first time in middle life, with no preconceptions at all"—she jotted down her "immediate impressions . . . in a series of letters to Charles Williams." She thought that "What Williams valued in the letters was . . . their witness to the excitement that Dante could produce, on a first reading, in a mind left naked to his assault." Williams told her he would like to use her comments in one of his critical works, but death forestalled him.[2]

Not content with repeated "top to bottom, bottom to top" readings in the Temple English edition of the *Divine Comedy,* Sayers in her fervid excitement taught herself—with typical industry—"to read the mediaeval Italian in a very few weeks' time, with the aid of Latin, an Italian Grammar, and the initial assistance of a crib." Understandably, in one place she speaks of her "mania" for Dante. Of course, in a sense all her previous life had been a preparation: her skill in languages, her successful apprenticeship as a writer in many genres, her bristling sensitivity to theology, her wide social awareness, her enormous reading in many fields.[3]

With the outbreak of war, Oxford University Press had been obliged to move its office and staff out of London. Charles Williams, therefore, resided in Oxford. There he was welcomed into the Circle of Inklings, which regularly met in C. S. Lewis's rooms at Magdalen. There he was invited to lecture and became both popular and influential. There he was honored by the conferral of a master's degree. And there, as a Master of the Affirmations, he received Sayers's exuberant letters. There, also, his friends began to prepare a volume of essays in his honor under the editorial direction of Lewis. But on 15 May 1945, just as the war was coming to its close, Williams died in Radcliffe Infirmary in Oxford.[4]

Williams's death was a shock to his friends. Lewis called this experience of loss the greatest he had yet known. Sayers, reviewing later in 1945 a play by Williams, wrote:

> By the passing of Charles Williams's fine and beautiful mind, Parnassus and the Church Militant are alike the poorer. It is true that our loss is his gain and that, to a spirit so compact of charity, release from the flesh is a release into power, exercised with a wider range and after a more direct manner.

Behind the obituary clichés, Sayers was attempting to express her feeling by the vocabulary and in the spirit of Williams's mystical and romantic theology.[5]

The fact is that Williams had not merely introduced her to Dante as a storyteller, even a great storyteller; he had also introduced her at the very right time to Dante as Poet of the Affirmation.

Interpreters of Williams are quick to point out the quality of romanticism inherent in his view. For Williams "the romantic experience" was not "an affirmation of emotional values to the exclusion of formal and intellectual ones," nor "a denial of the essential limitations of human nature." Rather, it was "a moment of vision, in which some image of the created universe is seen as embodying the transcendent God." His theology is anchored in the immanence of God: "The Way of Affirmation consists in . . . the acceptance, in love, of all things, not for their own sake, but as images however imperfect of the Divine." Sayers herself, in a lecture given in 1952 on "The Poetry of the Image in Dante and Charles Williams," elaborates upon this basic tenet:

> The sanction of the Affirmative Way lies in three great Christian doctrines: the first, which is inherited from Jewry, is the doctrine of a true creation. The visible universe is not an illusion, nor a mere aspect of Divinity, nor identical with God (as in Pantheism), still less a "fall into matter" and an evil delusion (as in the various Gnostic or Manichee cults). It is *made* by God, as an artist makes a work of art, and given a genuine, though contingent, real existence of its own, so that it can stand over against Him and know Him as its real Other. . . .
>
> The second doctrine is that of the Incarnation, whereby God Himself became manifest in mortal flesh. . . . From the Incarnation springs the whole doctrine of sacraments—the indwelling of the mortal by the immortal, of the material by the spiritual, the phenomenal by the real. . . .
>
> The third doctrine is the doctrine of the Trinity, which affirms that the Image actually exists within the very mystery of the Godhead Itself. Behind the Incarnation and the fleshly Image stands that ultimate mystery of the Divine Image, who is called also the Son and the Word. . . . It is because of this eternal presence of the Image within the Godhead that it is possible to pursue the Way of the Affirmation to the very confrontation of the soul with the immediate presence of God.

With her characteristic clarity Sayers says: "if the danger of the Way of Rejection is a solitary madness, the danger of the Way of Affirmation is precisely the worship of the images themselves—that is, idolatry." That kind of deviation would be "false" romanticism: "The false romantic makes the mistake of regarding the romantic experience as meant for him, instead of him for it."[6]

When in 1951 she wrote a short introduction to the second printing of Williams's *James I*—one of his lesser-known works—Sayers produced much more than sheer biography: her essay is bibliographical and critical. She boldly identifies Williams as "a genuinely original mind," and she finds his novels, theological books, critical works, and poetry forming "a closely connected unit." Among these, she considers *He Came Down from Heaven* "a key book," a handbook to Williams. As for the "purely historical works (such as *James I)*, Sayers underscores Williams's "acute sense of the living movement of history." He was "singularly free from that hypertrophied 'sense of period' on which our generation tends to pride itself rather too much, and which tends to inhibit judgment by turning all action in the past into a kind of 'costume-piece.' " Most important of all,"Williams never forgot that every age is modern to itself, and that this fact, or illusion, links it with our own."[7]

The same opinion appears in a letter she had written to Williams's son Michael on 2 December 1947:

> I am so glad that he was my guide to Dante—not only, I mean, for having been the stimulus which moved me to read the *Comedy* in the first place, but because the guide was he & no other. He had the great gift of making every author he touched alive & relevant, so that the great dead were never pushed back into a historical past but remained in his writing quick and vibrating with their own vitality & meaning. So many heavy monuments have been erected over Dante, & so many angry critical battles have raged round him that it is little wonder if lightness & humility have got lost. All these good earnest people mean well, & their work has its value; but they are apt to forget the two fundamental questions which, it seems to me, lie at the bottom of all good criticism: "What was this poet really trying to tell people?" & "What does all this mean to us, now?" As for the "metaphysical abstractions", surely the whole point is that to Charles they were not "abstractions", but concrete realities. His language was, I admit, sometimes difficult; but once one had grasped the structure of his thought, everything he said was an illumination.[8]

It is no wonder that when Sayers undertook the translation of Dante, she dedicated her version of the *Inferno* and of the *Purgatorio* to "The Dead Master of the Affirmations, Charles Williams." The readiness was all. She had met a master-spirit whose words were her lifeblood. It was this inspiration that chiefly gave vitality to her work and thought in the last years of her life.

Friendship with the Williams family came as a matter of course. Shortly after the publication of the memorial volume, Michael Williams wrote to Sayers to thank her for her contribution. She replied to his letter, "I am so very glad that you & your Mother like the essay & feel that there is something of your Father in it." By common agreement among the contributors, the royalties from the book were assigned to the Williams family, and after the first royalties had been received, Michael wrote another letter of thanks. On 29 September 1948 Sayers answered:

> I'm glad a little money has come in from the Essays—but I do wish it were more. The O.U.P. [Oxford University Press] are not very brilliant salesmen, I fancy. Still, such as it is, it is yours with my best love & that, I am sure, of all of us.

The Williamses, on their part, began to send to Sayers reprints of some of Charles's books as they appeared, and her gratitude was always keenly expressed—"I am looking forward very much to the *Plays*—thank you so much for sending me a copy"; "How sweet of you to send me *Shadows of Ecstasy*";

> Thank you so *very* much, darlings. I have been champing for years for *The Greater Trumps,* which I once possessed & which somehow vanished away from my shelves—sive dolo, seu jam Troiae sic fata ferebant [*Aeneid,* ii.34]—and left me lamenting. I recognised the writing on the parcel, & said to myself, "Can it be?" & it was! I am just going to sit down for a lovely evening with it, but I had to say thank-you first.

In her letters, Sayers encouraged friendship with Mrs. Williams and Michael by arranging visits, chatting about some of her activities, sending occasional gifts herself. This, early in December 1947:

> I should love to see you all again. I have to be in Town this coming weekend. Shall you by any chance be at home on Friday or Saturday evening? If so, could you send me a line to 24, Great James Street, W. C. 1., where I shall be from Thursday? I shall be immured all day in the B.B.C. Studios in Maida Vale, but free after about 6 p.m.

(In the BBC studios, Sayers was assisting in the preparation of a radio program which was to be aired at the end of February 1948. The program, Number 6 in the series of plays broadcast in the *Mystery Playhouse* under the title *The Detection Club,* was Sayers's own play—never published—"Where Do We Go from Here?")

The following spring to Michael:

We were very sorry you and your mother couldn't come to the Detection Club dinner, which was quite good fun. Also, as it was on the 3rd floor of the Café Royal, we knew nothing about the spectacular weather till it was all over, the rain having most considerately held off till we were in & cleared away before we came out. While there You were, doing your duty in the Steiner Hall & being flooded out for your pains. It is all very unjust, &, as your father used to say, there are a number of things we shall want Providence to explain to us some day.

In September 1948:

Alas! I shan't be able to go & hear Pat McLaughlin on the 3rd. Unfortunately I have to be in Town on the 7th, & I can't manage two visits so close together. On the 7th I have to go with a Deputation from St. Anne's to see a Bishop & Archdeacon about trying to keep the site of the House from being sold over our heads; & in the evening I've got a Detection Club meeting & dinner—so it's going to be rather an exhausting day.
. . . .
I would have written yesterday, but was knee-deep in a German translation of *Man Born*—typed with a very faint ribbon on the inferior blotting paper that passes for paper in Germany—& was exhausted by the end of the day.

At Christmastime 1953, Sayers sent off a gift to Mrs. Williams with a copy of her new juvenile, *The Days of Christ's Coming*. For Christmas 1955 she sent Mrs. Williams another gift—a small cushion—and later gave her news about the conference in which she had participated at Milland Place, Hampshire. Her letter was dated 4 January 1956.

I am very glad the cushion came at a useful moment—I always think those little ones that tuck into the small of the back are *rather* comforting—but it is very naughty of you to fall about, & not at all good of Poor Spire [the Williams pet]. And I am so sorry to hear of Michael's complication of troubles—I do hope he is now really better & that he will continue to be happy in his new job.
The people at Milland were really awfully nice, & I enjoyed myself there; so did Pat McLaughlin. We thought it was really brilliant of Miss Coupland to have gathered everybody together like that & arranged the thing all off her own bat, so to speak. I gather that she had only quite recently "discovered" Charles, & was prompted by nothing but an intense personal enthusiasm. I am sure she & her little lot are not predatory at all. One can't really blame people for getting together to discuss the work of an author who interests them—after all, that is what authors write books *for!*

Apparently, Mrs. Williams needed reassurance on the nature of the interest Miss Coupland had been taking in the works of Charles. She must have fretted over some possible infringement of copyright or the delving of people into the personal life of her husband, because then follows the strong statement by Sayers about people being forbidden to write biographies until the subjects are fifty years dead. Sayers adds one final word about a particular devotee of Williams: "I remember Mr. Cavaliero—I liked him very much, & feel sure that he is genuinely interested for the right reasons, & not one of the vultures."[9]

The Way of Affirmation was seductive to her intellect, but it was difficult to accept, "in love, all things, not for their own sake, but as images of the Divine." That took immense faith and practice. But she tried.

The friendship of C. S. Lewis and Sayers ripened during the closing war years, primarily because of their mutual esteem for Charles Williams. Lewis had become a fellow of Magdalen College, Oxford, in 1925, and he had also become a widely respected scholar even outside his own college. Besides numerous professional publications, his distinguished service included steady development of the English studies syllabus at Oxford. He had also experienced a conversion from atheism to Christianity, and as a consequence he had achieved a reputation as an apologist for his new faith. His precise logic and wit produced a natural affinity between him and Sayers.

It was Lewis who conceived of the Festschrift for Williams. Lewis was, after all, the leading spirit in the literary coterie known as the Inklings. Lewis, Williams, J. R. R. Tolkien, Nevill Coghill, Dom Bede Griffiths, Owen Barfield, and occasionally one or two others would meet once each week, take a meal together, and then in Lewis's rooms at Magdalen read and criticize each other's literary efforts. The Inklings were thus a male literary group. Sayers knew several of the members and was in their company upon occasion. But she was not a member of the Inklings.

Lewis seldom kept letters. There is, however, clear indication that Sayers wrote to him often. For example, on 10 December 1945, Lewis wrote her a note containing an interesting compliment while answering a query she had sent him about the proposed collection of essays for Williams:

> Although you have so little time to write letters you are one of the great English letter writers. (Awful vision for you—"It is often forgotten that Miss Sayers was known in her own time as an Author. We who have been familiar from childhood with the *Letters* can hardly realise" . . .) But I'm

not. No, Hopkins [Gerard Hopkins, nephew of the poet, friend and colleague of Williams at O.U.P.] is not contributing to the volume. A dear creature, though.

Those blue eyes of Sayers must have twinkled as she read this letter from Lewis. She undoubtedly composed a witty reply, saying that Lewis need not worry about *his* stature in letter writing. After all, the writer who had won a prize for *The Allegory of Love* and who had made a vast readership for his science fiction, his chronicles of Narnia, his *Screwtape Letters,* and numerous other highly admired apologetic writings need not lament any fancied exclusion from the world of "great" English letter writers.

She once wrote to Lewis about motivation in writing, and he replied:

> I don't think the difference between us comes where you think. Of course one mustn't do *dishonest* work. But you seem to take as the criterion of honest work the sensible *desire* to write, the itch. That seems to me precious like making "being in love" the only reason for going on with a marriage. In my experience the *desire* has no constant ratio to the value of the work done. My own frequent uneasiness comes from another source—the fact that apologetic work is so dangerous to one's own faith. A doctrine never seems dimmer to me than when I have just successfully defended it. Anyway, thanks for an intensely interesting letter.

Lewis, yet a bachelor, could not have known at the time of this letter—however well-advanced the friendship between himself and Sayers—that his simile on love and marriage must have touched Sayers as no other could have done.

In 1954 Lewis accepted a professorship at Cambridge, having been elected to a new chair in medieval and renaissance literature. If Sayers did not attend his inaugural lecture, she certainly read it upon publication. Professor Lewis's *De descriptione temporum* "added a new phrase to the colloquial jargon of the time, and many people could be heard for a while thereafter proclaiming stoutly that they were, or were not, specimens of 'Old Western Man'." Lewis had set forth the proposition that there was a greater gulf fixed between Christian and post-Christian periods than existed between any other two periods of history, and that he was a specimen of an anterior age, the Old Western Culture: "Ladies and gentleman, I . . . read as a native texts that you must read as foreigners." Needless to say, the views of the past held by Lewis were shared by Sayers.

On the tenth anniversary of the death of Charles Williams, 14 May 1955, these two friends jointly initiated public memorial services in London, Oxford, and Cambridge. They urged students of Williams's work living elsewhere to take steps to pay similar tribute.[10]

Almost as soon as it was known that Sayers was attempting in her new-found devotion to Dante a translation of the *Commedia*, she was prevailed upon to give a lecture. She started delivering lectures on Dante in August 1946 and continued until the spring of the year of her death, 1957. Most of the addresses were given under the auspices of the Summer School of Italian Studies at various university centers. Sayers spoke also to other groups and societies and on BBC programs. Her subjects are an indication of her rising interests in her study and translation of Dante: the narrative skill of the poet; Dante and St. Thomas Aquinas; Dante and Virgil; the "natural" imagery; the meaning of heaven, hell, and purgatory; the perennial relevance of great poetry; the comedy and the paradoxes of the *Comedy;* allegory; Dante and other poets; the art and demands of translation; the Beatrician vision.[11]

Dr. Barbara Reynolds, then lecturer in Italian studies at the University of Cambridge, met Sayers on the first of these occasions:

> My interest in Dorothy Sayers's work on Dante dates back to August 1946, when I attended a lecture she gave on Canto xxvi of the *Inferno* at a Summer School of Italian held at Jesus College, Cambridge. This was the first of a memorable series of lectures on the *Divine Comedy.* . . . It was evident from the beginning that she was bringing to Dante studies in this country a new and revitalizing force. . . . The most valuable and original service she performed for readers of Dante was to redirect attention to the literal meaning of the *Comedy.* This she did by commenting, in a stimulating and readable manner, on the story, or poetic reality, of the work. . . .
>
> In interpreting the allegory, Dorothy Sayers continually drew the reader's attention to the relevance of the *Comedy* to life.

Sayers wrote to her friend Norah Lambourne shortly after this first Dante lecture.

> I went this month to Cambridge to deliver a lecture on Dante to the Summer School of Italian Studies. Rather an ordeal, because the audience was made up of a) about 6 people who knew *all* about Dante—sitting, like sharks, just under the platform with their jaws wide open; b) about 50 people who knew more about Dante, & far more Italian, than I do; c) about 400 people who (to judge by the looks of them) had never even heard of Dante! However, I did fairly well, because, the acoustics of Jesus Hall being

> bad, & most of the other lecturers academic gentlemen who mumbled
> serenely along with their noses in their papers, I turned out to be the only
> lecturer whom, so far, the audience had been able to hear properly. Thus I
> had an unfair advantage—merely because, being no academic but a
> common popular soap-box lecturer, I didn't mind shouting at them in a
> loud & brassy voice, without regard for my own dignity or that of my
> subject. Which just shows that anybody who has anything to do with the
> stage rapidly goes to the dogs & starts showing off in public.

She was, of course, hard in her criticism of herself and also
wittily reassuring herself.[12]

Professor Lewis Thorpe, who "listened to her lectures on the
Divina Commedia given August after August to the Summer
Schools of the Society for Italian Studies," who even "checked
the galleys of those lectures," who "read her translations of
the *Inferno* and the *Purgatorio* and the masterly introductions
and explanatory notes which accompany them," "realized
more and more fully that here was [a] writer fully alive to the
Middle Ages in Europe, here was a fine literary craftsman who
with a creative and richly-stored mind was bringing into new
focus" the literature of medieval Italy.[13]

Dante was the center of reference, explicitly or implicitly, in
other addresses Sayers gave during the postwar years on
numerous occasions. In the summer of 1947 she spoke to
members attending a vacation course in education at Oxford
on "The Lost Tools of Learning," and "lost" was interpreted to
mean "since the Middle Ages." On 23 February 1951 she spoke
to the Royal Institution on "Dante's View of the Cosmos." She
compared and contrasted the cosmos as viewed by Sir Arthur
Stanley Eddington, the contemporary astronomer and physi-
cist, with that of Dante, emphasizing the hierarchical and
metaphysical differences between modern and medieval
times. Reference has already been made to her address "The
Poetry of the Image in Dante and Charles Williams," delivered
to the Chelmsford Arts Association in 1952. In the same year,
on 26 August, she appeared at the Annual General Meeting of
the Association for the Reform of Latin Teaching, having (as
she said in her opening statement) received from the society
"an invitation no less courteous than pressing," to speak on
the subject "Ignorance and Dissatisfaction." Latin study
brought in Dante. There were also lectures to the Oxford
Socratic Society (3 June 1954: "Poetry, Language and Ambiguity"); to the Training College, Darlington, County Durham

(10 November 1954: "The Writing and Reading of Allegory"); again to the Royal Institution (11 November 1955: "Oedipus Simplex: Freedom and Fate in Folklore and Fiction"); to the Oxford University Spectator Club (30 October 1956: "The Poetry of Search and the Poetry of Statement"); to the Oxford University English Club (6 March 1957: "The Translation of Verse"). On 9 July 1950 she spoke on the BBC *Third Program* on "Mediaeval Cosmology and the Imagination," and on 5 and 12 May 1952 she gave two additional talks on Dante for the *Schools Program.* As late as 12 December 1955, R. C. Walton sent a memorandum to BBC program-planners recommending further Dante talks by Sayers because he had heard her give three thirty-minute talks on Dante in St. Thomas's, Regent Street.[14]

Not content with reading and rereading of Dante, Sayers undertook also the translation of the *Divine Comedy.* When she wrote *The Devil to Pay,* she risked (and received) criticism for attempting to pick up after Marlowe and Goethe. Now she risked comparison with an immense array of scholars and poet-translators from Henry Francis Cary through Henry Wadsworth Longfellow, Charles Eliot Norton, Philip Henry Wicksteed, Melville Best Anderson, and Laurence Binyon, to name the most formidable among her predecessors. Sayers was indeed zealous, and with the encouragement of Penguin Books and its able editor, E. V. Rieu, her translation has reached millions of popular readers.

Sayers's translation of the *Inferno* was completed in May 1948 and published in November 1949. Recognizing that a translation of Dante is not Dante, she nonetheless sought to provide in English as much of the structure and tone of the original as she could. She stuck to *terza rima,* acknowledging all the attendant difficulties but determined to offer in this pattern the pace, flexibility, and fluidity of Dante. She tried to simulate in English Dante's Italian metrics. She decided that her commitment to a "modern English" translation had to be interpreted broadly in order to allow her to present as adequately as she could the rich variety of Dante's own style. To one item in her interpretation she clung tenaciously: Dante's humor must be shown in its entire range, from his "charming self-mockery" and "faintly ironic reflection" to his occasional burlesque.

That her introduction to the *Inferno* should carry echoes of some of her (subsequently published) lectures is understandable. She repeats the virtues of Dante as storyteller and master of swift verse. She discusses allegory, distinguishing the features of natural symbolism. She acknowledges Charles Williams as her guide. She develops a historical approach to Dante's world, offering the caveat that "The purely historical approach to a work of art can easily be overdone by the general reader" thus unwittingly dismissing the lasting relevance of that work of art. There is an adequate biographical outline: the Beatrice episodes; the Florentine Guelph-Ghibelline and White-Black feuds; the party purge resulting in the charges against Dante of barratry; the twenty years of exile; the mist of legend surrounding him thereafter. She fits in his writings, illustrating a point or two from the *Vita Nuova,* relating the *Convivio* and the *De Monarchia* to his personal and supranational visions, respectively, and the *Commedia* to both.

In the selection and arrangement of details in the biographical section, Sayers presents interpretations of Dante which reveal as much about herself as they do of the poet. To the salutation-from-Beatrice passage in the *Vita Nuova* she comments that "lovers will recognise an experience which is universal." "Not lovers only, but also all who have undergone the experience known as conversion, will recognise the frame of mind." About Dante's studies after the death of Beatrice in 1290 there are remarks which parallel Sayers's own self-discipline:

> As a young man, he had made himself familiar with the language and literature of Provence, on which all fashionable Italian verse was modelled. He now set himself to improve his Latin and extend his range. He read philosophy, theology, science (especially astronomy), and classical poetry, nosing his way into contemporary learning, as his eager, inquisitive mind led him. He was a voracious reader, with an invaluable gift of concentration. . . .

She cites with approval Boccaccio's report of Dante's habit of reading late into the night, judging it to have "a ring of truth" about it and risking immediate extrapolation—"Probably, like some other men of genius, he was imperfectly house-trained." She detects Dante's shortcomings as a statesman: "he had, indeed, three gifts hampering to the career of the practical politician: an unaccommodating temper, a blistering tongue, and an indecent superfluity of brains." How open to interpretation beyond Tuscany is this statement: "when one has turned forty, and is not particularly happy, one is apt to feel a false shame about one's earlier intimations of immortality"![15]

By September 1954 Sayers had completed translating the second *cantica* of the *Commedia*. It was published in May 1955. The *Purgatorio* volume primarily needed critical and theological introduction. Sayers felt it incumbent upon her to contest vigorously the psychology-oriented criticism of Dante dominated by the "mother-image." She reminds us that Dante was "nurtured upon the poetic doctrine of Courtly Love." The Sayers of "Are Women Human?" and "The Human-not-Quite-Human" lashes out here at all male-made mythology of women. "Women are not interested in sex," she thunders, "but in love-affairs; not in passion but in people; not in man but in men." There has always been "an Enigma of Woman," but "there is no corresponding Enigma of Man." "The sentiment, 'Man's love is of man's life a thing apart; 'tis woman's whole existence' is, in fact, a piece of male wishful thinking." "The great love-lyrics, the great love-tragedies, the romantic agony, the religion of beauty, the cult of the *ewig Weibliches,* the entire mystique of sex is, in historic fact, of masculine invention." Some of this heated polemic may seem to be only an indulgent aside on the part of Sayers, but it is also important to recognize that the very nature of Purgatory proper is discernment of true love: the first three cornices are devoted to the purging of love perverted, the fourth to the purging of love defective, and the upper three to the purging of excessive love of secondary goods. The psychology with which Dante handles these areas is not naive. As to the theological emphasis in the introduction, Sayers's direction is corrective, dispelling arch-Protestant bias and *outré* Catholic interpretations.[16]

Sayers did not live to complete her translation of the *Paradiso*. Only the first twenty cantos had been finished. "Of the remaining thirteen cantos, only one long section and a few fragments were found." She had not begun work on the notes, commentaries, or introduction. With some auspicious foresight, Sayers had corresponded and visited with Dr. Barbara Reynolds "over a period of eleven years, and particularly during the last three years of her life."

In conversations and in letters she discussed in detail her methods of translation, the reasons for her choice of diction, her preferences as to style and rhythm; sometimes she sent as many as ten or twelve renderings of a single passage, and frequently she wrote long letters almost wholly concerned with the technique of verse translation.

When Dr. Reynolds learned, after Sayers's death, that she had expressed the wish that her friend Barbara Reynolds should continue her work, she found that she had "accumulated a store of information, almost of instructions, as to how to proceed." Dr. Reynolds had access to Sayers's Dante notebooks and one or two of her unpublished lectures.[17]

Frequently Sayers sent portions of her Dante translations to friends as Christmas greetings in the postwar years. In 1946 she translated and privately printed the four *canzoni* of the "Pietra" group from Dante's *Convivio*. Printed in Witham, the little pamphlet (which Sayers called *The Heart of Stone)* was adorned by two wood engravings made by her friend Norah Lambourne. For Christmas 1949 Sayers sent to friends her privately printed translation of St. Bernard's Hymn to the Blessed Virgin from *Paradiso,* xxxiii.1-21.[18]

In 1965, Professor Lewis Thorpe published in *Nottingham Mediaeval Studies* (with the consent of Dorothy's son John Anthony Fleming) the Sayers translation of "The 'Terrible' Ode [*Cosi nel parlar voglio esser aspro*]."[19]

The quality of the Sayers translation of Dante has been disputed. The *Times* writers never altered their opinion, even in the obituary notice for Sayers: "The translations she published of *Inferno* and *Purgatorio* caught the directness of the original but failed, as Binyon did not, to catch the poetry." Her decision to render in English the *terza rima* of the *Commedia* made Sayers vulnerable to poetic limitation—in diction if in nothing else. But she approached her responsibility and sustained it with a conscientiousness no one can deny. She was among the first to recognize that translation always resists the translator; the translation is inevitably not the original. She labored consistently to arrive at adequacy: she turned some passages into multiple versions, always striving to catch not only "the directness of the original" but also the cadences and the connotative sensitivities of Dante. Dr. Reynolds endorsed the translation of Sayers in this way:

a poet who wrote for ordinary men and women has been relinquished by them to the learned, for whom he did not write. From this "seconda morte" erudition cannot resurrect him. . . . Dr. Sayers, who is both a trained scholar and a creative artist, brings her vitalising powers to the task of reviving before our eyes the living Dante, not the biographer's Dante, but the poet alive in his writing, "vivus per ora vivum".[20]

The first published Dante essay by Sayers appeared in the Charles Williams volume, *Essays Presented to Charles Williams*, published by Oxford University Press in 1947. C.S. Lewis speaks in the preface of Sayers as a "professional author," one who was part of "a fairly permanent nucleus among William's *literary* friends." The gist of her essay (". . . 'And Telling You a Story': A Note on *The Divine Comedy*") is that Dante is a superb storyteller, displaying exactness, proportion, "extraordinary" pace, adventure developed by "particularity."

Toward the end of October 1954, Dorothy Sayers's first collection of Dante essays, entitled simply enough *Introductory Papers on Dante,* was published. Dr. Barbara Reynolds wrote the preface, speaking enthusiastically of the work of the author. The author's own introduction wastes no time in getting to the business of identifying the allegorical character of Dante's work; recognizing the limitations of "contemporary criticism, whose hypertrophied historical sense and obsession with the psychology of the unconscious seem to compel it to thrust aside the poet's own account of himself and the avowed intention of his work in a frenzied search for the 'real' man and the 'real' meaning supposed to underlie them"; and commending the relevance of Charles Williams's "exploration of the long-neglected mystical signification" of Dante's poetry.

In May 1957, the second volume of Sayers's Dante studies appeared. *Further Papers on Dante* differs slightly, as the author notes in her preface, from the first volume.

The former studies presented a more or less closely connected study of the theological and ethical aspects of the *Commedia*. The present series is more heterogeneous in subject-matter, and pays, by and large, more attention to the literary and poetic aspects of Dante's work—so far as that may be done when addressing audiences of whom not all are acquainted with the Italian original.

The infectious enthusiasm for Dante is still there, and so also is the responsible writing.

There has been some posthumous publication of Sayers's Dante work. In 1963 Gollancz published *The Poetry of Search and the Poetry of Statement*, which contains several Dante essays. (John Anthony Fleming prepared the collection of essays contained in the volume, and Muriel St. Clare Byrne wrote the preface.) In 1965, Professor Lewis Thorpe published in *Nottingham Mediaeval Studies* the essay "The Art of Translating Dante."[21]

Dante, under Charles Williams's guidance, had become the last great love in Sayers's life. "If only *Hamlet* and *Lear*," she wrote poignantly in the last year of her life, "could rush upon one with the same unmuffled impact!"

> It is arguable that all very great works should be strictly protected from young persons; they should at any rate be spared the indignity of having their teeth and claws blunted for the satisfaction of examiners. It is the first shock that matters. Once that has been experienced, no amount of later familiarity will breed contempt; but to become familiar with a thing before one is able to experience it only too often means that one can never experience it at all. This much is certain; it is not age that hardens the arteries of the mind; one can experience the same exaltation of first love at fifty as at fifteen—only it will need a greater work to excite it. There is, in fact, an optimum age for encountering every work of art; did we but know, in each man's case, what it was, we might plan our educational schemes accordingly. Since our way of life makes this impossible, we can only pray to be saved from murdering delight before it is born.

How much unfolded from Sayers's vision of Dante at the right time and in the right place![22]

It would be misleading, of course, to suggest that Sayers had time for nothing but Dante and the Way of the Affirmation. These had surely become the core, but there were still the random experiences of life.

She had been commissioned to write a play for Lichfield Cathedral, commemorating the 750th anniversary of the beginning of cathedral construction in the Staffordshire borough. The play was to be the major attraction in the festival to be held at Lichfield Cathedral in June 1946. Sayers did not find inspiration in a strictly historical setting for this occasion. While she did include Dr. Samuel Johnson, Lichfield's most famous figure, she did not settle on an eighteenth-century topic. She turned aside from St. Chad and the misty beginnings of his bishopric. Addison, Garrick, and Erasmus Darwin were passed by. What she produced she entitled *The*

Just Vengeance. The title and theme, therefore, come from Dante. The accent in the structure and dialogue distinctly shows the influence of Charles Williams.

Sayers herself describes the work as "a miracle-play of Man's insufficiency and God's redemptive act, set against the background of contemporary crisis," specifically the crisis of the world war which had ended only one year previously. The play moves in "what may be called large blocks of action rather than in the swift to and fro of dialogue." The "important affirmations" are emphasized by repetition. The author anticipates the blurred chronology and fused character-identity which were to appear in Christopher Fry's *A Sleep of Prisoners* (1951). In Sayers's play, Biblical characters consort in a nonlinear pattern with Lichfield's Samuel Johnson, the Quaker George Fox, and any number of common people, including a modern airman.[23]

But while she was still putting finishing touches to the play in the end of February, a local distress claimed her attention. On Wednesday, 27 February 1946, the *Daily Sketch* splashed a sensational announcement before its readers' eyes that the Church of England would launch on Ash Wednesday, 6 March 1946, through Easter Sunday, 20 April, a "Campaign to Rid Soho of Crime."

In the biggest campaign of its kind ever launched in London the Church of England will set out on March 6 to clean up Soho, the criminal centre of the metropolis. Beginning with a convention that will run throughout Lent, from March 6 to April 20, it is planned to remove from Soho forever any immoral or criminal associations.

The Bishop of London will open the war on London's "bad lands" with an address at a public meeting in the Kingsway Hall on March 6. In the spring groups of church workers will walk through the streets of Soho, stopping here and there to pray or talk, and to send out disciples to rescue those in need. Later the movement is to spread through the capital.

At St. Anne's House and the Toc H Centre in Greek-street there are to be all kinds of meetings and discussions practically every evening, which will have a direct appeal to the whole of central London.

More than 100 men and women church workers who have been through the toughest struggles of the war with the troops will be drafted into Soho.

Dorothy Sayers, the playwright, will write "Thrillers" from the Bible, with modern dialogues and characterisation, which will be performed for Dean-street, Soho, audiences.

Already the work of rescuing men and women from London streets has begun, and a pioneer staff of clergymen and women helpers is now assisting hundreds of young men and women stranded in the capital.

> While I was talking to one of the priests last night two fainting girls were carried in from the snowy streets and given shelter and food.
>
> "We are not just giving them a roof here for one night; when they come here we make every effort to keep them from going back to the streets," said Father Petit Peire. "Many women and some men have turned from a life of crime to become Christians after resting here for a few days."[24]

This notoriously misrepresentative and sensationalist journalism sparked an almost-galvanic reaction from Sayers. At the very time *The Just Vengeance* was announced for June, here was an idiot reporter attributing "thrillers" from the Bible to be written by the distinguished religious playwright! She must have counted into the thousands to cool her indignation before writing the letter to the editor of *Daily Sketch* which appeared on the following Tuesday, 5 March 1946:

> May I clear up a misunderstanding about the Christian Mission to the Diocese of London, which opens to-morrow with a meeting in the Kingsway Hall at which I am speaking? The subject title of the Mission is: *Have You Understood Christianity?* and it has nothing whatever to do with "ridding Soho of crime," or cleaning up haunts of vice.
>
> The Mission is addressed to all London and its object is to give intelligent people an opportunity of hearing an orderly exposition of the Christian Faith and of asking as many questions as they like and having those questions intelligently discussed and answered.
>
> A great many people to-day find themselves living in a world which appears to make no sense. During this mission, which will last from Ash Wednesday to Easter Sunday, a number of Christian priests and laymen will make it their business to explain how the Christian revelation does "make sense" of the universe and of the lives of individual men and women.
>
> There will be services, lectures and discussions: and, in addition, the message of the Faith will be presented through the arts of drama, music, etc. Every effort will be made to deal with questions of to-day in terms relevant to the needs of twentieth-century people.
>
> The mission is being run from the parish of St. Thomas, Regent-street, and from St. Anne's Church House, 57, Dean-street, Soho, and all information can be obtained from St. Anne's Church House.
>
> In conclusion, may I make it quite plain that I am *not* writing "thrillers from the Bible," or anything of that kind? I am merely making a short speech at the opening meeting.[25]

At least one reader of the news article, Canon A. Linwood Wright of St. Mark's Vicarage, Leicester—only thirty miles from Lichfield, had already become very perturbed. What effect would this wretched sensationalist misinformation have on the June festival? Sayers wrote to Canon Wright on 21 March 1946, assailing in no uncertain terms the *Daily Sketch* reporter for his extravagant and unfounded language:

I am very sorry that you should have been misled by that preposterous article in the *Daily Sketch* (the perpetrator of which has, I understand, since been removed to a mental hospital). I contradicted it in the most emphatic terms on the following Tuesday. I am no more engaged in writing "religious thrillers" than I am involved in a campaign to "clean up Soho". All these sensational reports were the fantasy of a sick brain. I enclose a program of the London Mission, so that you may see what it really is all about. Nobody is going to harry prostitutes or swoop upon night-clubs, nor is anybody braving the inclemency of the English spring by street-performances. All that is happening is instruction, discussion, and the reading of certain religious and other classics in St. Thomas's Church.

My own job at the moment is translating the *Divine Comedy*—fortunately I did not mention *that* to the reporter, or he might have said I was composing a religious farce!

With many regrets that I cannot help you, and that you should have been (so to speak) led up the garden into a mare's nest.[26]

Obviously, therefore, Sayers had had some responsibility for giving information to the newspaperman on the London Mission, however unfortunate the interpretation.

The association of Sayers with St. Thomas's, Regent Street, the St. Anne's Society, Soho, and the Vicar, the Reverend Patrick McLaughlin, was a longstanding one. St. Anne's Society had as its continuing purposes to serve as an enquiry center; to serve as a play-producing society; to serve as a discussion club—nonbelievers and those of opposing faiths were welcomed to cross swords with others. Individuals like Sir Russell Brain, Mr. Osbert Lancaster, Mr. Michael Mac-Owan, Sir Harold Nicholson, Lord Pakenham, and Sir Herbert Read had participated in the discussions.

The spring of 1946 having passed by with its discontent, Sayers went to Lichfield near the end of May to attend rehearsals and to assist her friend the director, Frank Napier, in the production of the play. Norah Lambourne, who first met Sayers in 1945 when asked to design the costumes and to paint the set for *The Just Vengeance,* recalls that Sayers joined the company of actors, the producer, the composer, and the designer at Lichfield for the month prior to the production. All were housed in the Theological College in the close. Sayers took a keen interest in every aspect of the production. "She was a tower of strength and a great inspiration to everyone." There were some difficulties: the production required a large cast—some professional and many amateur actors; the regular services of the cathedral could not be interrupted for rehearsals; money and materials were in short supply, costumes being made from "unlikely" fabrics by a working party of volunteers from the town of Lichfield under Norah Lambourne's supervision. (England still had rationing of clothes and materials in 1946.)

But the festival began on time, running from 13 June through 29 June. The Midlands were "sodden and unkind," and the mayors who walked to their special service on 15 June paraded under umbrellas. Her Majesty Queen Elizabeth (the mother of Elizabeth II) attended the production on the same rainy day, and after the performance Sayers was presented to her. On 19 June 1946, Sayers wrote a hasty note to Val Gielgud, claiming that "the Queen was delighted, & so were the assembled archbishops, bishops & clergy; though I gather that the Sheriff's wife thought it blasphemous." Her friends from the BBC who attended thought the play moving and beautiful.

Sayers sent to Gielgud her own adaptation of *The Just Vengeance* for radio broadcasting early in 1947. The previous December she had written to him in a note of despair:

> No dramatic critics ever do seem to grasp what any play is *about*. I don't think it's all my fault—look at the incredible bosh they talk about *The Family Reunion*. They have no idea what *that's* "about". Even audiences are less stupid than they are.

She added: "I shall never succeed in explaining to anybody what *The Divine Comedy* is *about*." What she did not completely know was that her own infectious enthusiasm was indomitable.

Sayers always believed that *The Just Vengeance* was her best religious play. Although she worked diligently for a London production, it never came off. So now, *The Just Vengeance*, with its Dante overtones, was behind her. Dante, of course, persisted. On 13 January 1947 she wrote Gielgud again. "Dear Val,"

> what with Frank [Napier, the director of *The Just Vengeance*, who had been ordered abroad by his doctor], & the weather, & the strikes, & probably no food & the tobacco shortage & one thing & another, it is difficult not to become low in one's spirits. But I have acquired two 16th century Dantes, with woodcuts, & a fan in Australia sent us a magnificent cake for Christmas, so there are *some* alleviations.[27]

Similarly, she looked forward to her own outside commitments because of their Dante connections. Invited to chair a session of the annual meeting of the English Association of 3 July 1948, at which Sir Herbert J. C. Grierson was to speak, she wrote to Sir Herbert in April. She thanked him for the gift of his anthology *And the Third Day* and expressed her delight at the anticipation of meeting him at the July meeting of the association. "I am greatly looking forward to meeting you and thanking you in person," she said,

> and receiving from you valuable guidance in the task of verse-translation. As you know, I have rather rashly committed myself to grappling with the *Divine Comedy,* rushing in where so many better scholars and poets than myself have found the way hard to tread—and only hope that I may not end up in the vestibule of the Futile—or even lower down, among the Falsifiers!

She herself was the speaker at the annual luncheon, and her talk was on "Slipshod English." Her remarks were not printed. The editor of *English* wrote, after Sayers's death:

> A guest of the Association at one of the Annual Luncheons [presumably, 3 July 1948], she made, during the afterluncheon speeches, some pungent and stimulating observations on current English. In her capacity of entertainer, in the creation of first-class detective fiction, and of a religious playwright and classical scholar, Miss Sayers will be remembered as one of the century's leading women of letters.

If her "observations" were anything like her earlier "The King's English" (1935) and "Plain English" (1937), the combination of Sayers's insistence on accuracy and effectiveness and her lambent wit would indeed have regaled her audience.[28]

Activities and obligations continued to crowd her days, and she energetically continued to respond to requests and invitations as well as to scholarship. The year 1950 was a momentous year in her personal life. She was asked to rebut a famous scientist, to participate in a women's fashion show, to receive an honorary degree, to have her portrait painted, and to face the death of her husband.

The Yorkshire scientist Fred Hoyle (later knighted) had delivered through early September a series of BBC talks on the nature of the universe. In one outspoken talk he had coolly stated that there is no foundation for belief in God as the Creator of the universe. There were many indignant listeners—one London newspaper reported the situation under the caption "Heaven or Hoyle." Letters to editors charged the

BBC with giving preference to atheistic and left-wing propaganda. The atmosphere resembled the (much greater) furor aroused by Sayers's *The Man Born to Be King* in 1942.

Sayers might have been diffident of debating with a given scientist in the area of his discipline, but she was not at all shy when it was a matter of *verbal* reliability. T. S. Gregory arranged the rebuttal program for the BBC. On 30 August 1950 Sayers had written to him:

> As I said to you over the telephone, I dare say I can manage to do 15 minutes' criticism of Mr. Fred Hoyle's rather ill-informed notions about Christianity. Choose your own title, remembering to make it clear that I have only been asked to deal with Mr. Hoyle, and am not expected to review the whole subject of the relations between religion and science in this somewhat inadequate space of time!

The BBC arranged to have Professor Herbert Dingle and Sayers speak on Tuesday evening, 26 September 1950, each for fifteen minutes. Since this was customarily the time for the "Light Programme," broadcasts for young people, some discontented listeners read into the scheduling further BBC malicious maneuvering. Why were not Professor Dingle and Miss Sayers scheduled for the 9:15 *Home Service Program,* the hour during which Mr. Fred Hoyle had aired his "fantastic theories"? Nonetheless, the report is that Dingle and Sayers, speaking on "The New Cosmology," gave "two slashing attacks on Fred Hoyle's recent series of talks." The radio critic for the *Manchester Guardian* thought that the best of recent talks "were two criticising Frcd Hoyle's broadcasts on the universe, by Professor Dingle and Dorothy L. Sayers." Archibald Kenyon, radio critic for the Leeds *Yorkshire Post,* agreed and added that Sayers "had a sharp enough rap at scientists who . . . 'begin to discuss religion without seeming to know the meaning of words which Christians use.' "[29]

There was a bizarre occasion in Sayers's career near Christmastime 1950. Mrs. Doris Langley Moore, Yorkshire author, sponsored on the afternoon of 5 December a "Vista of Fashion through Two Hundred Years" with two uneven purposes in mind: to prove that the average Victorian waists were no smaller than those of the mid-twentieth century, and to encourage a plan for a London Museum of Costume. The Queen and Princess Margaret attended the production at New Theatre, and Mrs. Langley Moore secured actresses and writers, as well as art students and dressmaking students from London schools, to model some of the dresses from over one thousand in her own private collection. The author, whose book *The Woman in Fashion* had been published in the previous year, provided a running commentary on the parade from her seat at side-stage. "Three high-lights of the afternoon," wrote Helene Williams for a women's column, "were the appearance of Miss Beatrice Lillie in a fin-de-siècle evening gown with a fan to point one of her inimitable ditties; Dr. Dorothy Sayers as the leader of a Suffragette demonstration (Edwardian); and, in the grand finale, Dame Edith Evans, looking regal in a genuine and most magnificent Court dress of the same period." Sayers was apparently typecast. Her tailor-made outfit probably varied only a little from the costume she normally wore. To judge from reports and photographs made of Sayers at the time, it is probable that her waistline, also, helped to bear out Mrs. Langley Moore's thesis that not all Victorian ladies were wasp-waisted.[30]

From the early 1920s Sayers had felt the spur of fame. Disdainful as she might justifiably have become of those who sought only chatty gossip-column items, she genuinely was gratified by the respect she had won.

During the spring of 1950 she accepted an invitation from her old employer S. H. Benson, Ltd., to unveil the plaque in the Benson reception area which commemorates her writing of *Murder Must Advertise.*

On 24 May 1950 she was accorded further distinction. Sayers stood in front of the chancellor of The University of Durham to hear a citation read conferring the Doctorate of Letters upon her *honoris causa.* The Public Orator of the university displayed a fitting blend of wit and gravity as he presented the author.

> Mr. Chancellor, I have the honour to present to you Dorothy Leigh Sayers, Master of Arts of Somerville College, Oxford.
> An examination of the claims of Miss Sayers to appear before us today must raise a preliminary doubt whether this is quite the sort of platform upon which she should be standing. The Documents in the Case, unobscured by Clouds of Witness, cannot be dismissed as Five Red Herrings in establishing this point. Long before the evidence of Unnatural Death, which had itself come out before Lord Peter Viewed the Body, there could be no doubt Whose Body had been in question. In the Teeth of the Evidence, even after the Unpleasantness at the Bellona Club—and it will be

remembered that this did not follow but preceded the notorious Gaudy Night—Miss Sayers publicly took the unfortunate view that a book called Murder Must Advertise had no personal application. As for her victim, before anyone could Have His Carcase, Strong Poison proved to be present: and it is my feeling that there would have been no need to cite the Nine Tailors or to take the case further had not Hangman's Holiday intervened.

But Miss Sayers is an adept in triumphantly disspelling dark clouds of suspicion, and it may be fairly asserted that her detective novels have collectively given more pleasure to educated readers than any since Conan Doyle's immortal series. Both authors present the personality and circumstances of their characters so vividly that the accessory details sometimes count for even more than the main story. By this subtle means their stories become vehicles of their own attitude to society and its problems, material and moral: and a penetrating criticism of these matters is implanted in the guise of an idle tale.

This breadth of outlook and of human sympathy is well known to be in Miss Sayers the basis of a moral strength, in which a lively and uncompromising Christianity is the central core. At a given moment novels were laid aside in favour of an earlier interest in religious truth and this was expressed in a stream of stimulating essays and plays and at length in a vigorous and painstaking verse translation of Dante's *Inferno*. We have in Miss Sayers not only an artist, but a moralist who uses her art to convey a message with passionate desire to make it tell. And the Doctorate of Letters now to be conferred upon her expresses our admiration of her art, gay or grave, and a deep regard for her sincerity.

This academic honor was most gratifying. It had been fifty years since her father had taken her onto his lap to begin her acquaintance with Latin, and the intervening years had marked her indomitable pursuit of quality and conviction— Godolphin, Somerville, Hull, Oxford, Les Roches, and London: *ad astra per aspera.*

The chancellor of Durham at the time was George Macaulay Trevelyan, C.B.E., O.M., who had had a distinguished career at Cambridge as professor of modern history and Master of Trinity College. He stepped into the chancellorship in 1949, retired in 1957, and died in 1962. To him Sayers had sent a copy of her translation of the *Inferno,* and it was the evidence of her Dante scholarship primarily that prompted Trevelyan to recommend her for the degree.[31]

Earlier that year, Sayers had been asked by Sir William Oliphant Hutchison, president of the Royal Society of Portrait Painters until his death in 1970, to sit for a portrait. It was exhibited first in October 1950 at the Royal Glasgow Institute of the Fine Arts. Sir William met Sayers in London, either in the early 1930s or just after World War II when he had a studio there (though he resided mostly in Edinburgh). The paths of Sir William and the Flemings doubtlessly crossed in Galway, also, during the Flemings' summer holidays.

Atherton Fleming died on 9 June 1950. He would have been sixty-nine years old the following November. The death certificate states simply that death came from cerebral hemorrhage, abetted by hypertension.

Early in April 1949 he had been ill enough to take to his bed. Sayers wrote to her friend Norah Lambourne on 26 April that the doctor had found "Mac" that first time in a "kind of giddy & unco-ordinated state," much to her relief. "No doubt," she wrote about doctors, "they are only too well accustomed to wives' descriptions of patients' symptoms, & discount them automatically." The doctor expressed alarm at "Mac's" blood pressure, but, as Sayers wrote to her friend, "Mac" invented "a whole set of excuses for not going to Chelmsford to be overhauled." She added that she had told "Mac" they *were* only excuses, "& that even in they changed the venue to London, it would only produce a fresh set of reasons for not going!" In the privacy of the letter to a friend, Sayers wrote of her own frustration:

> The trouble, of course, with blood-pressurey people who have *uncontrolled tempers,* is that they may work themselves up into a stroke at any moment. But one can't do anything about it, because nobody else can control their tempers for them. But at any rate the Doctor knows now exactly what the situation is, & is doing what he can to cope.

Apparently "Mac" *was* persuaded within a few days to undergo a complete physical examination, because on 11 May 1949 Sayers wrote to Norah Lambourne again: "Nobody has been able to find anything wrong with Mac's inside! So there we are!"

Fleming had been responsible for bringing on his own condition. He had the reputation in Witham of frequently drinking to excess. His visits to the public houses signalized his withdrawal. In one pub he pounded the piano keys because he was not waited on promptly enough. He often had to be assisted home. "Put me to the rail," he would say, and some one would help him to the wrought-iron fencing which he could follow, supporting himself to his own door. In one pub he had been identified in his hearing as "the husband of Dorothy Sayers," and he haughtily left the place never to return.

Dorothy was with "Mac" at the time of his death. She must have reviewed the twenty-five years of her marriage and accepted humbly the less-than-perfect image of the divine in him. An affirming charity was there. The touching evidence of it is the word she offered—surely she alone—on the death certificate for his occupation: *Artist.* A sensitive man broken by World War I—"the gruff warrior with tears in his eyes"— his chief creative efforts had flowed over words and ballet (he saw everything done by Pavlova) and cookery and photography and painting. Artist did not seem inappropriate.

Fleming's body was taken to Ipswich for cremation, and a friend later took the ashes to his native Scotland. That friend, stopping at Biggar in Lanarkshire, felt reassured when his automobile was parked in front of the Fleming Arms. Instantly he had the good feeling that "Mac" had come home. The ashes were scattered in the churchyard the next morning.[32]

Death, like war, is not a final catastrophe. Sayers was an independent woman. She had already been commissioned to do another religious play; she had not completed her work on Dante; and there were necessary diversions.

On 24 August 1950, she wrote to her friend who had carried "Mac's" ashes to Scotland: "Thank you so much for your letter, & for your great kindness in enabling me so easily to fulfill poor old Mac's last wishes." Her letter was sent from Townhill in Chilton, Aylesbury, two months after Fleming's death, and she reported that she was taking a little holiday, the first since before the war. She was traveling by car with Muriel St. Clare Byrne, "visiting places of interest & working in three plays at Stratford-on-Avon (by good luck of knowing the Management)." Earlier in the month she had stopped in Exeter to give two lectures on Dante to the Summer School of Italian Studies. Barbara Reynolds noticed on that occasion that Sayers was again wearing earrings for the first time in a long while.

Three days before the death of Atherton Fleming the first public announcement was made of the play Sayers had promised to write for the borough of Colchester as part of its entertainment during the 1951 Festival of Britain. In the *Colchester Gazette* of that date amateur actors were encouraged to offer themselves for audition for small parts in

Sayers's "specially-written Festival play, 'The Emperor Constantine.' " By mid-1950, therefore, Sayers's play was certainly well roughed out.

As one of the most famous writers in Essex, Sayers was a logical choice for the writing of a play drawn in part from the legendary and historical backgrounds of the eastern county. She had acquired extensive knowledge of the role played by the Romans in the history of Britain. Typical of her singleness of purpose, however, she was not about to write for the Colchester festival a mere chronicle nor to brush up slightly on her knowledge of the Romans in England. Also, somewhat disappointed by the reception of *The Just Vengeance,* she decided not to venture again too far into expressionism. Realism would be the technique of the play.

Sayers recognized that in accepting the commission to write the play for the Colchester Festival she had to pay respect to some of the old Essex legends. Thus, when she summarizes the mixed details about Constantine's mother handed down through the centuries, she acknowledges those legends:

> His mother was that Helena who was later canonised as St. Helena, and whose finding the True Cross in Jerusalem is commemorated in the Church's calendar on the third day of May. It was said by some, both then and now, that she was [Constantine Chlorus's] concubine, a woman of humble origin—a barmaid, indeed, from Bithynia. But an ancient and respectable tradition affirms, on the other hand, that she was his lawful wife, a princess of Britain, daughter of the local chieftain "King" Coel of Colchester, whose legend, distorted by time, is preserved in the nursery song of "old King Cole". If this is so—*and Colchester will hear no word to the contrary*—she may well have been a Christian from her birth; for in the 4th century there was already a Christian church, with a Christian bishop, at Colchester.

But Sayers is more interested in Constantine than she is in his reputed mother. In the preface to the published play she comes directly to the point:

> The reign of Constantine the Great is a turning-point in the history of Christendom. Those thirty years, from A.D. 306, when he was proclaimed Augustus by the Army of Britain at York, to A.D. 337, when, sole Emperor of the civilised world, he died at Nicomedia in Asia Minor, exchanging the Imperial purple for the white robe of his baptism, saw the emergence of the Christian ecclesia from the status of a persecuted sect to power and responsibility as the State Church of the Roman Empire. More important still, and made possible by that change of status, was the event of A.D. 325: the Council of Nicaea. At the first Great Synod of East and West, the Church declared her mind as to the Nature of Him whom she worshipped.

The briefest of prologues (in which Old King Cole appears) is followed by act I, in which we see how Constantine became Emperor of the West. Act II portrays the steps by which he became Emperor of the East, and so of the whole Empire. Act III is entitled "The Empire of Christ." A short epilogue pulls together the main symbols of the play.

The Emperor Constantine was presented in the Playhouse Theatre, Colchester, 3-14 July 1951. The production took three and three-quarter hours. Apparently, audiences responded in terms of their capacity to follow the career of Constantine and to keep pace with the theological argument. The dramatic critic of the *Times* was not impressed.

> This piece seems to have been written less in the spirit of a stage chronicle than in that of a pageant. It has 26 scenes and 93 characters; it takes nearly four hours to perform. In no other sense is it a big work. Constantine's life is presented in much historical and legendary detail, but he remains in the end little more than the spectacular hero of a pageant.
>
> Sometimes a single detail—for instance, the feigned reluctance with which the young general accepts the army's nomination as Augustus—is the pretext for a whole scene. This might be all very well in the open air, but the effect in the theatre is to make it difficult to see the wood for the trees. At the other extreme Miss Sayers endeavours to compress the Arian controversy into a brief and heated discussion at the Council of Nicaea; and only minds versed in theological technicalities can keep up with the disputants' telegraphese. The chronicle is written throughout in modern idiom. . . . Fortunately the largely amateur cast, led by Miss Veronica Turleigh [who created Harriet in *Busman's Honeymoon*] and Mr. Ivan Brandt, gives the piece an unflaggingly good performance. Mr. John Izon's production treats every scene with zestful skill, and the long evening is smoothly decorative.

On the other hand, the *Church Times* reviewer considered the play "a mighty chronicle," swift-moving, keeping the audience "alert." He—and most of the audience at the premiere performance on 3 July—did not find "the disputants' telegraphese" annoying. Instead,

> The fact that the play did not ever pall, was not the least of its virtues. Apart from a few trivial first-night difficulties over curtains, it moved swiftly through its thirty-two years of history from A.D. 305 to 337, and many of the twenty-six scenes ended in the laughter of the people of Colchester—thus proving Miss Sayers's contention that history and theology can be fun. Especially theology; for if the author has painted her enormous canvas with a commixture of stagecraft, history and theology, the greatest of these is theology; and, as it happened, the theology contained the most entertainment value. . . . Intrigue, warfare and the spice

of humour kept the audience alert. . . . Miss Sayers has proved that she knows how to make a discreet use of the modern idiom.

The last act was far and away the best. This was the Empire of Christ, and it is not irreverent to say that this was where the fun really began. Miss Dorothy Sayers "enjoys" her religion. Here she positively made her audience enjoy it too.

Monday, 3 July 1951, was a day of sweltering heat, but that did not deter the distinguished audience at the premier performance, including the bishop and the mayor of Colchester. After the performance, the audience called for the author. Sayers "took a curtain call, and received the plaudits of an enthusiastic theatre." One viewer remembered Sayers's stateliness as she stood in a long, dark velvet dress wearing a strand of pearls.

Six years afterward, the columnist for the *Church Times,* reminiscing at the time of Sayers's death, recalled the same occasion differently.

I have a very lively memory of her at the first night of her dramatic chronicle about the Emperor Constantine, at Colchester. She was standing in a box, wearing a white overall, and surveying the action with an awful scrutiny. What a night that was. I was sitting next to a critic who had been with me a year or two before at the Oberammergau Passion Play. He looked apprehensively at his programme. "This isn't a play," he said, "it's a pageant. It will be as long as Oberammergau!" It was certainly long. I left some time before it was finished, but still did not get back to London before the early hours of the morning. But she had certainly succeeded in her objective of making drama out of dogma.

Colchester had received the whole production, but a shortened version of the play (with a new title: *Christ's Emperor)* was presented in London at St. Thomas's Church, Regent Street, for a season of three weeks from 5 February 1952. The part of Constantine was again acted by Mr. Brandt, and Sayers herself (assisted by Graham Suter) directed the production. Norah Lambourne designed the settings and costumes for both the Colchester and London productions.

Dr. James Denholm of Witham, Sayers's physician, was asked by the dramatist during the time she was composing the play several questions which reveal her interest in realism. "What," she first asked him, "did a razor look like in Roman times?" (She had the barbershop scene in mind—a symbolic anticipation of the Council of Nicaea scene.) Then she asked: "About how heavy would be a human head carried on a spear?" (She had in mind the last scene of act I when the head of Maxentius is carried in upon the stage in such fashion.)

It is worthy of note that during the Festival of Britain that year not only was Sayers's new play, *The Emperor Constantine,* presented in Colchester, but other plays by Sayers were also presented in various localities as part of the Festival celebrations. *The Zeal of Thy House* was repeated in Canterbury that June. At St. John's Church, Waterloo Road, episodes from *The Man Born to Be King* were presented from 13 through 30 August. In mid-September, *The Zeal of Thy House* was part of Chatham's Festival entertainment. In Plymouth, Kensington, Dorchester, Worthing, Southampton, and Thornhill there were productions of these same plays by Sayers. There were even productions of *Busman's Honeymoon* in many places in the provinces and a presentation of her radio play *He That Should Come* by the St. Andrew's Society in Taunton in January.[33]

Sayers had not yet completed the *Purgatorio* volume in the Dante translation, but she managed to work in numerous lectures or addresses for other occasions. Newspapers and magazines give fugitive evidence of some of this activity.

Eric Keown in *Punch* of 21 February 1951 begins an article by saying: "Two years ago Miss Dorothy Sayers, addressing members of the Church Assembly, said that all her life people had connected Christianity with bad art, and that what was really damaging to church art was a genteel imbecility and sheer technical incompetence."

A *Manchester Evening News* item on 19 March 1951 announced that several Manchester delegates of the British Drama League would be going up to London for their annual conference in May and would participate in discussions of plays led by Robert Atkins, Christopher Fry, Norman Marshall, Dorothy Sayers, Henry Sherek, and others.

The *Church of England News* announced in March 1951 that the Canterbury Festival season—18 July through 10 August—would include lectures by Dame Sybil Thorndike and Dorothy Sayers. (An American professor, Rosamond Kent Sprague, heard Sayers on that occasion on 20 July 1951:

She spoke to a captivated audience on "Change-ringing." I remember two particular things about the content of the lecture. The first was that she informed us that she had got up the subject of campanology for the specific purpose of writing *The Nine Tailors*. . . . Secondly—and I am sure that no one there could possibly forget this—she divided us into three groups, each group to represent the note of a different bell, and set us to work to illustrate the lecture. Not only was this an excellent teaching device, but everyone enjoyed it—we were *creating* something.)[34]

In January 1952 she was elected Vicar's Warden of St. Thomas's, Regent Street. Her main responsibility was the traditional one: to work with the People's Warden in making preparations for services, assigning seats to parishioners, and keeping order during the services—"if necessary—giving offenders into custody."

Many people have seen her go round with the alms-dish. She was often at that intellectural centre, St. Anne's, Soho, and she liked to drop in there for informal conversation, regardless of time. She was certainly a "character." She would not suffer fools gladly.[35]

On 8 May 1952, she wrote to Norah Lambourne about the pressure of activities, citing obligations at the Detection Club, activities at St. Anne's House, and Dante programs for the BBC.[36]

Late the month before, Sayers had attended a party for Georges Simenon, the Belgian detective-story writer. Noel Whitcomb, columnist of the *Daily Mirror,* reported an impression and a snatch of conversation:

The party was mostly made up of novelists.

I was talking to Mr. Herbert Read, poet and critic, when he introduced me to Miss Dorothy Sayers.

She is a large woman with a voluminous overcoat, and a pork-pie hat jammed four-square on her head.

"What a pity, Miss Sayers, that you find time no more to write those delightful detective stories," I remarked.

Miss Sayers swept me with a glance that was clearly inquiring what I had done with the body.

"The more people badger me to do so, the less I feel inclined," she barked. "Why should I write for the income tax man?"

The sweeping glance may have been a reconnoitering move. Was this newsman about to misrepresent, misquote, misinterpret for the press? The authentic word *badger* is there, however. As to her closing question, she was a widow with no dependents, able to live comfortably on book and play royalties, lecturing fees, and the occasional article for publication. She was not extravagant in personal tastes. The freehold in Witham was clear. John Anthony Fleming was twenty-eight years of age and independent. (When she died five years later she left an estate in excess of £35,000.) In so far as income was concerned, she had made an accurate appraisal and protest. But—more important —there was still work to do on Dante.[37]

Nevertheless she still divided her time. Late in November 1952, the Letters-to-the-Editor column of the *Times* was lamenting the "school projects" of children who were encouraged to write to very busy professional people to seek assistance on topics on which no (or very limited) preparatory study and research had been given. R. d'E. Atkinson, of the Royal Observatory in Greenwich, for example, had bemoaned on 21 November that school children had been writing to the Royal Observatory (wretchedly generalized requests with deplorable spelling) requesting all the information that could be given on "astronimy," the planet Mars, or even the universe. Sayers sympathetically heard the lament of Mr. Atkinson and offered her own testimony:

> Sir,—Let me assure your correspondents that students unable or unwilling to do any work for themselves are by no means peculiar to this country; neither do they confine their attention to such useful and improving subjects as textiles and the universe. It is by no means unusual for me to receive from some young person in an American or Continental place of learning, announcing that the writer has undertaken a thesis (save the mark!) on me and my works: will I kindly explain what I mean by (here follows a list of queries, all of which could be answered by a little intelligent study of the Creed, the Lord's Prayer, and the Ten Commandments), and will I further oblige with a few pages of bright and chatty autobiography?
>
> Doubtless the choice of theme is prompted by the notion that it is easier to pump a live mouse than to anatomize a dead lion; but why any school or university should allow this kind of thing to pass for "research" I cannot imagine. It looks as though literary criticism would come to bear in the future, even more than it does now, a disquieting resemblance to the gossip columns of the less responsible portion of the popular Press.

Sayers's understandable perplexity at the encouragement of such procedures sets her apart as one of the few independent worker-scholars of the generation.[38]

Perhaps her perplexity was one reason why she set aside valuable time to produce juveniles. Her wartime children's book *Even the Parrot,* for all its peculiarities, managed to go into additional printings. Now, in the last five years of her life, she completed more children's books. They all followed the same format as that marking *The Days of Christ's Coming,* which was prepared for the Christmas season 1953: brief text and illustration with pull-out portions of the *Adventkalendar* type, inculcational in purpose. (She wrote to Mrs. Charles Williams on 23 December 1953, enclosing *The Days of Christ's Coming:* "I sent off my cards early, so that people would have time to open all the little doors. . . .") On the title page she had given instructions: "THE PICTURE inside has twenty-seven numbered doors for you to open as the story goes along. . . ."

The second such work appeared late in March 1955. Entitled *The Story of Adam and Christ,* the picture represented a stained-glass church window, and the purpose was obviously to invite readers to recognize the symbolic interpretation of Scripture. The third juvenile was published in 1956: *The Story of Noah's Ark.* The pullouts encouraged children to find animals, birds, insects, reptiles, and even a dragon—"Yes, to be sure there were Dragons in the Ark, or there wouldn't have been one for St. George to fight with; but they are all dead now."

She completed two additional juveniles on this sort which were never published. One was "The Story of Easter," a summary of the Gospel account of the passion and resurrection of Christ. The other, "The Enchanted Garden," was an adaptation from Boiardo's *Orlando Innamorato.*[39]

She also still sought to contribute her mite from time to time to the community of scholars by writing to the journals. Now it was on "Adam's apple"; then it was a protest over a disputed translation of Aristotle's *Poetics;* once it was an innocuous correspondence on "enjambement." In 1953, she saw published a preface to G. K. Chesterton's *The Surprise.*[40]

Many years after the demise of her great-uncle Percival Leigh, who had been known as the "Professor" of *Punch,* she sent to *Punch* some comic satire of her own. Beginning with the 2 November 1953 issue, Sayers introduced Didymus Pantheon, M.A., Ph.D., professor of comparative irreligion in Mansoul University, Cosmopolis, on whom she hung a correspondence, a "Calendar of Unholy and Dead-Letter Days," a "colour-plate" from Blimey's *Monumental Monstrosities of the Age of Unreason*, sketches and "lives" of unheard-of "saints" (e.g., St. Lukewarm of Laodicea, SS. Ursa and Ursulina, St. Simian Stylites, and St. Supercilia), a hymn "For an Evening Service," maxims of "the Polar Cult," and "A Sermon for Cacophony-Tide." She has obvious fun with such items as the

"Beautification of St. Henna," "St. Marx the Evangelist," "the fiery loins of St. Lawrence [D.H.], "St. Sigmund (Freud) sub-Limine," the "Gratification of St. Gorge," "Commemoration of the Blessed Word Mesopotamia," and "St. Cloud the Obscure."[41]

She was not always so inspired. When she yielded in 1955 to an appeal to submit an article to the first volume of *World Theatre,* the bilingual (French, English) publication of the International Theatre Institute, she bungled. Her article, "Playwrights Are Not Evangelists," is ineffectual, flat, and unprofitable. She resisted attempts at being "badgered" into writing detective fiction; she ought also to have resisted those who badgered her into writing this article.

> The competent dramatist who has—for reasons best known to himself—been moved to explore a Christian theme finds himself subjected to intense pressure from ecclesiastical and educational quarters to "go and do it again," and especially to write the kind of play which is "needed", whether or not the spirit moves him to do so. This is all wrong. There is, to be sure, no harm in suggesting a theme for a play, but if the writer replies that it does not appeal to him, then it is both wicked and unwise to undermine his resistance by appeals to his vanity ("nobody could do it so well as you"), his missionary zeal ("you have so much influence"), or his duty to the brethren ("we look to you for help"). . . .
>
> No: let the workman look to the work. Evangelisation is not the proper concern of the playwright. It follows that I have no business to be writing this article (but I was over-persuaded, see above). . . .[42]

On Tuesday, 23 August 1955, Sayers planned to participate in the Charles Williams conference at Milland Place, Liphook, Hampshire; she was to deliver an address on "Charles Williams: A Poet's Critic."

Before she left for Hampshire, she noticed an article which appeared on Friday, 19 August 1955, in a column of the *Church Times:* "Portraits of Personalities." The personality portrait presented there was a garbled account of Sayers herself. Once again she must take time to correct the press. She was especially annoyed by one statement (full of clichés): "At Oxford," wrote the columnist, "her prowess led to hopes of a fellowship. These were not fulfilled—a cruel disappointment." A prickly response from Sayers appeared in the very next issue:

> Sir,—Allow me to inform you that I never at any time either sought or desired an Oxford fellowship. If anybody entertained such hopes on my

behalf, I am not aware of it, and if I disappointed anybody by my distaste for the academic life, that person has my sympathy. But I suspect that the "cruel disappointment" exists only in the romantic imagination of your columnist.

Neither was I "forced" into either the publishing or the advertising profession by the death of my parents, who were both alive and flourishing at the time, and for many years after. Nor do I quite understand why earning one's living should be represented as a hardship. (After all, even Oxford fellows have to do some work nowadays to justify their existence). "Intellectual frustration" be blowed! My generation had not much use for that word, and it was all very good fun while it lasted.

This much is true: that I was a scholar and a Christian both before and after I turned my hand to advertising copy or detective fiction. But I must respectfully decline to have this simple fact adorned with all this weeping willow and sentimental bric-a-brac.

(Quite likely, the columnist's version was a transposition of the author herself for Harriet Vane in *Gaudy Night,* without realizing how near he was to the pulse.)[43]

It was inevitable that Sayers's stalwart, not to say aggressive, defense of her faith would often rankle readers with different presuppositions or lesser assurance. Her persistent sniping at writers and thinkers she considered wrongheaded was also bound sooner or later to provoke contention. She—along with others—is subjected to vigorous criticism in Kathleen Nott's *The Emperor's Clothes,* which appeared 1953.

Miss Nott, herself a poet and novelist, was committed to the scientific method with a fervor matching Sayers's Christian commitment. To Miss Nott, the pronouncements of orthodoxy and faith made by T. S. Eliot, T. E. Hulme, Basil Willey, Graham Greene, C. S. Lewis, and Sayers were (in varying measure, of course) as liable to the charge of gullibility as the conduct of the defrauded emperor in the old *Märchenbuch.* One long chapter in Miss Nott's book carries a dubious compliment: it is entitled "Lord Peter Views the Soul." Elsewhere in the book there are asides (usually linking Sayers with Lewis) which ascribe vulgarity, coarse sensibility, fundamentalism, argumentativeness, ostentatious hauteur, and trickiness to Sayers. Once Miss Nott refers to the two writers Lewis and Sayers as "the Hallelujah Chorus," but she confesses that "Miss Sayers . . . often disarms one with her common sense." Basically, of course, Miss Nott simply could not accept theology as a branch of knowledge: "For there is no experimental check on theology." To her, science, reason, humanism are the only viable options for an intelligent person. Her term for all who prefer reference to God, faith, dogma, and original sin is "neo-scholastic."

Sayers came close to a rebuttal of Kathleen Nott in her lecture "Poetry, Language and Ambiguity," which she delivered to the Oxford Socratic Society on 3 June 1954. She exposes the vulnerability of words—their ambiguity—especially when disputants either do not see or simply refuse to accept common meanings. To take one example:

> When a scientist says that something "does not exist", he merely means (if you press him for a definition) that the thing in question is "not observable by any methods of which science takes cognisance" . . . Scientifically speaking, therefore, there is no very significant distinction between existing and not existing; and the expression "God does not exist" boils down, scientifically speaking, to "God is not observable by scientific methods"—a proposition which need not keep the most nervous theologian awake o' nights. . . .
>
> But for the theologian, the term "existent" does not mean "observable by the methods of physical science", nor yet "observable by observers on this planet". He starts from quite different assumptions. For him, God alone can be said to exist unconditionally, and is the pre-supposition behind all being. . . . Whatever observables contingently exist do so in virtue of being sustained in God's mind. "God is" thus means exactly what it says, and no other subject can thus stand without predicate. . . .

One may label this "neo-scholasticism," but the label does not dismiss the thought.

> It is still frequently said that there is today a quarrel between science and religion. I do not think myself that this is where the real conflict lies. Pure religion has, in fact, a good deal in common with pure science—or with what used to be called, charmingly and in some ways more accurately, Natural Philosophy. What they have chiefly in common is humility. Science which is philosophic in the original meaning of the word—which desires only knowledge—calls for humility in the face of the facts. Religion—and poetry in so far as it is religious—calls for humility in the face of unconditioned reality. Both are the servants of truth, and they have no good reason to hate or fear one another.[44]

For Epiphany 1957 Sayers was "persuaded" to write an article for the *Sunday Times* on a topic which for her was surely question-begging: "The Great Mystery: My Belief about Heaven and Hell." The editor opened his brief explanation of the nature of the series (in which Sayers appeared first) by saying: "The survival of the soul or spirit after death is one of the great mysteries of man's existence." "Mystery" she knew in many meanings; and *"my* belief" could easily enough be converted to "what *Christians* believe." "Survival"? Well, she handled that in context.

With an echo from *The Mind of the Maker* (and a pervasive metaphor) she began her article with remarks on time and space:

> we must first rid our minds of every concept of time and space as we know them. Our time and space have no independent reality: they belong to the universe and were created with it.

Like any novel you may take down from the shelf, the story it tells "may cover the events of a few hours or of many years; it may range over a few acres or the whole globe." But "all that space-time is contained within the covers of the book, and has no contact at any point with the space-time in which you are living." These factors derive solely from the mind of the maker. *Eternity* and *infinity* are the terms that mark the total unlikeness of "real existence" to anything experienced in a time-space universe.

> All this was understood and insisted on by instructed Christians up to the end of the Middle Ages (e.g., by Boethius in the sixth century and Dante in the fourteenth). It was only after the Reformation and the Renaissance of Learning that childishly literal notions of a localised Heaven extended in measurable time began to creep out of popular mythology into the minds of educated people.

Thus intelligent Christians today "do not very much care for the term 'survival,' which suggests a continuation along the old lines of space and time."

> So that when we die, it is not as though the characters and action of the book were "continued in our next" like a serial; it is as though they came out from the book to partake of the real existence of their author.

Destiny is chosen: "God *sends* nobody to Hell: only a wicked ignorance can suggest that He would do to us the very thing He died to save us from." "Neither can He force any soul into beatitude against its will: for He has nothing but Himself to give it, and it is precisely the light of His presence which the self-centred soul can know only as burning and judgment." About the "end of the world" Christians know very little; we are also limited in our knowledge of the "resurrection-body." "In any case, we need not puzzle our wits to find a time and place for it within the universe, because, in the end of time, that universe 'shall be rolled together as a scroll' (that is, as a reader shuts up a volume when he has finished with it), and God will write a new book."

Approaching her sixty-fourth birthday, Sayers must have found the task of producing this article a *memento mori.* But she was too self-possessed to think of her own death as a step into mystery; rather, it would indeed be "as a reader shuts up a volume when he has finished with it."[45] And, of course, her continuing study of Dante meant that death would not take her by surprise—except in the unreal time-space of this universe.

There was one old chore, even older than the commitment to Dante, that she wanted to complete. On 6 March 1957, Sayers spoke in Oxford on "The Translation of Verse," and she included a revealing comment:

> Shortly after going down, I embarked on a translation of the *Song of Roland,* in the original metre, but in rhyme instead of assonance. I still have it. It is very bad. I completed the task much later—in assonance this time, and I hope with better results. It was nice to get something finished that had been lying about for forty years or so.

Penguin did not publish her *Song of Roland* until September, but of course she had worked it over for months before it was sent to the publisher. The *chansons de geste,* to be sure, were a part of the climate of Dante's world. It is fascinating to see that with the *Paradiso* two-thirds translated Sayers felt compelled to devote herself also to the starkness and the directness of Roland.

> So he rides out, into that new-washed world of clear sun and glittering colour which we call the Middle Age (as though it were middle-aged), but which has perhaps a better right than the blown summer of the Renaissance to be called the Age of Re-birth . . . a world with which we have so utterly lost touch that we have fallen into using the words "feudal" and "mediaeval" as mere epithets for outer darkness. Anyone who sees gleams of brightness in that world is accused of romantic nostalgia for a Golden Age which never existed. But the figure of Roland stands there to give us the lie: he is the Young Age as that age saw itself.

The figure of Roland was indeed appropriate. He was always there in her mind now, perhaps keeping company with the figure of Beatrice.[46]

As late in her life as July 1957 Sayers wrote to a friend that "pressure of other business" had kept her from completing

another old project, the biography of Wilkie Collins. She added
that she still hoped one day to finish it, "if and when old age
brings leisure."[47]

For her, to be "still moving into another intensity" was an
enduring commitment. By training and interest Sayers was at
home in the realm of the spirit. With the fresh curiosity of a
child she possessed the critial mind of a superior intelligence
and the wit of a balanced soul.

She had become careless, however, in some respects. She
had begun to put on weight from overeating. Barbara Reynolds recalls going to tea with her in the 1950s and saying,
"We eat those things we ought not to eat and leave uneaten
those things which we ought to eat." Sayers quickly quipped,
"And there is no health in us." Norah Lambourne spent two
Christmas holidays with the Flemings, and in 1953 Miss
Lambourne and her mother shared Christmas again with
Sayers. "My recollections of those occasions are of welcome,
warmth, the scent of log fires; a tall sparkling candle-lit tree in
the entrance hall and, of course, delicious food."[48]

Sayers also smoked too much. She would go through a pack
of Senior Service cigarettes in an evening. Dr. James Denholm, who attended the Flemings from 1948 until their deaths,
remembers the immense copper ashtray—probably made from
a small washtub—which stood beside Sayers's reading chair:
it was always piled with cigarette-ends and ashes.

The austere postwar years did not always provide sufficient
physical comfort. Casual visitors in winter often found Sayers
at work in the boiler room of the Witham house because there
was inadequate heat elsewhere. There she would receive such
visitors, offering them a glass of Amontillado sherry, her
favorite. When she had to go out on slight errands, she piled on
herself extra sweaters and coats.

Sayers found it easier and easier to stay at home. In 1952 she
had entertained plans to visit Italy, for it had been many years
since she had stood in the land of Dante. The translating and
the lecturing were inviting such a voyage, and there was a new
reason. She had written to Norah Lambourne: "I really must
go *sometime* to Ravenna, having become suddenly obsessed
(as if I hadn't enough to cope with already) by a novel about
Dante & his daughter, which has been simmering for some
time at the back of my mind." She wrote, however, that she

had temporarily abandoned the notion: "there is too much to do, & if I went away I should only end by being devil-driven for the rest of the year." But she was confident in the postponement.[49]

Her regular commitments kept her extremely busy. In the Witham cottage she worked most of the time in her library on the first floor at the front of the house. Working on the *Paradiso,* she made copious jottings—neat and well-organized—in several notebooks. Mrs. Joyce Wallage, sister of her wartime secretary Kathleen Richards, did her secretarial work. When she had to go to Colchester or to Cambridge, Jack Lockwood frequently chauffeured her; seldom did she chat with him, however, because she always had things to read. When she did want to have a little relaxation in the evening, she worked on a large jigsaw puzzle from her sizeable collection.

Barbara Reynolds once persuaded Sayers to accompany her on a visit to Professor Geoffrey L. Bickersteth, emeritus professor of English literature at Aberdeen, at his home in retirement at Chichester. (Professor Bickersteth had published a translation of the *Paradiso* in *terza rima* in 1933; two editions of his translation of the complete *Comedy* were to appear—one in 1955, one in 1965.) It was his later published opinion that Sayers was "too much inclined to scan Italian verse in the way that she scanned English verse" and that "she frequently supposed Dante to be expressing himself humourously . . . when neither his actual words nor the context afford the slightest ground for the supposition." Yet he conceded that she was "a brilliant, witty and captivating defender of her own interpretation of Dante." Apparently the visit between the two Dante scholars was pleasant.[50]

After their call on Professor Bickersteth, the two friends visited Dr. Reynolds's aunts in Chichester. Sayers was as much at home with them, cordial and gracious, as she had been with Professor Bickersteth.

The day was not over. Sayers, in her turn, asked Barbara Reynolds to go with her to call upon Dr. George K. Bell, the bishop of Chichester. And there, too, she was a completely relaxed visitor.

Many of her friends and acquaintances preceded her in death. At the end of 1955, Dr. Cyril Garbett, the archbishop of

York (of whom she had written Val Gielgud toward the conclusion of *The Man Born to Be King*— "the poor dear Archbishop of York . . . he's not a bad old stick, really") died also. Then in May 1957 she must have read in the newspapers that Professor Gilbert Murray had died at the age of ninety-one. In August 1957 it was Monsignior Ronald Knox, for almost thirty years a fellow member in the Detection Club, and now a very distinguished churchman and scholar himself. On 12 December 1957, just five days before her own death, Sayers learned of the death of Harcourt (Billy) Williams.

It was on 13 December that she had been in Cambridge as a guest of Barbara Reynolds (i.e., Mrs. Lewis Thorpe). There had been a family luncheon at the Blue Boar; Dr. Reynolds's father, husband, and children were all there. Sayers had become noticeably slow-moving, "reminding one," says Dr. Reynolds, "of a figure in a Millet painting." During the afternoon she insisted on going out to purchase a recording of Beethoven's *Fifth Symphony* for Adrian Thorpe, Dr. Reynolds's son. As the two ladies were walking through the street, Dr. Reynolds spoke casually about her children's study and their teacher, Mrs. Eric Whelpton. The name came stabbing back across the years. Sayers turned aside to look into a shopwindow.

On Sunday, 15 December 1957, Val Gielgud had tea with Sayers in Witham. After her death he recalled:

> Only a few days ago I had tea with Dorothy Sayers in her Essex home, and I find it very difficult to realise that I shall never see her again. She was her usual brisk, vital, amusing, almost exuberant self, full of plans for the future, and typically a little impatient that people should still expect her to revert to the writing of detective stories; that they should not realise that by instinct, preference, and training she was a scholar and an expert on the French of the Middle Ages. . . . She was positive, as only an inherently shy person can be. And behind a facade occasionally forbidding there was an immense friendliness.

That same weekend Norah Lambourne stayed with Sayers, returning to her home in London on Sunday evening.[51]

On Monday, 16 December, she went up to London to do more Christmas shopping. She ordered a magnum of Amontillado to be sent to the Thorpes in Cambridge. She spent the night in London.

On Tuesday she took the train to Witham in late afternoon, took a taxi to her home, and entered it for the last time in the early evening darkness. Just inside the closed door she slumped, dying quickly of a coronary. There was no one present to help her. Her body was discovered by her secretary the following morning.

The newsmen, of course, tried to surround her death with mystery. Some reporters garbled the data of her life. One news item invented a sinister discovery of the body—*the gardener* had come upon her body *in the bedroom!* Even the post-mortem was sensationalized although it was only required because Dr. Denholm had not attended her within the pre-scribed number of days before Sayers's death. No foul play. No blunt instrument. No intrigue.[52]

The funeral was private. After the cremation, her ashes were deposited beneath the floor tiling of the tower of St. Anne's, Soho, adjoining St. Anne's House. Until the spring of 1978 there was no marker, simply a different color of tile in the floor. There is not even yet free access to the tower. Like the unknown people who pause for a few moments in the garden which surrounds the tower, Dorothy Leigh Sayers's resting place is almost anonymous.

Early in January 1958, a memorial service for Sayers was conducted in St. Margaret's Church, Westminster. The arch-bishop of Canterbury was represented, six robed bishops were in the sanctuary, as were the dean of Canterbury and the archdeacon of Rochester. A canon officiated; the lessons were read by Val Gielgud and Judge Gordon Clark; a panegyrick written by Professor C. S. Lewis was read. Among others present were several additional members of the clergy; titled men and women; professors; writers; official representatives of universities, scholarly organizations, drama organizations, parish councils, and publishing companies. The hymn se-lected for the service was more appropriate than anyone knew. It was Abelard's hymn, "O Quanta Qualia."[53]

In the privacy of friendship, Raf de la Torre (who had been *Persona Dei* in the Lichfield play) spoke not only for himself when he wrote to Norah Lambourne after learning of the death of Sayers: "a really great yet supremely humble woman who happened to possess an original sense of fun which delighted all her friends and true admirers . . . that lovely person—gone before her work was finished."[54]

"Full of plans for the future" was the way Val Gielgud had reported Sayers. It is perhaps fitting, as Professor Thorpe has written, that "the very last words she wrote are a letter explaining how she *intended*" to write for him an article "On Translating *La Chanson de Roland.*" The letter reached him "just twelve hours after her death." She had also promised to speak during the 1958 Canterbury Festival.[55]

Dorothy Leigh Sayers knew full well that all men's labors are interrupted. William of Sens had told her so distinctly. So did the Man born to be King. Even Dante, though he completed his story about the Love which moves the sun and the other stars, left life—Sayers well knew this—with an incomplete dream.

Notes

All dates of births, marriages, divorce, deaths, and wills come from certified copies of entries in British files.

Preface

1. DLS to Mrs. Charles Williams (4 Jan. 1956), in the possession of Wheaton (Illinois) College Library.

2. James Sandoe, "Contributions toward a Bibliography of Dorothy L. Sayers," *Bulletin of Bibliography*, XVIII (May-August, 1944), 76-81; Robert B. Harmon and Margaret A. Burger, *An Annotated Guide to the Works of Dorothy L. Sayers* (New York: Garland Publishing Co., 1977).

Chapter One

1. DLS, "A Vote of Thanks to Cyrus," in *Unpopular Opinions* (London: Gollancz, 1946), p. 23.

2. DLS, "Ignorance and Dissatisfaction," *Latin Teaching: The Journal of the Association for the Reform of Latin Teaching*, XXVIII (October 1952), 69. This essay was reprinted (under a new title: "The Teaching of Latin: A New Approach") in DLS, *The Poetry of Search and the Poetry of Statement* (London: Gollancz, 1963), pp. 177-99.

Joseph Foster, *Alumni Oxonienses,* IV, 1260; *Crockford's Clerical Dictionary* (through 1928). Mr. Sayers's use of Latin in the Cathedral had not been confined to propaedeutics. Just a year and a half before DLS's birth, he had assisted in the installation (in Latin) of Dr. Francis Paget as dean of Christ Church College and the Cathedral in succession to Dean Henry George Liddell. See Oxford University *Herald,* 23 Jan. 1892, p. 7.

3. Helen Mary Leigh Sayers was born 26 June 1856 in Shirley Warren, Milbrook, then the County of Southampton, later (for legal purposes) named Hampshire. She had one brother, Alexander Haslop Leigh, and one sister, Mabel Leigh.

Henry Sayers's father, Rev. Robert Sayers, was vicar of Ratby cum Groby from 1881 until 1892, having previously served the parish of Tittleshall, Norfolk, during the long incumbency of Rev. the Hon. Kenelm Digby. Henry had been born in Tittleshall on 19 July 1854. His mother was Anna Breakey Sayers.

4. DLS, "Ignorance and Dissatisfaction," p. 69-70. The rectory has now been pulled down.

DLS, *The Lost Tools of Learning* (London: Methuen, 1948), p. 15. This essay was reprinted in DLS, *Poetry of Search and the Poetry of Statement,* pp. 155-76.

5. Alan Villiers, "Inland Cruise of the Eastern Counties," *This England* (Washington, D.C.: National Geographic Society, 1966), p. 372; Nikolaus Pevsner, *Bedfordshire and the County of Huntingdon and Peterborough* (Harmondsworth, Middlesex: Penguin, 1974), p. 211.

6. DLS, "Ignorance and Dissatisfaction," pp. 70, 73.

7. DLS to Dr. James Welch (5 Nov. 1940), BBC Written Archives Centre, Caversham Park, Reading.

8. DLS, "A Vote of Thanks to Cyrus," pp. 23, 24.

9. DLS, "Ignorance and Dissatisfaction," pp. 73, 74.

10. DLS, *Begin Here: A War-Time Essay* (London: Gollancz, 1940), p. 30. DLS to Dr. Welch (21 Dec. 1940), BBC Archives. Some information was given to me by Mrs. Evelyn Compline Bedford, Christchurch.

11. Pevsner, *Bedfordshire,* p. 210. See also: William Page, ed., *A History of Huntingdonshire,* 2 vols. (London: St. Catherine, 1926), II, 153-58.

Obituary for Rev. Henry Sayers, *Wisbech Standard,* 28 Sept. 1928, p. 5. Page, *History of Huntingdonshire,* II, 157, notes that there were eight bells in the ring (so also in *The Nine Tailors),* the eighth bearing the inscription: "Henry Sayers, Rector, and Arthur David Godfrey, sometime warden, gave me, MCMX."

12. DLS, *The Mind of the Maker* (New York: Harcourt, Brace, 1941), pp. 149-50. DLS to Dr. Welch (7 Dec. 1940), BBC Archives.

13. DLS, "The Fen Floods: Fiction and Fact," *Spectator,* 2 Apr. 1937, p. 611.

14. DLS, *Lost Tools of Learning,* p. 15.

15. Information about the Godolphin period has been obtained largely from the issues of *Godolphin School Magazine* published during the period (and also the issue—Sept. 1958—containing the DLS obituary) very kindly made available to me by a former secretary of the school, Miss P. Adkins; and from Miss Ivy Phillips, St. Morvah, Throwleigh, Okehampton, who was in school (and in the same House) with DLS during the years 1909-1911. Items of special interest may be found in the following issues: (1) the Oakhurst entertainment, No. 42 (Spring Term 1909), p. 17; (2) a kindergarten play, No. 43 (Summer Term 1909), p. 15; (3) DLS trans. of Leconte de Lisle's "La Mort du Soleil," No. 45 (Spring Term 1910), p. 11; (4) DLS rev. in French of *L'Avare,* No. 44 (Autumn Term 1909), pp. 17-18; (5) DLS sonnet "To Sir Ernest Shackleton and His Brave Companions," No. 47 (Autumn Term 1910), p. 21; (6) DLS sonnet on excavations at Old Sarum, "Captivo Ignoto" (Autumn Term 1910), p. 25; (7) DLS, "Ode, from the French of P. Ronsard" and DLS poem "Duke Hilary," No. 49 (Summer Term 1911), pp. 17-18; and (8) DLS rev. of productions of Labiche's *La Poudre aux Yeux* and Molière's *Les Précieuses Ridicules* in French, No. 50 (Autumn Term 1911), p. 28.

Miss Phillips writes that she never heard nicknames used at Godolphin because Miss Douglas banned them; also that DLS did *not* suffer a complete breakdown as a result of her illnesses.

16. DLS, "Target Area," *Fortnightly,* 161, NS 151 (Mar. 1944), 181-84. The poem appeared the same month in *Atlantic Monthly,* 173 (Mar. 1944), 48-50.

17. DLS to Dr. Welch (5 Nov. 1940), BBC Archives.

18. Muriel St. Clare Byrne and Catherine Hope Mansfield, *Somerville College 1879-1921* (Oxford: University Press, 1927), p. 15 et passim; *Handbook to the University of Oxford: Oxford University Calendar; Somerville College, Oxford, Report, 1912-1913,* passim; and *1913-1914,* p. 83.

Memorandum to Under-graduates on Matriculation, Oct. 1922, lists the obligations of Oxford male students.

19. DLS, "Ignorance and Dissatisfaction," pp. 74-75; DLS, "The Translation of Verse," in *The Poetry of Search and the Poetry of Statement* (London: Gollancz, 1963), p. 127.

20. DLS, *The Song of Roland* (Baltimore: Penguin, 1957), p. 45.

21. DLS, "Ignorance and Dissatisfaction," p. 72; DLS, *Begin Here,* pp. 105-6.

22. DLS, "Translation of Verse," p. 127.

23. DLS, "Ignorance and Dissatisfaction," p. 72.

24. *Somerville College, Oxford, Report, 1912-1913, and Calendar, 1913-1914,* p. 83.

25. DLS, *Op. I* (Oxford: Blackwell, 1916), p. 4.

26. Vera Brittain, *Testament of Youth: An Autobiographical Study of the Years 1900-1925* (Bath: Cedric Chivers, 1971), pp. 94-104.

27. C. S. Lewis, *Surprised by Joy: The Shape of My Early Life* (London: Geoffrey Bles, 1955), pp. 173-74.

28. Brittain, *Testament of Youth,* pp. 105, 106; Vera Brittain, *The Women at Oxford: A Fragment of History* (London: Harrap, 1960), p. 123.

29. Charis V. Frankenburg, *Not Old, Madam, Vintage* (Lavenham, Suffolk, 1975), pp. 62-63, 66.

30. Vera Farnell, *A Somervillian Looks Back* (privately printed by Oxford University Press, 1948), quoted in V. Brittain, *Woman at Oxford,* p. 123.

31. Brittain, *Women at Oxford,* pp. 122, 123; Brittain, *Testament of Youth,* p. 106.

32. Frankenburg, *Not Old,* pp. 66, 67.

33. A copy of the Going-Down Play was kindly supplied to me by Miss Dorothy Hanbury Rowe.

34. DLS to Dr. Welch (21 Dec. 1940), BBC Archives.

35. DLS, "What Is Right with Oxford?" *Oxford* (Summer 1935), p. 37.

36. DLS, "Eros in Academe," *Oxford Outlook,* I (June 1919), 112, 113, 114-15, 110, 111.

37. DLS, *Op. I,* p. 21. "Now that we have gone down" is published in the same volume, p. 70, and simply titled "To M. J." The initials stand for Muriel Jaeger, a college friend and later also a novelist.

38. DLS to Dorothy H. Rowe (8 Oct. 1915), in the recipient's possession. (Hilda is a sister of Miss Rowe.)

39. D. K. Roberts, ed., *Titles to Fame* (London: Nelson, 1937), p. 240: "From 1916 until 1922 she taught in a school in Hull, worked at publishing in Oxford, spent some time in France and did a number of odd jobs in London." Mr. S. W.

Hobson, Chief Education Officer for the City and County of Kingston upon Hull, informed me that "This lady was not employed by the Kingston upon Hull Education Committee but she had some connection with the Hull High School for Girls, an independent school" (correspondence dated 24 March 1971). The secretary of Hull High School for Girls, Tranby Croft, Anlaby, Hull, however, wrote (28 April 1971): "I have made a search of the records available here, dating back to 1915, and I regret that I can find no trace of any reference to Miss Sayers." But Miss D. M. Nicholson, Head Mistress of Newland High School, Kingston upon Hull, in a letter (dated 16 Oct. 1975) to Miss Dorothy Rowe indicates that "the fact that Miss Sayers spent a period at the school was something that was commonly known at the time."

DLS, *The Lost Tools of Learning* (London: Methuen, 1948), pp. 1-2.

40. DLS, "Ignorance and Dissatisfaction," p. 79.

41. *Times,* 1 Jan. 1958, p. 13; *Sunday Times,* 9 Sept. 1934, p. 8; Mrs. Dorothy Cross, Cliff Road, Hornsea.

42. *Times,* 1 Jan. 1958, p. 13; interview with Miss Wallace, 20 May 1971; letter from Miss Wallace, 26 Jan. 1975.

43. DLS, "Hymn in Contemplation of Sudden Death," *Oxford Magazine,* 5 Nov. 1915, p. 37; DLS, "Epitaph for a Young Musician," *Oxford Magazine,* 25 Feb. 1916, p. 212; DLS, "Matter of Brittany," *Fritillary* (I have been unable to locate copies of this periodical, but see p. [8], *Op. I,* where acknowledgment appears); DLS, "Lay," *Oxford Poetry 1915* (Oxford: Blackwell, 1915), pp. 50-57; DLS, "To the Members of the Bach Choir on Active Service," *Oxford Magazine,* 18 Feb. 1916, p. 194; DLS, "Icarus," *Oxford Magazine,* 5 May 1916, p. 286.

44. DLS, "The Last Castle," *Op. I,* pp. 32-46.

45. Brittain, *Oxford Poetry 1919,* p. 6; Byrne: *Oxford Poetry 1917,* p. 2; Graves: *Oxford Poetry 1917,* pp. 24, 25; Huxley: *Oxford Poetry 1915,* p. 27, *1916,* pp. 29-30, 31, 32, *1917,* p. 33, *1918,* pp. 33, 34; Tolkien: *Oxford Poetry 1915,* p. 64.

Oxford Poetry 1910-1913, eds. G. D. H. C[ole]., G. P. D[ennis]., and W. S. V[ines]. (Oxford: Blackwell, 1913), pp. xiv, xv, xviii.

46. DLS, "Fair Erembours," *Oxford Poetry 1917* (Oxford: Blackwell, 1917), pp. 52-53.

47. DLS, "Pygmalion," *Oxford Poetry 1918* (Oxford: Blackwell, 1918), pp. 46-48.

48. DLS, "For Phaon," *Oxford Poetry 1919* (Oxford: Blackwell, 1919), p. 50.

49. DLS, "Sympathy," *Oxford Poetry 1919,* p. 51.

50. DLS, "Vials Full of Odours," *Oxford Poetry 1919,* p. 52.

51. Eric Whelpton, *The Making of a European* (London: Johnson, 1974), pp. 126, 128.

52. DLS, "Rex Doloris," *New Witness,* 26 Apr. 1918, p. 519. See Maisie Ward, *Gilbert Keith Chesterton* (Harmondsworth, Middlesex: Penguin, 1958), p. 217.

53. *Times Literary Supplement,* 21 Nov. 1918, pp. 570-71.

54. *The New Decameron,* 2 vols. (Oxford: Blackwell, 1919, 1920), I, 1-28; II, 76-81.

55. DLS, "Eros in Academe," *Oxford Outlook,* June 1919, pp. 110-16; DLS, *Strong Meat* (London: Hodder and Stoughton, 1939), pp. 9-10; DLS, *Creed or Chaos?* (London: Methuen, 1947), p. 14n.

56. Interview with Miss Doreen Wallace, 20 May 1971; *Times,* 1 Jan. 1958, p. 13; "Woman Edgar: Country Parson's Daughter," *Daily Express,* 28 Feb.

1934. See also: Brittain, *Women at Oxford,* p. 123; Whelpton, *Making of a European,* p. 128.

57. DLS to Leonard Green (29 Aug. 1919), in the possession of the Humanities Research Center, University of Texas.

58. Whelpton, *Making of a European,* p. 138.

59. Janet Hitchman, *Such a Strange Lady* (London: New English Library, 1975), p. 52.

60. Whelpton, *Making of a European,* p. 138; correspondence dated 5 May 1975.

61. See n. 57.

62. DLS, *Clouds of Witness* (London: Gollancz, 1969), p. 300.

63. In addition to her literary pursuits, DLS also played the viola in a small string orchestra at the school.

64. Whelpton, *Making of a European,* pp. 131, 139, 140, 141.

65. DLS, "What Is Right with Oxford?" p. 41.

Chapter Two

1. Vera Brittain, *The Women at Oxford* (London: Harrap, 1960), p. 156.

2. Probate on Henry Sayers's will was granted at Peterborough, 22 Oct. 1928.

3. DLS, "Obsequies for Music," *London Mercury,* III (Jan. 1921), 249-53.

4. D. K. Roberts, ed., *Titles to Fame* (London: Nelson, 1937), p. 240; letter from Miss Beaumanoir Hart dated 6 Mar. 1976.

5. DLS, "The Poem," *London Mercury,* III (Oct. 1921), 577.

6. Letter from Mrs. Heather Harper, Staff Manager, S. H. Benson, Ltd., dated 13 Apr. 1971. See also DLS to editor, *Times,* 24 Nov. 1938, p. 15.

7. DLS, *The Mind of the Maker* (New York: Harcourt, Brace, 1941), p. 77; DLS, "The Psychology of Advertising," *Spectator,* CLIX (19 Nov. 1937), 896-98; DLS, *Murder Must Advertise* (London: Gollancz, 1971), pp. 128, 70; DLS, "The Psychology," p. 898.

8. Robert Graves and Alan Hodge, *The Long Week-End: A Social History of Great Britain 1918-1939* (London: Faber and Faber, 1940), pp. 300-301.

9. DLS, "Gaudy Night," *Titles to Fame,* ed. D. K. Roberts; rpt. in *The Art of the Mystery Story,* ed. H. Haycraft (New York: Grosset & Dunlap, 1946), p. 208.

10. Ibid.

11. "Dorothy L. Sayers Reveals Origin of Lord Peter Wimsey," *Harcourt, Brace News,* 15 July 1936, pp. 1-2.

12. DLS, *Whose Body?* (London: Gollancz, 1971), pp. 219, 56, 21n, 22n.

13. Ibid., p. 20.

14. *Daily Mail,* 24 Dec. 1957, p. 1. Miss Shrimpton was still living on 13 Apr. 1939 and residing at the Sidelings, Westcott Barton, according to DLS's will.

15. DLS, *Clouds of Witness* (London: Gollancz, 1969), p. 47.

16. John Cournos, *Autobiography* (New York: G. P. Putnam's Sons, 1935), pp. 175-76, 177-78, 183, 187, et passim. Alfred Satterthwaite, Cournos's stepson, does not think Cournos was the father of DLS's child, but he admits (from his knowledge of the letters) that Cournos had treated her "scurvily," and that the letters are "recriminatory" (correspondence dated 30 Aug. 1975).

17. Mrs. Ann Schreurs, Fleming's second daughter, suggests that the fault was entirely that of DLS who did everything to keep Fleming from meeting his own children. (Notes communicated to the DLS Historical and Literary Society, Witham. Essex, in the summer of 1976.) Nevertheless, she supplies evidence indicating that Fleming himself was constantly remiss.

18. DLS to Dr. James Welch (20 Nov. 1943), BBC Archives.

19. The sisters were Grace Mary and Maude; the brothers were Oscar, John Maconochie, Hugh James, Edgar, Edmund, and Edward.

20. Some details on Fleming's youth and early journalistic career were supplied by Muriel St. Clare Byrne in an interview on 19 Apr. 1971. I have been able to locate two articles by him in *Land and Water* ("Motor Topics," 1 Aug. 1914, pp. 842, 844, 846; "The Advent of the Shooting Season," 8 Aug. 1914, pp. 914, 916, 918, 920).

Hendy, *Gourmet's Book of Food and Drink* (London: John Lane, Bodley Head, 1933), pp. 131, 165-66, 167, 168, 183.

21. Schreurs, Notes (see n. 17).

22. Three articles under his byline appear in *Daily Chronicle*—"From 'The Daily Chronicle' Special Correspondent, A. Fleming": 10 Oct. 1914, p. 2; 17 Oct. 1914, p. 3; 22 Oct. 1914, p. 2. The war book claims the same byline.

The Ministry of Defence Library, Central and Army, supplied an outline of Fleming's military career (memo from Mr. C. A. Potts, 7 Apr. 1971).

Capt. Atherton Fleming, *How to See the Battlefields* (London: Cassell, 1919), p. 42.

23. Schreurs, Notes.

24. DLS, *Clouds of Witness,* pp. 179, 178, 60, 55.

25. DLS, *Unnatural Death* (London: Gollancz, 1969), pp. 245, 42, 37, 226, 229-30, 98, 181, 59, 183, 184, 188, 186, 91, 43, 197.

The title of this work in the U.S.A. was *The Dawson Pedigree.* See R. Philmore and J. Yudkin, "Inquest on Detective Stories," *Discovery,* I (Apr.-Dec. 1938), 28-32; *Sunday Times,* 18 Sept. 1927, p. 8 and 25 Sept. 1927, p. 8.

26. *Times Literary Supplement,* 21 Jan. 1928, p. 468; F. W. Bateson, ed., *Cambridge Bibliography of English Literature,* 5 vols. (Cambridge, 1941-1957), III, 480-82; DLS, Introduction to *The Moonstone,* by Wilkie Collins (London: Dent, 1944).

Alexander Woolcott, in Foreword to the Modern Library edition of *The Moonstone* and *The Woman in White* (New York, 1937), refers to Sayers's projected study of Collins; her "book would be the first considerable word on the subject, but I am oppressed by a doubt that she will ever get around to finishing it" (pp. vii-viii). The Houghton Library of Harvard University possesses four DLS letters to Woolcott (7 Nov. 1930, 16 May 1931, 1 Nov. 1936, 22 Oct. 1941). The Humanities Research Center of the University of Texas possesses an extensive collection of the DLS materials on Wilkie Collins. See E. R. Gregory, *Dorothy L. Sayers's Wilkie Collins* (Toledo, Ohio: Friends of the Library, 1977).

27. John Rhode, ed., *Detection Medley* (London: Hutchinson, 1939), p. 7; Maisie Ward, *Gilbert Keith Chesterton* (New York: Sheed & Ward, 1943), pp. 550-52. After Chesterton, first Berkeley and then Sayers became president of the Detection Club.

28. H. Haycraft, ed., *The Art of the Mystery Story* (New York: Grosset & Dunlap, 1946), p. 71.

Some DLS letters seeking copyright permission for inclusion of various authors' selections in the First Series may be found in The Humanities Research Center of the University of Texas and in the library of Northwestern University.

In the States, the First Series appeared in 1929 under the title *Omnibus of Crime;* the contents differ from the British edition because of copyright problems. The Introduction was reprinted in A. S. Burack, ed., *Writing Detective and Mystery Fiction* (Boston: The Writer, 1946, 1947) under the caption "Detective Fiction: Origins and Development," pp. 3-48. A partial reprint of the Introduction, entitled "A Sport of Noble Minds," was published in *Saturday Review of Literature,* 3 Aug. 1929, pp. 22-23, and in *Life and Letters Today,* IV (Jan. 1930), 41-54. A Gollancz advertisement in *Sunday Times,* 29 July 1929, boasted that printing of Series I had reached nearly 130,000 copies.

29. DLS, *The Unpleasantness at the Bellona Club* (London: Gollancz, 1969), pp. 15, 16, 95.

30. DLS, *Lord Peter Views the Body* (London: Gollancz, 1928). "The Adventurous Exploit of the Cave of Ali-Baba" is the final story in the collection.

31. *Wisbech Standard,* 21 Sept. 1928, p. 7. Probate of Henry Sayers's will was announced in the *Times* on 14 Nov. 1928, p. 19.

32. Many details have been supplied by Mrs. Evelyn (Compline) Bedford, Christchurch. Mrs. Sayers's will, which was dated at Christchurch Rectory on 30 March 1928 (six months before her husband's death), bequeathed to her daughter "absolutely" all she possessed when she died.

In Nov. 1975 the Witham home, completely renovated, was publicly memorialized. Mrs. Eileen Bushell of Witham and Countryside Society was largely responsible for the achievement, and Ian Carmichael unveiled the plaque. After renovation, the house was designated for preservation by a ceremony on 15 Nov. 1976 jointly organized by the Witham and Countryside Society and Essex County Council

Admirers of Ian Carmichael's portrayal of Wimsey in the BBC television programs should read his article "The BBC through a Monocle" in *Murder Ink: The Mystery Reader's Companion,* ed. Dilys Winn, (New York: Workman, 1977), pp. 109-12.

33. The verso of the title page of DLS, ed., *Tristan in Brittany* (London: Benn, 1929) gives July as the month of completion; publication was in September. See *Modern Languages,* I (June 1920), 131, 142-47; and I (Aug. 1920), 180-82. The letters to Sir John Squire, editor, *London Mercury,* pertinent to this endeavor are in U.C.L.A. Library. See *Times Literary Supplement,* 30 Jan. 1930, p. 74.

34. Certain Members of the Detection Club, *The Floating Admiral* (London: Hodder and Stoughton, [1931]). Sayers wrote the Introduction; G. K. Chesterton, a Prologue; and chapters were provided by the following in order: Canon Victor L. Whitechurch, G. D. H. and M. Cole, Henry Wade, Agatha Christie, John Rhode, Milward Kennedy, Dorothy L. Sayers, Ronald A. Knox, Freeman Wills Crofts, Edgar Jepson, Clemence Dane, and Anthony Berkeley.

Anthony Berkeley, Milward Kennedy, Gladys Mitchell, John Rhode, Dorothy L. Sayers & Helen Simpson, *Ask a Policeman* (London: Arthur Barker, [1933]).

Margery Allingham, Anthony Berkeley, Freeman Wills Crofts, Ronald Knox, Dorothy Sayers, Russell Thorndike, and Ex-Supt. Cornish, *Six against the Yard* (London: Selwyn and Blount, 1936).

Dorothy L. Sayers, Freeman Wills Crofts, Valentine Williams, F. Tennyson

Jesse, Anthony Armstrong, David Hume, *Double Death: A Murder Story* (London: Gollancz, 1939). "Supervised and with a Preface by John Chancellor."

John Rhode, ed., *Detection Medley* (London: Hutchinson, [1939]). Contributors were A. A. Milne, Margery Allingham, H. C. Bailey, E. C. Bentley, Nicholas Blake, J. Dickson Carr, G. K. Chesterton, Agatha Christie, G. D. H. and M. Cole, J. J. Conington, Freeman Wills Crofts, Carter Dickson, Edgar Jepson and Robert Eustace, R. Austin Freeman, Anthony Gilbert, Lord Gorell, Ianthe Jerrold, Milward Kennedy, E. C. R. Lorac, Arthur Morrison, The Baroness Orczy, E. R. Punshon, Dorothy L. Sayers, Henry Wade, Hugh Walpole. In the States this volume was published under the title *Line-up* by Dodd, Mead in 1940. The DLS contributions to this volume: "The Haunted Policeman" and "Striding Folly."

35. Dr. Eustace Robert Barton was a member of the staff of the Gloucester Mental Hospital at the time of his assistance to DLS. He had, of course, assisted other writers with his scientific knowledge. Wheaton (Illinois) College Library contains some of his letters to DLS; in addition to his help (not always accurate, according to his own confession) in *Documents,* he was to aid DLS in *Have His Carcase.* His elusiveness to the researcher is summarized by Hugh Greene, ed., *The Rivals of Sherlock Holmes* (New York: Pantheon, 1970), pp. 14-15. See Harold Hart, "Accident, Suicide, or Murder? A Question of Stereochemistry," *Journal of Chemical Education,* LII (July 1975), 444. Also: *Sunday Times,* 20 July 1930, p. 6; 27 July 1930, p. 7; 3 Aug. 1939, p. 5.

36. Interview with Dorothy H. Rowe, 14 Aug. 1975; Hendy, *Gourmet's Book of Food and Drink,* p. 183: "I have before me a breakfast bill-of-fare from the *Mauretania*—it is dated May 4, 1931. Here is what they gave us for breakfast. . . ."

37. DLS, "A Sport of Noble Minds," *Saturday Review of Literature,* 3 Aug. 1929, pp. 22-23; *Life and Letters Today,* IV (Jan. 1930), 41-54.

DLS, "The Present Status of the Mystery Story," *London Mercury,* XXIII (Nov. 1930), 47-52.

Great Unsolved Crimes (London: Hutchinson, 1935): a compilation of articles which originally appeared in *Evening Standard* during Oct. and Nov. 1934. DLS's contribution, which appeared in *Evening Standard,* 6 Nov. 1934, pp. 26-27, was entitled "The Mysterious Telephone Call." See, also, her review of George Goodchild and C. E. Bechhofer, *The Jury Disagree,* in *Sunday Times,* 18 Nov. 1934, p. 7.

Helen Simpson, Margaret Cole, Dorothy L. Sayers, John Rhode, E. R. Punshon, Francis Iles, and Freeman Wills Crofts, *The Anatomy of Murder: Famous Crimes Critically Considered by Members of the Detection Club* (London: John Lane, Bodley Head, 1936): DLS's "The Murder of Julia Wallace" appears on pp. 157-211.

DLS, "The Dates in *The Red-Headed League,*" *Colophon,* V (June 1934), eight unnumbered pages; rpt. in DLS, *Unpopular Opinions* (London: Gollancz, 1946), pp. 168-78. In the latter volume, DLS explains the ploy: "The game of applying the methods of the 'Higher Criticism' to the Sherlock Holmes canon was begun, many years ago, by Monsignior Ronald Knox, with the aim of showing that, by those methods, one could disintegrate a modern classic as speciously as a certain school of critics have endeavoured to disintegrate the Bible" (p. 7).

DLS, "Holmes' College Career," in *Baker-Street Studies,* ed. H. W. Bell (Morristown, N.J.: The Baker Street Irregulars, 1934), pp. 3-34; rpt. in *Unpopular Opinions,* pp. 134-47, also in *Baker Street Journal* (1947), pp. 279 ff., and in the 1955 rpt. of *Baker-Street Studies.*

DLS, "Dr. Watson's Christian Name," *Queen Mary's Book for India* (London: Harrap, 1943), pp. 78-82; rpt. in *Unpopular Opinions,* pp. 148-51; also in Edgar W. Smith, ed., *Profile by Gaslight: An Irregular Reader about the Private Life of Sherlock Holmes* (New York: Simon and Schuster, 1944), pp. 180-86.

DLS, "Dr. Watson, Widower," *Unpopular Opinions,* pp. 152-68.

The manuscript beginning of DLS's "The Modern Detective Story," labeled "Sesame Imperial Club, 27.10; 36," is in the possession of Wheaton (Illinois) College Library.

DLS, "Other People's Great Detectives," *Illustrated,* 29 Apr. 1939, pp. 18-19.

38. DLS to Mr. Fielden (28 Mar. 1934), BBC Archives; DLS to Antony Brown (19 May 1954), BBC Archives.

39. DLS to Rev. J. G. Williams (19 May 1941); DLS to Eric Fenn (4 Apr. 1941); DLS to Eric Fenn (16 May 1943); DLS letters declining participation in various programs may be found in her correspondence with BBC officials in Aug. and Oct. 1946; Apr., May, and June 1948; May 1949; July 1952; Sept. 1953; and May 1954; DLS to Dr. Welch (20 May 1943); DLS to Eric Fenn (14 Dec. 1942); DLS to Mr. Lambert (4 Feb. 1931), BBC Archives.

40. For example, in 1931 it was "Consider Your Verdict" and "Conversation in the Train," and in 1932 it was "Trials and Sorrows of a Mystery Writer." In 1936 it was an adaptation of "The Man with the Copper Fingers"; in 1938, "The Learned Adventure of the Dragon's Head"; in 1941, "Absolutely Elsewhere"; in 1943, "The Man with No Face," "The Man Who Knew How," "Striding Folly," and "Suspicion"; in 1944, "The Inspiration of Mr. Budd." The play *Busman's Honeymoon* was aired as early as Feb. 1937. Adaptations of, or readings from, her novels: *Gaudy Night,* 1947; *Whose Body?,* 1947-1948; *The Nine Tailors,* 1954; *Murder Must Advertise,* 1957.

41. DLS, "Gaudy Night," in *Art of the Mystery Story,* pp. 209, 120-11. DLS, *Strong Poison* (London: Gollancz, 1970), pp. 53, 141, 143.

42. Miss Muriel St. Clare Byrne pointed this out to me and showed me an oil portrait in her possession signed by Fleming as "Pigalle." See also the 1942 line-drawing portrait of DLS made and signed by Fleming as "Pigalle." The BBC Written Archives Centre contains numerous evidences of the Flemings' holidays in Kirkcudbright.

43. DLS, *Have His Carcase* (London: Gollancz, 1971), pp. 173-74, 448, 7.

44. S. H. Benson, Ltd., is located at 129 Kingsway, London, and the plaque may still be seen in the reception area.

DLS, "Gaudy Night," in *Art of the Mystery Story,* pp. 209-10; DLS, *Mind of the Maker,* pp. 77, 118-20.

See *Sunday Times,* 19 Feb. 1933, p. 11; and 26 Feb. 1933, p. 9; *Times Literary Supplement,* 2 Mar. 1933, p. 149; *Saturday Review of Literature,* 6 May 1933, p. 581. H. Haycraft *(Murder for Pleasure,* [New York: Biblo and Tannen, 1969], p. 260) says that DLS's *Murder Must Advertise,* "published in her writing prime and easily one of her two or three finest books, was lucky to reach 9,000 copies in its original American edition."

45. DLS, *The Nine Tailors* (London: Gollancz, 1972), pp. 4, 25, 68, 79.

"Technicalese," in *The Mystery Writer's Handbook,* ed. Herbert Brean (New York: Harper, 1956), pp. 64-65.

Carolyn Heilbrun, "Sayers, Lord Peter and God," *American Scholar,* XXXVII (Spring 1968), 325; *Evening News,* 10 Nov. 1950; *Times* (Braintree and Witham), 2 Nov. 1950, p. 5.

46. "Woman Edgar: Country Parson's Daughter: Who Found that Poetry Didn't Pay," *Daily Express,* 28 Feb. 1934.

47. The DLS letter accepting the invitation of Mrs. Belloc Lowndes is in the collection of the Humanities Research Center of The University of Texas. Two DLS letters to Hugh Walpole (24 Apr. 1933, 30 Apr. 1933), written when she was secretary of the Detection Club, and another (3 Jan. 1940), in reply to a request of Walpole (then Sir Hugh), are in the collection of the Humanities Research Center of The University of Texas.

Christopher Morley, "The Bowling Green," *Saturday Review of Literature,* 7 July 1934, p. 795.

BBC Written Archives Centre.

48. DLS, "Gaudy Night," in *Art of the Mystery Story,* p. 212; DLS, "What Is Right with Oxford?" *Oxford,* Summer 1935, pp. 34-41; *The Ninth Annual Supplement of the Association of Senior Members to the Report of the College* [Somerville, Oxford], 1933 to 1934, contains a précis of the DLS talk under the caption "Impressions of the Gaudy of 1934."

49. Carolyn Heilbrun, "Sayers, Lord Peter and God," p. 330.

50. DLS, "Gaudy Night," in *Art of the Mystery Story,* p. 211.

51. "Biographical Note Communicated by Paul Austin Delagardie."

52. DLS, "Gaudy Night," in *Art of the Mystery Story,* pp. 220-21; C. W. Scott-Giles, *The Wimsey Family* (London: Gollancz, 1977), pp. 13-25.

53. DLS to C. W. Scott-Giles (15 Apr. 1936), in the recipient's possession.

54. "Biographical Note Communicated by Paul Austin Delagardie," passim.

55. DLS, "Gaudy Night," in *Art of the Mystery Story,* pp. 208-21; DLS, *Gaudy Night* (London: Gollancz, 1972), pp. 5, 482, 8, 9, 10, 13, 241-42, 322.

Sunday Times, 10 Nov. 1935, p. 7; 24 Nov. 1935, p. 9; 29 Dec. 1935, p. 5; 19 Jan. 1936, p. 9; 19 Apr. 1936, p. 9.

Harcourt, Brace News (15 July 1936, p. 2) indicated that the sales of *Gaudy Night* were greater than those of any previous Wimsey novel. See also Frank Swinnerton, *The Georgian Literary Scene* (London: Heinemann, 1935), pp. 448, 450.

56. DLS and Muriel St. Clare Byrne, *Busman's Honeymoon: A Detective Comedy in Three Acts* (London: Gollancz, 1937), pp. 7-9. *Times,* 17 Dec. 1936, p. 14; *Sunday Times,* 19 Sept. 1937, p. 4. BBC Written Archives. See "Talk of the Day," *Evening News,* 15 July 1939, p. 6.

57. The beginning of the manuscript of *Thrones, Dominations* may be found in the Wheaton (Illinois) College Library. See n. 40.

58. See especially the following issues: 3 Feb. 1935, p. 9; 10 Feb. 1935, p. 7; 17 Feb. 1935, p. 9; 24 Feb. 1935, p. 7; 3 Mar. 1935, p. 9; 10 Mar. 1935, p. 9; 17 Mar. 1935, p. 9; 24 Mar. 1935, p. 9; 7 Apr. 1935, p. 9; 14 Apr. 1935, p. 9; 21 Apr. 1935, p. 7; 28 Apr. 1935, p. 9; 12 May 1935, p. 9; 19 May 1935, p. 9; 26 May 1935, p. 9; 2 June 1935, p. 9; 9 June 1935, p. 7; and "Letters to the Editor," 3 Mar. 1935, p. 10; 10 Mar. 1935, p. 14; 17 Mar. 1935, p. 11. The italicized passage is from the issue of 30 Dec. 1934, p. 6.

59. Mary Ellen Chase, "Five Literary Portraits," *Massachusetts Review,* III (Spring 1962), 514-15.

60. DLS, "Aristotle and Detective Fiction," *English: Journal of English Association,* I (1936), 21-35; rpt. in DLS, *Unpopular Opinions* (London: Gollancz, 1946), pp. 178-90.

See *Times,* 24 June 1935, p. 12; *English,* IV (Summer 1943), 169-70; and XII (Spring 1958), 10.

61. Eustace Portugal, "Death to the Detectives!" *Bookman,* 84 (Apr. 1933), 28.

62. Noel Stock, *The Life of Ezra Pound* (Harmondsworth, Middlesex: Penguin, 1970), p. 405.

63. Heilbrun, "Sayers, Lord Peter and God," p. 324; Q. D. Leavis, "The Case of Miss Dorothy Sayers," *Scrutiny,* VI (1937), 334-40. See J. Raymond, "White Tile or Red Plush?" *New Statesman,* 30 June 1956, p. 756.

64. DLS, *Mind of the Maker,* pp. 49-50.

Chapter Three

1. Cyril Ray, "Death of Miss Dorothy L. Sayers," *Manchester Guardian Weekly,* 26 Dec. 1957. See: Pamela Frankau, "Personality Parade," *Daily Mirror,* 10 Feb. 1937, p. 11; DLS, "Chekhov at the Westminster," *New Statesman and Nation,* XIII (27 Feb. 1937), 324; John G. W. Roebuck, "Letter to Editor," *Times,* 23 Mar. 1937, p. 17; DLS, "The Fen Floods: Fiction and Fact," *Spectator,* 2 Apr. 1937, pp. 611-12; DLS, "Ink of Poppies," *Spectator,* 14 May 1937, pp. 897-98; DLS, "Plain English," *Nash's Pall Mall Magazine* (1937), rpt. in DLS, *Unpopular Opinions* (London: Gollancz, 1946), pp. 81-89; DLS, "The Psychology of Advertising," *Spectator,* 19 Nov. 1937, pp. 896-98; DLS, *An Account of the Lord Mortimer Wimsey, The Hermit of the Wash* (Oxford, 1937); DLS, "The Wimsey Chin," *Times,* 4 Dec. 1937, p. 15.

2. Margaret Babington, "Letter to Editor," *Times,* 9 Jan. 1958, p. 14; DLS, *The Zeal of Thy House* (London: Gollancz, 1937), p. 7.

3. Laurence Irving, Preface to *The Zeal of Thy House,* by DLS, p. 6. William Stubbs, ed., *The Historical Works of Gervase of Canterbury,* 2 vols. (London: Longman, 1879), I, 20. See the unpublished doctoral dissertation of Marian Baker Fairman, "The Neo-Medieval Plays of Dorothy L. Sayers," Diss. University of Pittsburgh 1961.

4. *Church Times,* 18 June 1937, p. 745; *Times,* 14 June 1937, p. 12.

5. DLS, *The Mind of the Maker* (New York: Harcourt, Brace, 1941), p. 207.

6. DLS to Dorothy H. Rowe (15 Apr. and 25 Apr. 1937), in the recipient's possession.

7. *Church Times,* 18 June 1937, p. 745.

8. DLS, *Zeal of Thy House,* pp. 33, 34, 49, 96, 104; *Church Times,* 18 June 1937, p. 745.

9. *Times,* 30 Mar. 1938; *Sunday Times,* 26 June 1938.

10. *Church Times* (see n. 7), and *Times,* 14 June 1937, p. 12.

11. "Religion in the Theatre," *Church Times,* 8 Apr. 1938, p. 893. *The Zeal of Thy House,* newly designed by Norah Lambourne, was presented at the 1949 Canterbury Festival. Christopher Hassal directed, and E. Martin Browne was in charge of production.

12. DLS to R. A. Scott-James (22 Nov. 1938), in the collection of the Humanities Research Center of the University of Texas.

13. DLS to V. Gielgud (18 Nov. 1938), BBC Archives.

14. *Modern Languages, A Journal of Modern Studies,* XX (Oct. 1938), 1; and XX (Mar. 1939), 97. Frank Swinnerton, *The Georgian Literary Scene: A Panorama* (London: Heinemann, 1935), p. 448.

15. DLS, "The Haunted Policeman," *Harper's Bazaar* (Feb. 1938), pp. 62, 130-35.

16. *Times,* 21 Nov. 1938, p. 13; and 24 Nov. 1938, p. 15. An unexpected correspondence ensued over the appropriateness of DLS's quotation from the Latin New Testament: 26 Nov. 1938, p. 13; 30 Nov. 1938, p. 15.

17. DLS, "The Greatest Drama Ever Staged," *Sunday Times,* 3 Apr. 1938, p. 20; 10 Apr. 1938, p. 18; 17 Apr. 1938, p. 8; 8 May 1938, p. 12. The editorial was reprinted (along with "The Triumph of Easter") in pamphlet form (London: Hodder and Stoughton, 1938) and went through five printings by November 1938. (See Hodder and Stoughton advertisement in *Sunday Times,* 13 Nov. 1938, p. 6.) It also appears as the first of the collected essays in *Creed or Chaos?* (London: Methuen, 1947), pp. 1-6.

18. *Sunday Times,* 17 Apr. 1938, p. 10.

19. DLS, "Are Women Human?" in *Unpopular Opinions* (London: Gollancz, 1946), pp. 106, 107, 113. This address (along with "The Human-Not-Quite-Human"—also printed in *Unpopular Opinions)* was published with an Introduction by Mary McDermott Shideler (Grand Rapids, Mich.: Eerdmans, 1971).

20. DLS, *He That Should Come* (London: Gollancz, 1939), pp. 5, 9-10; rpt. in DLS, *Four Sacred Plays* (London: Gollancz, 1948). *Times,* 27 Dec. 1938, p. 15; *Church Times,* 30 Dec. 1938, p. 723. See also DLS, "Nativity Play," *Radio Times,* LXI (2 Oct. 1938-7 Jan. 1939), 13.

21. "Death of Miss Dorothy L. Sayers," *Manchester Guardian Weekly,* 26 Dec. 1957.

22. *Times,* 6 Jan. 1939, p. 7.

23. *Times,* 16 Feb. 1939, p. 11.

24. *Sunday Times,* 10 September 1939, p. 8.

25. DLS, *The Devil to Pay* (London: Gollancz, 1939), pp. 11. 54, 55. DLS to Dorothy H. Rowe (previous to June 1939), in the recipient's possession. *Church Times,* 16 June 1939, p. 656; James Agate, "Faust in the Haymarket," *Sunday Times,* 23 July 1939, p. 4. See also: *New Statesman and Nation,* XVIII (29 July 1939), 177-78; *Theatre Arts Monthly,* XXIII (Oct. 1939), 706-7. DLS made several comments on her play in a lecture given in 1945: "The Faust Legend and the Idea of the Devil," *Publications of the English Goethe Society,* NS XV (for 1945, published in 1946), 1-20; rpt. in DLS, *The Poetry of Search and the Poetry of Statement* (London: Gollancz, 1963), pp. 227-41. See DLS "Letter to the Editor," *Church Times,* 4 Aug. 1939, p. 110.

26. DLS, *Strong Meat* (London: Hodder and Stoughton, 1939), p. 27. Both "Strong Meat" and "The Dogma Is the Drama" were reprinted in DLS, *Creed or Chaos?* (London: Methuen, 1947), pp. 14-24.

27. DLS, "The Dogma Is the Drama," *Strong Meat,* pp. 32-33.

28. *Church Times,* 28 July 1939, p. 100 [advertisement].

29. *Times,* 1 Aug. 1939, p. 15. This is the early announcement of the Coventry meeting.

30. The will of DLS is on file in Somerset House.

31. DLS, "Wimsey Papers," *Spectator,* 17 Nov. 1939, pp. 672-74; 24 Nov. 1939, pp. 736- 37; 1 Dec. 1939, pp. 770-71; 8 Dec. 1939, pp. 809-10; 15 Dec. 1939, pp. 859-60; 22 Dec. 1939, pp. 894-95; 29 Dec. 1939, pp. 925-26; 5 Jan. 1940, pp. 8-9; 12 Jan. 1940, pp. 38-39; 19 Jan. 1940, pp. 70-71; 26 Jan. 1940, pp. 104-5.

32. Charles Smyth, "Church, Community and State," *Spectator,* 17 Nov. 1939, p. 687; 1 Dec. 1939, p. 782; 8 Dec. 1939, p. 820; 15 Dec. 1939, p. 869; 22 Dec. 1939, p. 904; 29 Dec. 1939, pp. 934-35; 5 Jan. 1940, p. 19. Following DLS's last letter is a terse, bracketed editorial note: "We cannot continue this correspondence."

33. DLS, *Begin Here: A War-Time Essay* (London: Gollancz, 1940), pp. 11. 31, 151, 152. DLS's work looks back upon Peter Drucker's *The End of Economic Man,* V. A. Demant's *The Religious Prospect,* Charles Williams's *He Came down from Heaven,* and Christopher Dawson's *Beyond Politics.* See *Times Literary Supplement,* 27 Jan. 1940, p. 48; *Church Times,* 9 Feb. 1940, p. 100.

34. DLS, *The Man Born to Be King: A Play-Cycle on the Life of Our Lord and Saviour Jesus Christ* (London: Gollancz, 1943), p. 9.

35. DLS, "Divine Comedy," *Unpopular Opinions* (London: Gollancz, 1946), pp. 20-21; first published in *Guardian,* 15 May 1940, p. 128.

36. *Man Born to Be King,* pp. 9-16. See, for example, *Daily Mirror,* 11 Dec. 1941, p. 8; *Daily Telegraph and Morning Post,* 11 Dec. 1941, p. 5; *News Chronicle,* 11 Dec. 1941, p. 3; *Evening News,* 11 Dec. 1941, p. 2; *Daily Mail,* 11 Dec. 1941, p. 3.

37. *Journals of the House of Commons,* 376 (19 Dec. 1941). cols. 2233-34; and 377 (21 Jan. 1942), col. 379.

38. *Man Born to Be King,* p. 40. See the advertisement in, for example, *Daily Telegraph and Morning Post,* 24 Dec. 1941, p. 3; and also the comment in 6 Jan. 1942, p. 4.

39. *Man Born to Be King,* p. 39; Charles Smyth, *Cyril Forster Garbett, Archbishop of York* (London: Hodder and Stoughton, 1959), p. 211. The records of the BBC Archives contain full information on the broadcasts.

40. Val Gielgud, *Years of the Locust* (London: Nicholson and Watson, 1947), pp. 79, 110-11, 89; *Man Born to Be King, p. 38.*

41. See Robert Speaight, *The Christian Theatre* (London: Barnes & Gates, 1960), pp. 129-30, 4.

42. Gielgud, *Years of the Locust,* pp. 177-78. See also his *British Radio Drama 1922-1956* (London: Harrap, 1957), pp. 170-73. *Man Born to Be King,* p. 39.

43. The files of correspondence at the Written Archives Centre, BBC, Caversham Park, Reading, are of course invaluable. Quotations from, or references to, the following correspondence are made in the course of my discussion: DLS to Dr. Welch (23 July 1940); Note to Dr. Welch from C. (no date, but the writer has seen the DLS letter to Welch); DLS to Derek McCulloch (11 October 1940); McCulloch to DLS (22 Oct. 1940); DLS to McCulloch (25 Oct. 1940); DLS to Miss May Jenkin (22 Nov. 1940)—"Trisagion of A & M" refers to a hymn-tune in the Anglican hymnbook, *Hymns Ancient and Modern;* McCulloch to DLS (26 Nov. 1940); DLS to McCulloch (28 Nov. 1940): DLS to Dr. Welch (28 Nov. 1940); McCulloch to Dr. Welch (11 Dec. 1940); Dr. Welch to

DLS (4 Dec. 1940); Dr. Welch, Internal Circulation Memo (31 Dec, 1940); DLS to Dr. Welch (7 Dec. 1940); Rev. Eric Fenn to Miss M. T. Candler (21 Jan. 1941); Dr. Welch to Miss Candler (24 Mar. 1941); Dr. Welch to C. H. D. (29 Feb. 1940).

44. DLS to Val Gielgud (13 Jan. 1942, 27 Jan. 1942, 9 Feb. 1942, 22 Sept. 1942), BBC Archives.

45. B. E. Nichols to DLS (16 Oct. 1942, 5 May 1943); DLS to Mr. Nichols (22 Oct. 1942); DLS to Miss Ethel Eaves (5 Nov. 1942, 6 Jan. 1944, 17 Mar. 1944), BBC Archives.

See, among numerous diverse criticisms of *The Man Born to Be King: Times Literary Supplement,* 19 June 1943, p. 28 (and the editorial, p. 29); G. W. Stonier, "Miss Sayers's Christian Drama," *New Statesman and Nation,* XXVI (10 July 1943), 28; Murray Roston, *Biblical Drama in England: From the Middle Ages to the Present Day* (London: Faber and Faber, 1968), pp. 296-98; William V. Spanos, *The Christian Tradition in Modern British Verse Drama* (New Brunswick, N.J.: Rutgers, 1967), passim. A cleric, writing to the *Times* on 9 July 1943, suggested that "Miss Sayers's broadcast plays, *The Man Born to Be King,*" should "be reverently read in all schools at least once during a pupil's career" (p. 5).

46. DLS to Sir Hugh Walpole (3 Jan. 1940), in the possession of the Humanities Research Center of the University of Texas.

47. DLS, "The Technique of the Sermon," *Spectator,* 2 Feb. 1940, p. 150; DLS, "The Contempt of Learning in 20th Century England," *Fortnightly,* 153, NS 147 (Apr. 1940), 373-82.

DLS, "Creed or Chaos?" was issued as a pamphlet by Hodder and Stoughton in June 1940 and rpt. in *Creed or Chaos? and Other Essays in Popular Theology* (London: Methuen, 1947), pp. 25-46. At least two readers of the address found it well written. Hilaire Belloc, writing on 4 July 1940 to his closest friend among professional soldiers, Major General Guy Dawnay (1878-1952), said: "I have read Miss Sayers' pamphlet, and I agree with you that it is very well written, for especially is it concise." (Nevertheless, Belloc felt that the address was lacking in an essential point for Roman Catholics: "There is no answer to the question *Quid de ecclesia?* Which may be put more sharply, *Ubi Christus?")* See Robert Speaight, ed., *Letters from Hilaire Belloc* (London: Hollis & Carter, 1958), pp. ix, 292-93. Because in this address DLS had quoted critically from an article in *Spectator* written by Dr. W. B. Selbie, former principal of Mansfield College, Oxford, a correspondence erupted in that periodical: see 2 Feb. 1940, 12 and 19 July 1940 (in the last of which there is a letter by DLS).

DLS, "Notes on the Way," *Time and Tide,* 15 June 1940, pp. 633-34; and 22 June 1940, pp. 657-58.

DLS, "Vox Populi," *Spectator,* 2 Aug. 1940, p. 117.

DLS, "Pot *versus* Kettle," *Time and Tide,* 10 Aug. 1940, pp. 826, 828; 24 Aug. 1940, p. 863; 31 Aug. 1940, p. 884; 7 Sept., 1940, p. 906.

48. *Times,* 10 Apr. 1940, p. 6; *New Statesman and Nation,* XIX (13 Apr. 1940), 493; *Time and Tide,* 13 Apr. 1940, p. 392. The MS of the play, with the original title *Cat's Cradle,* is in the possession of Wheaton (Illinois) College Library.

49. I should like to acknowledge the kindness and generosity of Mr. Wolf Suschitzky, who made available to me a choice of his DLS-porcupine portraits.

50. DLS, "Notes on the Way," *Time and Tide,* 15 June 1940, pp. 633, 634.

51. DLS, "For Albert, Late King of the Belgians," *Life and Letters To-day,* XXVI (July 1940), 36.

52. DLS, "The English War," *Times Literary Supplement,* 7 Sept. 1940, p. 445. (See a consistently patriotic stance in the DLS letter to *Times,* 24 Aug. 1940, p.5.) "The English War" was included in *The Best Poems of 1941* (which I have not seen) and in Brian Gardner, ed., *The Terrible Rain: The War Poets 1939-1945* (London: Methuen, 1966), pp. 45-47.

53. DLS, *The Mysterious English* (London: Macmillan, 1941), pp. 3, 15, 24.

54. DLS to Sir Richard Maconachie (13 July 1940), in the BBC Archives. See Kenneth Clark, *The Other Half* (New York: Harper & Row, 1977), pp. 1-41.

55. DLS, "Helen Simpson," *Fortnightly,* 155, NS 149 (Jan. 1941), 54-59. The visit of DLS to Helen Simpson's home was undoubtedly the visit "a short time ago" to the Isle of Wight mentioned in *The Mysterious English* (p. 15). See Helen Simpson, "Cart Canvassing," *Fortnightly,* Dec. 1938. Earlier in 1940 Simpson gave a BBC broadcast (subsequently published in *A Woman Looks Out* by Lutterworth Press, London, 1940) in which she acknowledges DLS as the source of her thinking.

56. *Malvern, 1941: The Life of the Church and the Order of Society* (London: Longmans, Green, 1941), pp. vii-xv, 1-8, 57-78.

57. DLS to Val Gielgud (24 Feb. 1941), BBC Archives.

58. DLS, "The Religions behind the Nation," in *The Church Looks Ahead: Broadcast Talks* (London: Faber and Faber, 1941), pp. 67, 68, 72.

59. DLS, "Vocation in Work," in *A Christian Basis for the Post-War World: A Commentary on the Ten Peace Points* ed. A. E. Baker (London: Student Christian Movement, 1942), pp. 88n., 7-8, 89, 94, 102, 103.
Prepared about the same time was DLS's short essay "Living to Work," which she said was commissioned for "a Sunday evening B.B.C. 'Postscript' " but was "suppressed" before it appeared, "on the heterogeneous grounds that it appeared to have political tendencies, and that 'our public do not want to be admonished by a woman' " (*Unpopular Opinions,* pp. 7, 122-27). Miss Mary S. Hodgson, Written Archives Centre, BBC, informed me (in correspondence dated 18 Aug. 1972) that the DLS talk was postponed because the prime minister spoke on that day at 9:00 P.M. But see G. R. Barnes to DLS (1 Sept. 1941), BBC Archives.

60. DLS, "The Church in the New Age," *World Review,* Mar. 1941, pp. 11-15; "The Church in War's Aftermath," *Living Age,* 360 (July 1941), 441-45.

61. DLS, "Forgiveness and the Enemy," *Fortnightly,* 155, NS 149 (Apr. 1941), 379-83; *Unpopular Opinions,* p. 7.

62. The bishop's letter was dated 14 Apr. 1941 and was reprinted, along with the invited responses, in *Fortnightly,* 155, NS 149 (June 1941), 555-56. The bishop and his proposal are presented in Rolf Hochhuth's "documentary" drama *Soldiers.*

63. DLS to Mr. Ackerley (5 Dec. 1931); Dr. J. Welch to DLS (10 July 1940, 24 Aug. 1940); DLS to Dr. Welch (2 Jan. 1941), BBC Archives.

64. DLS, *Mind of the Maker,* pp. 3-17, 35, 38-41, 42, ix; *Times Literary Supplement,* 9 Aug. 1941, p. 382; see also the editorial on the same page. *Church Times,* 19 Sept. 1941, p. 537; C. S. Lewis, rev. of *The Mind of the Maker, Theology,* Oct. 1941, pp. 248-49. See also C. S. Lewis, *Miracles: A Preliminary Study* (London: Geoffrey Bles, 1947), p. 118; Samuel M. Zwemer, "The Doctrine of the Trinity," *Moslem World,* XXXV (Jan. 1945), 1-5.

The four promised volumes in "Bridgeheads" include Denis Browne, *A New Charter for Medicine;* U. Ellis-Fermor, *Masters of Reality;* M. St. Clare Byrne, *Privilege and Responsibility;* and G. W. Pailthorpe, *The Social Value of Surrealism.* On pp. 23-24 of DLS, *Why Work? An Address Delivered at Eastbourne April 23rd 1942* (London: Methuen, 1942) there is a statement of purpose:

> We live in a world increasingly specialised, analytical, and disintegrated. As man has achieved more and more mastery in separate spheres of his activity, he has grown less and less capable of relating his achievements to any coherent social purpose or philosophy of life. Money is divorced from real wealth, knowledge from understanding, politics from conduct, labour from creation, belief from experience: "we have driven the living imagination out of the world." If the whole fabric of society is not to collapse into chaos, we must either submit to an artificial uniformity imposed by brute force, or learn to bridge for ourselves these perilous gaps which sunder our behaviour from reality. This series of books is an attempt to establish a few Bridgeheads, by means of which the remakers of civilization may throw forward their pioneering works.

Besides DLS, *Mind of the Maker,* U. Ellis-Fermor's book is announced as published, the others still "in preparation." A. P. Herbert's *The Point of Parliament* had become the third volume in the Bridgeheads series by 1946.

65. DLS to Dr. Welch (23 July 1940); DLS to Val Gielgud (1 Apr. 1941); DLS to Gielgud (22 July 1941), BBC Archives.

66. David A. Jasen, *P. G. Wodehouse: A Portrait of a Master* (New York: Mason & Lipscomb, 1974), pp. 172-83; P. G. Wodehouse, *The Performing Flea: A Self-Portrait in Letters* (Harmondsworth, Middlesex: Penguin, 1961), p. 130.

67. *Times,* 20 Aug. 1941, p. 5; 23 Aug. 141, p. 5; 26 Aug. 1941, p. 5.

68. DLS, *The Other Six Deadly Sins* (London: Methuen, 1943), p. 3. The essay is reprinted in *Creed or Chaos?,* pp. 65-88. A slightly tangential correspondence arising from DLS's Public Morality Council address appears in *Church Times,* 31 Oct. 1941, p. 633; 14 Nov. 1941, p. 673; 21 Nov. 1941, p. 688; 7 Nov. 1941, p. 754.

69. DLS, "Christian Morality," *Unpopular Opinions,* pp. 9-12.

70. DLS, "How Free Is the Press?" *Unpopular Opinions,* pp. 129-32.

71. *Daily Telegraph and Morning Post,* 6 Jan. 1942, p. 4.

72. I am indebted to Stanley H. Horrocks, Borough Librarian, Reading, for supplying to me specific details about the occasion of DLS's 13 Feb. 1942 address in Reading. The address is published in *Unpopular Opinions,* pp. 43-58. DLS to Val Gielgud (16 Feb. 1942), BBC Archives.

73. DLS, *Why Work? An Address Delivered at Eastbourne April 23rd, 1942* (London: Methuen, 1942); rpt. in *Creed or Chaos?* pp. 47-64. "Platform," *Sunday Pictorial,* 13 Jan. 1943, p. 4.

74. DLS, "Lord, I Thank Thee," *Britain,* I (Nov. 1942), 37-41. I have not seen this publication, but the poem appears in Storm Jameson, ed., *London Calling* (New York: Harper, 1942), pp. 293-98, a volume specially directed to an American audience. DLS to Derek McCulloch (5 Nov. 1940), BBC Archives.

75. The poem on Fatima was sent to Mr. Moralee, who worked for DLS during the time of the pigs, and kindly supplied by him.

76. "War Cat" was published in *Time and Tide,* 4 Dec. 1943, p. 994, and in

Mona Gooden, comp., *The Poet's Cat: An Anthology* (London: Harrap, 1946), pp. 95-98. "For Timothy in the Coinherence," *Listener and B.B.C. Television Review*, 15 Mar. 1973, p. 337; Rosamond K. Sprague, *A Matter of Eternity* (Grand Rapids, Mich.: Eerdmans, 1973), pp. 138-39. Val Gielgud, *Years in a Mirror* (London: Bodley Head, 1965), pp. 196-97. DLS to Mrs. Charis Barnett Frankenburg (July 1948), in the recipient's possession.

77. DLS, *Strong Meat,* p. 14. DLS to Robert Speaight (24 July 1943), in the possession of Boston University Library. DLS to Val Gielgud (16 Aug. 1943, 2 Jan. 1943), BBC Archives.

Atherton Fleming shared the admiration of DLS for Gielgud. In 1942 he had made two portrait photographs of Gielgud, one of which was on display at the United Artists show that year.

78. *English,* IV (Summer 1943), 169-70.

79. DLS, "Aerial Reconnaissance," *Fortnightly,* 160, NS 154 (Oct. 1943), 268-70.

80. The three addresses have been printed in *Unpopular Opinions:* "The Gulf Stream and the Channel," pp. 59-66; "They Tried to Be Good," pp. 97-105; "The Human-Not-Quite-Human," pp. 106-16.

81. Gielgud, *Years in a Mirror,* p. 93. DLS to Val Gielgud (4 Jan. 1944), BBC Archives.

82. DLS, "Target Area," *Fortnightly,* 161, NS 155 (Mar. 1944), 181-84; *Atlantic Monthly,* 173 (Mar. 1944), 48-50.

83. Frederick Laws, "Tolerance the Essence of Criticism," *John o' London's Weekly,* 24 Mar. 1944, p. 247; and 7 Apr. 1944, p. 16. A reader requested "the famous equation," and DLS supplied it in the issue of 19 May 1944, p. 77. In the same issue (p. 78) she corrected an earlier correspondent on another matter: "Frankenstein was not the name of the monster, but of the poor mutt who made the monster."

84. DLS, *Even the Parrot: Exemplary Conversations for Enlightened Children* (London: Methuen, 1944). This work ran to at least two reprints: I have seen a "Third edition" (1945). See *Times Literary Supplement,* 25 Nov. 1944, p. 574.

85. DLS, ed., *The Moonstone,* by Wilkie Collins, (London: J. M. Dent, 1944). See *Times Literary Supplement,* 4 Nov. 1944, p. 535.

86. Garet Garrett, *A Time Is Born* (Oxford: Blackwell, 1945), pp. v-ix. Edward Peter Garrett (1878-1954), who changed his name to Garet Garrett, was an American writer; he produced novels, financial reports for the *New York Times* and the *Wall Street Journal,* editorials for *Saturday Evening Post, New York Times,* and *Tribune,* and several free-lance articles.

87. DLS, "Towards a Christian Aesthetic," in *Our Culture: Its Christian Roots and Present Crisis* [Edward Alleyn Lectures, 1944], ed. V. A. Demant (London: S.P.C.K., 1947), pp. v-vi, 50-69; rpt. in *Unpopular Opinions,* pp. 29-43; rpt. in *The New Orpheus: Essays toward a Christian Poetic,* ed. Nathan Scott (London: Sheed, 1964), pp. 3-20. The character and history of the Edward Alleyn Foundation are described in C. W. Dugmore, ed., *The Interpretation of the Bible* [Edward Alleyn Lectures, 1943] (London: S.P.C.K., 1944), pp. v-vii.

88. DLS, "The Faust Legend and the Idea of the Devil," *Publications of the English Goethe Society,* NS XV (1945), 1-20. This volume was actually published in 1946; rpt. in DLS, *The Poetry of Search and the Poetry of Statement* (London: Gollancz, 1963), pp. 227-41.

Chapter Four

1. Alice Mary Hadfield, *An Introduction to Charles Williams* (London: Robert Hale, 1959), p. 156.

2. Charles Williams, *The Figure of Beatrice: A Study in Dante* (London: Faber and Faber, 1943). *Essays Presented to Charles Williams* (London: Oxford University Press, 1947), pp. 1-2. DLS, *Introductory Papers on Dante* (New York: Harper & Brothers, 1954), p. xvi. Anne Ridler, ed., *Charles Williams: The Image of the City and Other Essays* (London: Oxford University Press, 1958), p. xxvii.

It is inaccurate to speak, as some have done, of DLS as a full member of the Inklings, the coterie which gathered an evening a week in C. S. Lewis's rooms at Magdalen College. See W. H. Lewis, ed., *Letters of C. S. Lewis* (London: Geoffrey Bles, 1966), pp. 287-88. But see *Essays Presented to Charles Williams,* p. v.

In the Charles Williams letters possessed by Wheaton (Illinois) College Library, there are interesting references to DLS. See the Williams letters for 10 Feb. 1944, 29 Apr. 1944, 12 July 1944, 24 Aug. 1944, 7 Sept. 1944.

3. DLS, "Ignorance and Dissatisfaction," *Latin Teaching: The Journal of the Association for the Reform of Latin Teaching,* XXVIII (Oct. 1952), 79; DLS, *Further Papers on Dante* (London: Methuen, 1957), p. 104.

4. *Essays Presented to Charles Williams,* pp. v-xiv.

5. Ibid., pp. xiii-xiv. DLS, "A Drama of the Christian Church," *International Review of Missions,* XXXIV (1945), 430-32.

6. John Heath-Stubbs, *Charles Williams* (London: Longmans, Green, 1955), pp. 15-16, 18. DLS, "The Poetry of the Image in Dante and Charles Williams," in *Further Papers on Dante* (London: Methuen, 1957), pp. 187-88, 204.

7. DLS, Introduction to *James I,* by Charles Williams (London: Arthur Barker, 1951), pp. ix, xii, xiii.

8. DLS to Michael Williams (2 Dec. 1947), Wheaton (Illinois) College Library. See also: DLS, "Charles Williams: A Poet's Critic," in *The Poetry of Search and the Poetry of Statement* (London: Gollancz, 1963), pp. 69-90.

9. DLS to Michael and Mrs. Williams (24 May 1948, 28 June 1948, 29 Sept. 1948, 5 May 1950, 23 Dec. 1953, 4 Jan. 1956), Wheaton (Illinois) College Library.

10. W. H. Lewis, ed., *Letters of C. S. Lewis* (London: Geoffrey Bles, 1966), pp. 1-26, 208, 209, 287, 299. Roger Lancelyn Green and Walter Hooper, *C. S. Lewis: A Biography* (London: Collins, 1974). C. S. Lewis, "De descriptione temporum," in *Selected Literary Essays by C. S. Lewis,* ed. Walter Hooper (Cambridge: University Press, 1969), pp. 1-14. *Times,* 14 May 1955, p. 9.

11. The published lectures may be found in the following: DLS, *Introductory Papers on Dante* (New York: Harper, 1954); DLS, *Further Papers on Dante* (London: Methuen, 1957); DLS, *The Poetry of Search and the Poetry of Statement* (London: Gollancz, 1963); DLS, "The Beatrician Vision in Dante and Other Poets," and DLS, "On Translating the *Divina Commedia,*" *Nottingham Mediaeval Studies,* II (1958), 3-23, 38-66.

12. DLS and Barbara Reynolds, trans. *The Divine Comedy: III. Paradise,* by Dante (Harmondsworth, Middlesex: Penguin, 1962), p. 9. DLS to Norah Lambourne (27 Aug. 1946), in the recipient's possession.

13. Lewis Thorpe, ed., *Nottingham Mediaeval Studies,* II (1958), 1.

14. DLS, *The Lost Tools of Learning* (London: Methuen, 1948). (The bulk of this address was also published in *Hibbert Journal,* XLVI [Oct. 1947], 1-13; the entire article was reprinted in DLS, *Poetry of Search and the Poetry of Statement,* pp. 155-76.) DLS, "Dante's View of the Cosmos," *Proceedings of the Royal Institution,* XXXV (1951), 43-67; rpt. in DLS, *Further Papers on Dante,* pp. 78-101. DLS, "The Poetry of the Image in Dante and Charles Williams," in *Further Papers on Dante,* pp. 183-204. DLS, "Ignorance and Dissatisfaction," pp. 69-92; the article was reprinted under a new title—"The Teaching of Latin: A New Approach," in DLS, *Poetry of Search and the Poetry of Statement,* pp. 177-99. DLS, "Poetry, Language, and Ambiguity," in *Poetry of Search and the Poetry of Statement,* pp. 263-86. DLS, "The Writing and Reading of Allegory," in *Poetry of Search and the Poetry of Statement,* pp. 201-25. DLS, "Oedipus Simplex: Freedom and Fate in Folklore and Fiction," *Proceedings of the Royal Institution,* XXXVI (1955), 215-34; rpt. in DLS, *Poetry of Search and the Poetry of Statement,* pp. 243-61. DLS, "The Poetry of Search and the Poetry of Statement," in *Poetry of Search and the Poetry of Statement,* pp. 7-19. DLS, "The Translation of Verse," in *Poetry of Search and the Poetry of Statement,* pp. 127-53. The BBC items may be found in the BBC Written Archives Centre, Caversham Park, Reading.

15. DLS, trans., *The Divine Comedy: I. Hell* (Harmondsworth, Middlesex: Penguin, 1949), pp. 9-66. See: Lord Kennet's review in *Sunday Times,* 8 Jan. 1950, p. 3; *Times Literary Supplement,* 4 Apr. 1950, p. 224; 12 Dec. 1958, p. 721; Gilbert F. Cunningham, *The Divine Comedy in English,* 2 vols. (Edinburgh: Oliver and Boyd, 1966), II, 212-20.

16. DLS, trans., *The Divine Comedy: II. Purgatory* (Harmondsworth, Middlesex: Penguin, 1955), pp. 9-71.

17. DLS and Barbara Reynolds, trans., *The Divine Comedy: III. Paradise* (Harmondsworth, Middlesex: Penguin, 1962), pp. 9-52.

18. DLS, trans., *The Heart of Stone, Being the Four* Canzoni *of the "Pietra" Group, Done into English . . . from the Italian of Dante Alighieri (1265-1321)* (Witham, Essex: Clarke, 1946). DLS, trans., *St. Bernard's Hymn to the Blessed Virgin in the Rose of Paradise,* by Dante (1949).

19. DLS, "The 'Terrible' Ode [*Cosi nel parlar voglio esser aspro*]," *Nottingham Mediaeval Studies,* IX (1965), 42-54. See in the same issue DLS, "The Art of Translating Dante," 15-31.

20. Barbara Reynolds, Preface to *Introductory Papers on Dante,* by DLS (New York: Harper, 1954), pp. vii-viii.

21. C. S. Lewis, ed., *Essays Presented to Charles Williams* (London: Oxford University Press, 1947), pp. v, 1-37. DLS, *Introductory Papers on Dante,* p. xvi. DLS, *Further Papers on Dante,* p. v. DLS, *Poetry of Search and the Poetry of Statement.* DLS, "The Art of Translating Dante," *Nottingham Mediaeval Studies,* IX (1965), 15-31.

22. DLS, *Further Papers on Dante,* pp. vi-vii.

23. The completed Lichfield Cathedral Festival plans were announced by 13 May 1946 in the *Times,* p. 7. DLS, *The Just Vengeance: The Lichfield Festival Play for 1946* (London: Gollancz, 1946), pp. 9, 10.

24. *Daily Sketch,* 27 Feb. 1946, p. 8. "Toc H": a society committed to Christian fellowship and service; the signallers' former T + H, for Talbot

House, started by Rev. T. B. Clayton in Ypres Salient in 1915 in memory of Gilbert Talbot.

25. *Daily Sketch,* 5 Mar. 1946, p. 2.

26. DLS to Canon Wright (21 Mar. 1946), in the possession of Wheaton (Illinois) College Library.

27. The mingled fortunes of St. Anne's were discussed in a continuing correspondence in the *Times* in the summer of 1953; see especially the issue of 8 Aug. 1953, p. 9. Letter from Miss Lambourne (29 Feb. 1976). *Times,* 17 June 1946, p. 6. DLS to Val Gielgud (19 June 1946, 12 Dec. 1945, 13 Jan. 1947), BBC Archives. The staging of the drama took place in the western end of the nave and was three- tiered, suggesting the appearance of a medieval mystery play. Miss Kathleen Richards (DLS's secretary at the time) received word from DLS of her safe arrival in Lichfield "intact" with all her "bags and bottles in good order"; DLS requested Miss Richards's help in forwarding (if available in "the big cabinet in the far library" and not moth-eaten) a parcel of white flannel for use in the production (the letter undated but obviously previous to 18 June 1946). In another note DLS asked Miss Richards to bring with her to Lichfield on 22 June (when she would be the author's guest) an M.A. gown, cap, and hood—"the larger, older, and shabbier" of two gowns, "the red-lined hood & the little square flat cap" (not the mortarboard)—which she needed for the procession on Sunday, 23 June 1946. See *Church Times,* 21 June 1946, p. 365. Surprisingly, W. V. Spanos *(The Christian Tradition in Modern British Verse Drama* [New Brunswick, New Jersey: Rutgers, 1967]) writes this work off merely as a pageant.

28. *Times,* 5 July 1948, p. 6. *English,* XII (Spring 1958), 10. DLS to Sir Herbert Grierson (26 Apr. 1948), in the possession of the National Library of Scotland, Edinburgh.

29. *London Star,* 20 Sept. 1950; *News Chronicle,* 21 Sept. 1950; *Radio Times,* 22 Sept. 1950, p. 22; *Yorkshire Post,* 29 Sept. 1950; *Sunday Times,* 1 Oct. 1950; *Evening Standard,* 6 Oct. 1950; *Manchester Guardian,* 9 Oct. 1950; *Free-thinker,* 3 Dec. 1950. DLS to T. S. Gregory (30 Aug. 1950), BBC Archives.

30. *London Star,* 14 Nov. 1950; *Birmingham Gazette,* 16 Nov. 1950; *Truth,* 24 Nov. 1950, p. 547; *Sheffield Telegraph,* 6 Dec. 1950; *Yorkshire Post,* 6 Dec. 1950; *Country Life,* 20 Dec. 1950.

31. The copy of the University of Durham citation was graciously supplied to me by Mr. W. Morrow, the chief clerk of the university, on 2 April 1971.

32. *Scotsman,* 9 Oct. 1950; *Glasgow Herald,* 7 Oct. 1950; *Glasgow Record,* 9 Oct. 1950; *Glasgow Herald,* 27 Oct. 1950; a photograph of the portrait appears in *Scotsman,* 7 Oct. 1950. Some details have very kindly been supplied to me by R. E. Hutchison, Esq., the elder son of Sir William, keeper of the Scottish National Portrait Gallery, Edinburgh.

DLS to Norah Lambourne (26 Apr. 1949, 11 May 1949), in the recipient's possession.

33. A copy of the DLS letter to her friend (24 Aug. 1950) is in my possession; I have been asked to withhold his name.

Colchester Gazette, 6 June 1950, p. 1. DLS, *The Emperor Constantine: A Chronicle* (London: Gollancz, 1951), pp. 5, 7, 8. *Times,* 4 July 1951, p. 8; *Church Times,* 6 July 1951, p. 433; and 27 Dec. 1957, p. 5; *Times,* 11 Jan. 1952, p. 6; DLS, "Constantine—Christ's Emperor," *Everybody's Weekly,* 16 Feb. 1952, pp. 15, 20. Conversation with Dr. James Denholm, 23 Jan. 1976.

Stage, 19 Apr. 1951; *Chatham News,* 26 Jan. 1951; *Scotsman,* 25 Apr. 1951; *London Star,* 21 Sept. 1950; *Thames Valley Times,* 20 Sept. 1950; *Richmond Times,* 23 Sept. 1950; *Richmond Herald,* 23 Sept. 1950; *Somerset County Herald,* 27 Jan. 1951; *Hendon Times,* 23 Feb. 1951; *Hampstead Express,* 23 Feb. 1951; *Dewsbury Reporter,* 10 Apr. 1951; *Somerset County Herald,* 3 March 1951; *Southampton Southern Echo,* 9 Mar. 1951; *Brixton Free Press,* 16 Mar. 1951.

As part of the Festival of Britain, the National Book League invited DLS to lecture in the Victoria and Albert Museum on 16 Aug. 1951 *(Bookseller,* 3 Mar. 1951, p. 348).

34. Eric Keown, "Towards Better Choirs," *Punch,* 21 Feb. 1951, p. 242; *Manchester Evening News,* 19 Mar. 1951; *Church of England News,* 16 Mar. 1951; Rosamond K. Sprague, *A Matter of Eternity* (Grand Rapids, Mich.: Eerdmans, 1973, pp. 13-14.

35. *Church Times,* 27 Dec. 1957, p. 5.

36. DLS to Norah Lambourne (8 May 1952), in the recipient's possession.

37. *Daily Mirror,* 26 April 1952, p. 5.

38. *Times,* 21 Nov. 1952, p. 7; and 26 Nov. 1952, p. 9.

39. DLS, *The Days of Christ's Coming* (London: Hamish Hamilton, 1953); a second edition (without the pullouts) was published in 1960. DLS, *The Story of Adam and Christ* (London: Hamish Hamilton, 1955). DLS, *The Story of Noah's Ark Retold* (London: Hamish Hamilton, 1956). The manuscripts of the two unpublished juveniles ("The Story of Easter" and "The Enchanted Garden") are in the possession of the Wheaton (Illinois) College Library.

40. *Sunday Times,* 1 May 1949, p. 5. *Times Literary Supplement,* 11 Dec. 1953, p. 801; 8 Jan. 1954, p. 25; 15, 29 Jan. 1954, pp. 41, 73; 5 Feb. 1954, p. 96; 12 Feb. 1954, p. 105. *Times Literary Supplement,* 3 Feb. 1956, p. 69. DLS, Preface to *The Surprise,* by G. K. Chesterton (New York: Sheed and Ward, 1953). These sources are only representative and not a complete accounting of the work of DLS during this period. For example, see another letter to the editor by DLS, *Times Literary Supplement,* 27 Mar. 1953, p. 205 [a comment on Binyon's translation of Dante].)

41. DLS, "Calendar of Unholy & Dead-letter Days," "Cosmic Synthesis," "The Pantheon Papers," "For an Evening Service," *Punch,* 2 Nov. 1953, pp. 16-19; DLS, "More Pantheon Papers," *Punch,* 6 Jan. 1954, p. 60; DLS, "More Pantheon Papers," 13 Jan. 1954, p. 84; DLS, "The Polar Synthesis: A Sermon for Cacophony-Tide," *Punch,* 20 Jan. 1954, p. 124. "For an Evening Service" was also published in *Christian Century,* LXXXI (3 Nov. 1954), 1329.

42. DLS, "Playwrights Are Not Evangelists," *World Theatre,* I (1955), 61-66.

43. DLS, "Charles Williams: A Poet's Critic," pp. 69-90. *Church Times,* 19 Aug. 1955, p. 8; 26 Aug. 1955, p. 10.

44. Kathleen Nott, *The Emperor's Clothes* (London: Heinemann, 1953), pp. 5, 8, 43, 48, 59, 68, 76, 106, 253-98. The work was reprinted by Indiana University Press in 1958. See *Commonweal,* 22 Apr. 1955, pp. 83-84. DLS, "Poetry, Language and Ambiguity," pp. 266, 267, 276-77.

45. DLS, "The Great Mystery: My Belief about Heaven and Hell," *Sunday Times,* 6 Jan. 1957, p. 8. The editor noted in the following issue (13 Jan. 1957) that many readers responded to DLS's article, although only one letter was published and that one took modest exception to a point in DLS's argument. Subsequent guest-contributors included Bertrand Russell, Sir Basil Hen-

riques, the Abbot of Downside, Air Chief Marshal Lord Dowding, Bishop Wand, the Aga Khan, Lt. Col. R. E. Key, Christopher Humphrey, Dr. W. E. Sangster, Arabinda Basu, and Prof. E. N. da C. Andrade. The series ran from Jan. through Mar., and Hodder and Stoughton compiled the articles for publication before the end of 1957 under the title *The Great Mystery of the Hereafter: A Symposium. Time* magazine was impressed by DLS's article: see "Mystery Story," *Time,* 21 Jan. 1957, pp. 36-38.

46. DLS, "The Translation of Verse," p. 127. DLS, trans., *The Song of Roland* (Harmondsworth, Middlesex: Penguin, 1957), p. 17. She acknowledges the aid of Mildred K. Pope, with whom she first read *Roland* at Oxford over forty years before, and, among others, the assistance of Professor Lewis Thorpe, who had "patiently vetted the whole translation line by line" and saved her from "numerous slips and mistakes." See *Times Literary Supplement,* 25 Oct. 1957, p. 646; also, *Nottingham Mediaeval Studies,* II (1958), 1; also, R. C. Johnston, "Hoese 'Boot' in the 'Chanson de Roland', Line 641," *Modern Language Review,* XLVIII (July 1963), 391-92.

47. The DLS letter (July 1957) is in the possession of the Humanities Research Center of The University of Texas.

48. Correspondence with Miss Lambourne, 29 Feb. 1976.

49. DLS to Norah Lambourne (8 May 1952), in the possession of the recipient.

50. Geoffrey L. Bickersteth, "Letter to the Editor," *Times Literary Supplement,* 12 Dec. 1958, p. 12.

51. Val Gielgud, "Literature's Loss," *Sunday Times,* 29 Dec. 1957.

52. See, for example, *Evening News,* 18 Dec. 1957, p. 1; *Daily Mail,* 19 Dec. 1957, p. 1; *Daily Express,* 18 Dec. 1957. Even the *New York Times,* 19 Dec. 1957, p. 29, credited the gardener with finding her body.

53. *Times,* 16 Jan. 1958, p. 12.

54. The letter of Raf de la Torre to Norah Lambourne is in the possession of the recipient.

55. Lewis Thorpe, ed., *Nottingham Mediaeval Studies,* II (1958), 2.

Largely because of the efforts of The Dorothy L. Sayers Literary and Historical Society of Witham, Essex, a memorial appeal was launched and sustained to place an appropriate tablet on the ground floor of St. Anne's Tower, Soho in the spring of 1978. The tablet reads:

In memory of DOROTHY LEIGH SAYERS, D. Litt., Scholar and Writer, Churchwarden of this Parish 1952-1957, born 13 June 1893, died 17 December 1957, whose ashes lie beneath this tower. "The only Christian work is good work well done."

Index